5/28/80 - ST

Genealogical Data Relating
to the
GERMAN SETTLERS
OF PENNSYLVANIA
and Adjacent Territory

From Advertisements in German
Newspapers Published in Philadelphia
and Germantown, 1743-1800

BY EDWARD W. HOCKER

Indexed by Thomas L. Hollowak

Baltimore
GENEALOGICAL PUBLISHING CO., INC.
1980

PREFACE

HIS UNUSUAL COMPILATION has lain in typescript in the library of the Germantown Historical Society since 1935. It abounds with the kind of curious and out-of-the-way information likely to be helpful to those wishing to augment their knowledge of their German ancestry, for which reason we are delighted to bring out the first published edition of the work.

Arranged by newspaper, and thereunder by date of publication, this work contains abstracts of paid notices, advertisements, and articles pertaining to German settlers in Pennsylvania during the period 1743 to 1800, the data deriving variously from death notices, advertisements for runaway servants, offers of property for sale and lease, offers of goods and services, notices of arrival and removal in the Pennsylvania area, advertisements of letters received and awaiting delivery, and notices placed by persons seeking news of relatives and friends, which sometimes designate place of residence in America and birthplace in Germany.

In compiling this material, Mr. Hocker confined his searches to the five principal German newspapers published in Germantown and Philadelphia during the 1743-1800 period, extracting only data of genealogical import and rejecting what was otherwise irreducable or irrelevant to his object. The papers used were Christopher Sower's Germantown Newspaper, 1743-1762 (*Pennsylvanische Geschicht-Schreiber,* later called *Pennsylvanische Berichte*); Henry Miller's *Staatsbote,* 1767-1779; *Philadelphische Zeitung,* 1756-1757; *Philadelphische Correspondenz,* 1781-1800; and *Germantauner Zeitung,* 1785-1790.

As it has some bearing on the valuation of the book as a research aid, we might point out that Edward Hocker was the librarian of the Germantown Historical Society and the author, among other publications, of *Germantown, 1683-1933,* and was therefore admirably suited to the task of searching the local papers for genealogical signposts.

Our publication is a verbatim rendering of the original typescript, to which we have added an index of names. Our thanks to Professor Don Yoder for bringing the work to our attention.

Genealogical Publishing Co., Inc.

EXPLANATORY

Spelling of proper names was subject to many variations in
Pennsylvania in the eighteenth century. The same person was
likely to spell his name differently at different times.
Furthermore, printers were at the mercy of wretched manuscript.
Christopher Sower added this postscript to an advertisement in
his newspaper of April 9, 1762:
"If this is distorted the writer is to blame. Sometimes the purport of a communication may be guessed. But
not so with names. Please write names and places plainly."
Hence in using the index it is desirable to consult every
possible variation of the name sought. Personal names appear
as printed in the newspapers. Geographical names usually are
in modern form.
Where only names and addresses are given the advertisements
from which they are taken usually concern stray cattle or other
matters without genealogical value. Names and addresses without further data appear only for the period not covered by the
tax lists in the Pennsylvania Archives.
Certain lists of names mentioning birthplaces are from advertisements of letters received from Germany and awaiting delivery in Philadelphia. The postal facilities being primitive,
it was the custom to address letters intended for settlers in
care of a newspaper publisher or a merchant.
The suffix "in" attached to a family name indicates the
female. Thus the wife or daughter of a man named Hoffman would
be named Hoffmanin.
As redemptioners had to serve four to six years without pay
and often under hard taskmasters, the twentieth century in-
vestigator hardly considers it to their discredit if they mani-
fested sufficient spirit to run away.

NOTES ON LOCALITIES

Unless otherwise evident, places mentioned are in Pennsyl-
vania.
Skippack comprised not only the present Skippack Township in
Montgomery County, but all the region along Skippack Creek.
Falckner Swamp was in the neighborhood of the present New
Hanover Township, Montgomery County.
Methacton was the vicinity of Worcester Township, Mont-
gomery County.
Goshenhoppen was the Perkiomen Valley north of Schwenks-
ville. The lower part was Old Goshenhoppen, and the upper part
New Goshenhoppen.
Manatawny was in the vicinity of the creek of that name,
northwest of Pottstown.
Oley was the extensive territory in Berks County, northwest
of Boyertown.
Saucon was along Saucon Creek, south of Bethlehem, in North-
ampton and Lehigh Counties.
Swatara Creek is a branch of the Susquehanna River flowing
through Berks, Lebanon and Dauphin Counties.

Great Swamp was in southwestern Bucks County.
Quitopahilla was in the present Lebanon County.
Conococheaque was in Maryland, near Hagerstown.
Anweil was in northern New Jersey.

PENNSYLVANISCHE GESCHICHTS-SCHREIBER

Published in Germantown, Pennsylvania, now part of Philadelphia, by Christopher Sauer (Saur, Sower). The name of
the paper was later changed to Pennsylvanische Berichte.

April 16, 1743

Martin Mueller, merchant (peddler?), died suddenly. Those
owing him in Lancaster County are requested to make payment to
Emanuel Zimmerman, and in Philadelphia and Bucks Counties to
John Wister, Philadelphia.

Georg Adam Weidner, Oley (Berks County), wants a workman
for his tile kiln.

Ludwig Huenge, Franconia Township, on Skippack Creek.
(Montgomery County).

June 16, 1743

Rudolph Diebendoerffer, in service in New Jersey, lost his
life while with his master. This is to notify his mother,
Barbara Diebendoerffer, of his death. Further information may
be had from Jacob Beck, in New Jersey, or from Mr. Clem, the
barber, in Philadelphia.

Johann Casper Repp, "aus der Wetterau von Dauernheim,"
arrived in this country six years ago, and then notified his
sister, Anna Maria Reppin, also to come. She arrived last
autumn and is now in Germantown, and she seeks news of her
brother.

Johannes Schuppi, bookbinder, from Hamburg, is now located
in Strawberry alley, Philadelphia.

September 16, 1743

Hansz Dettweiler, Skippack, offers for sale two proper-
ties in Bedminster Township, Bucks County, on Deep Run.

Jacob Hoffman, Skippack, near Jacob Reiff (Montgomery
County).

October 16, 1743

Mathes Egner, Macungie (Lehigh County).

Jacob Biedert, Tulpehocken (Berks County).

November 16, 1743

Philip Traut, Cocalico Township, near Ephrata (Lancaster
County).

December 16, 1743

Walter Luis, New Hanover Township, on the Schuylkill, (Montgomery County), offers for sale 50 acres on Oley road, nine miles above Trappe, near Melcher Hoch.

January 16, 1744

Daniel Womelsdorf, on Manatawny Creek (Berks County), operator of a fulling mill, wants to employ a newly arrived wool weaver.

Georg Diri, on French Creek (Chester County), offers a reward for the return of his runaway horse to Johannes Schrack, Trappe.

H. Rieger, doctor of medicine, Lancaster.

February 16, 1744

Michael Weyermann, on North Wales road, on Neshaminy Creek, in "Hetwil" (Hatfield?) Township (Montgomery County).

March 16, 1744

Jacob Falmer, Tulpehocken (Berks County), offers a fulling mill for rent.

Jacob Fischer, Skippack road, Whitpain Township, nine miles from Germantown (Montgomery County).

April 16, 1744

Jacob Friedrich Rieger, Lancaster.

May 16, 1744

Hansz Jerg Knoedler, Frankford (Philadelphia).

July 16, 1744

Georg Kastner, Whitpain Township (Montgomery County), advertises that his German servant, Conrad Wied, ran away. He is 30 years old.

Johann Nickel Haupt, merchant in Great Swamp (Bucks County).

September 16, 1744

Johann Otto Iserloh, Falckner Swamp (Montgomery County); wife, Anna Maria.

Philip Schuetz, Lancaster.

October 16, 1744

Melcher Sueszholtz, Goshenhoppen (Montgomery County).

December 16, 1744

Christian Schneider, Goshenhoppen, known as Juden Schneider, urges payment of debts due him.

Wilhelm Jansen, Skippack (Montgomery County).

Michael Hartlein, near Oley, on Chestnut Hill (Berks County).

January 16, 1745

Joh. Peter Grosz, Lebanon.

February 16, 1745

Balthaser Heiderick, Frederick Township (Montgomery County), near Hansz Mueller.

March 16, 1745

Valentin Steinmetz announces that he will discontinue collecting money for the erection of a stone church in Saucon, as a wooden meeting house is to be built six miles away, under the direction of Valentin Steinmetz, Johann Georg Reinhart, Johannes Appel, Henrich Croszman, Conrad Walb, Johann Andreas Erdmann, Johann Peter Marstaeller, Mathias Oder, Johann Georg Bossel, Michel Seider, Christian Kaubt, Balthaser Beil, Frantz Rusz and Michel S

Jacobus Gerardus Becker, doctor of medicine.

Christian Schneider, Goshenhoppen, expects to remove from the vicinity in five weeks.

Georg Wittman, Cocalico Township (Lancaster County).

April 16, 1745

Henrich Stoehr, Lancaster County, on Little Muddy Creek, offers a grist mill for sale.

May 16, 1745

Johann Gottlieb Graeuninger, born at Erlingen, near Sinsheun, arrived in this country in 1738, with his brother, Martin. They were separated, and Johann Gottlieb, who is now in Anweil (New Jersey), seeks news of his brother.

Jacob Schlauch, Saucon, three miles from Bethlehem.

June 16, 1745

Johann Georg Schneider, saddler, Lancaster, is about to remove to the New York Region.

August 16, 1745

Christoffel Bayer, Allemangel (Albany Township, Berks County); wife, Maria Chatarina.

September 16, 1745

Peter Conrad, New Hanover Township (Montgomery County), advertises that his German servant, Carl Witt, ran away. He is a smith by trade and 30 to 40 years old.

Maria Judith, born at Pfaffenhoffen, Wurtemberg, seeks her brother-in-law, Jacob Legler.

October 16, 1745

Jacob Weickert, the old wheelwright of Tulpehocken (Berks County).

Leonhart Schnaebeli, on Swatara Creek, near Hansz Brechbiel.

Christian Mueller, Allemangel (Albany Township, Berks County).

November 16, 1745

Henrich Hausser came from Switzerland to Philadelphia two years ago. He and his wife were sick on the ship, and he died. Their children were indentured, and the mother lost trace of them. She has since located three of the children, and she now seeks information about her son, Caspar, who is 10-11 years old.

Johann Nickel Sauer arrived in this country two years ago. While he was sick his children were indentured. He asks for information about them: Georg Wilhelm, 13-14 years old, and a daughter 21 years old.

Henrich Ruth, Lower Salford Township (Montgomery County).

Johannes Frey, Skippack (Montgomery County).

December 16, 1745

Alexander Johannes Rent wrote to Germany telling his "Baasze" (aunt or cousin), Anna Maria Rentin, to come to him in Pennsylvania. She crossed the ocean two years ago, with her husband, Philip Odenwaelder, a smith, and she now seeks the aforesaid Rent.

Jesaia Guschua, near Great Swamp (Bucks County).

January 16, 1746

Georg Wuerffel, Conestoga, on Pequea Creek (Lancaster County).

Michael Grosz, Lancaster.

Johannes Nicol, Conestoga, on Pequea Creek (Lancaster County).

Andreas Bayer, Frederick Township, near Johannes Miller (Montgomery County).

Conrad Schwartz, Lancaster.

Philip Setzler, Trappe.

Sebastian Graff, Lancaster.

February 16, 1746

Gottfried Lehman, potter, Germantown.

Henrich Huber, Macungie (Lehigh County).

March 16, 1746

Johannes Schneider, Skippack, a half mile from Henrich Funck's mill (Montgomery County).

Jonas Osborn, harness shop, Front street corner of Arch, Philadelphia.

April 16, 1746

Andreas Keppler, Falckner Swamp (Montgomery County).

May 16, 1746

Daniel Mackinet's widow, Lancaster.

June 16, 1746

Johann Dietrich Ort, who sharpens tools, recently arrived from Germany and is now in Lancaster but intends removing to York. He will be in Lancaster for business every court day.

Daniel Beneset, store, opposite the St. George inn, Second street, Philadelphia.

Ulrich Spinner, Great Swamp, two miles from Peter Walbert (Bucks County).

Jacob Dettweiler, Perkasie, on Deep Run, in Bedminster Township (Bucks County).

Christian Schwartz, Perkasie (Bucks County).

Abraham Sayler, on Perkiomen Creek (Montgomery County).

June 16, 1746

Georg Dietrich Held, Oley (Berks County).

Andreas Sadosky, Amity Township (Berks County).

July 16, 1746

Wilhelm Fischer, "auf Gagusi," Heidelberg Township.

Jacob Koch, over the Perkiomen Creek, in Providence Township (Montgomery County).

Nicholas Bucher, Lancaster.

Georg Schwab, York.

August 16, 1746

Peter Metz, Johannes Metz and Vallentin Metz, brothers, were indentured five years ago. Peter is now free and seeks his brothers.

Matheas Groh, on Little Swatara Creek (Lebanon or Berks County).

September 16, 1746

Five years ago at Christmas a widow complained to a man on the street in Philadelphia that she had many small children and could not pay for their passage on the ship. The man took one child and paid part of the passage costs. He took the child, a boy of 8, to his home, 30 miles distant, to consult his wife on the matter of retaining the boy. The mother did not get the man's name, and she now wishes to hear from him. The boy, named Christian Meyer, is now 13 years old. He was born in Meisenheim, "auf dem Dandes Hoff." The mother lives with the Welsh in Montgomery Township (Montgomery County), with Henrich Kremer.

John Spencer, Philadelphia, advertises that his German servant, Maria Elisabeth Korin, 22 years old, ran away.

Joseph Crellius, sign of the Hand and Feather, Second street, Philadelphia.

Hansz Zimmerman, on Cocalico Creek, Lancaster County.

October 16, 1746

Peter Heibe, Manatawny (Berks County).

Heinrich Klein, Lancaster.

Leonhart Schnaebeli, Swatara Forks.

November 16, 1746

Michel Gebert, Brenson's Furnace, advertises that his servant, Johann Ludwig Weiss, 30 years old, ran away.

Peter Conrad the younger, near Conrad Weiser, Tulpehocken (Berks County).

Arrent Hessert, store, Letitia court, Philadelphia.

Henrich Walter, dyer, Lancaster.

Peter Joerger, at Barr's furnace.

December 16, 1746

Sigmund Haenle, on Swatara Creek (Dauphin or Lebanon Counties).

Peter Walber, New Goshenhoppen.

January 17, 1747

Conrad Schweighausen, from Basel, living in Philadelphia, on Third street, adjoining Thomas Maeyer, potter, is going to Switzerland and will return. He will carry letters and attend to legacies. He sells Schweitzer tea.

Nicholas Kennel, beer brewer, Lancaster.

Christian Krall, Upper Milford Township (Lehigh County).

Rolland Schmitt, Bethlehem.

February 17, 1747

The house of the well known Friedrich Ocks (Ax), in Germantown, was burned.

April 16, 1747

Johannes Kuecheler, Conestoga (Lancaster County), near Hansz Graff, indentured his son Christoph for his passage costs. The son was transferred from one master to another and the father lost trace of him. He now seeks news of his son. He was last known to be with Robert Batz (Bates).

Ulrich Scherer, on the Schuylkill, at Poplar Neck; wife, Maria Aebel.

Carl Ludwig Essig, Philadelphia, on October 16 last became security for Henrich Mueller, unmarried, for the payment of his passage costs from Amsterdam; now Mueller has disappeared.

Hansz Christian Mueller, over the Susquehanna on Codorus Creek (York County), offers his mill for sale.

May 16, 1747

Simon Klaar arrived in this country six years ago and was indentured as a servant. His sister Barbara became free two years ago, and she seeks her brother.

Henrich Braband, a Swiss, two years ago was captured by Spaniards but was soon released. He seeks his brother Jacob, who is in this land, having come from Zweybruecken in 1743. Notify Jacob Bauman, Germantown.

Johann Von Vossen, Skippack (Montgomery County).

August Henrich Kuntzman, Falckner Swamp (Montgomery County).

Mathias Gmaehlin, glazier, Methacton, Worcester Township (Montgomery County).

Christian Bauer, Tulpehocken (Berks County).

July 16, 1747

Reinert Vogdes, residing on the side lands of Germantown, back of John Gorgas, near Antoni Williams, on the street which is to be laid out from Chestnut Hill to Luken's mill, advertises his farm for sale. Apply to him or to Jann Jansen, saddler, Germantown.

Jacob Rincker, a Swiss, arrived in this country four years ago and still has a year to serve. His mother, who is free and lives near Germantown, seeks information about him and asks that he come to see her and his brothers, Caspar and Henrich, living with Thomas Lorentz, four miles from Merion Meeting House, across the Schuylkill (Montgomery County).

August 16, 1747

John Jarrett, Horsham Township (Montgomery County), advertises that a German servant, Lorentz Husar, 20 years old, ran away; he has probably gone toward Tulpehocken.

Gertraut Schnaeuzin seeks her son, Conrad Schnauz.

October 16, 1747

Christian Mayer, Methacton (Montgomery County).

Jacob Hollinger, Lancaster.

November 16, 1747

Stadian Ebelin, a young man, son of a carpenter, from Deinheim, near Oppenheim, came to Pennsylvania in 1744. His parents want to hear from him.

Notice is given of the settlement of the estate of Geret in Haeven (DeHaven) and his drowned son Ebert, by Dietrich and Sara Welcker, administrators.

November 16, 1747

Johann Dewald Bauer, from Gauersheim, five miles from
Worms, came to Pennsylvania four years ago with his sister,
Maria Elisabeth, and his "Basze" (cousin or aunt), Anna
Barbara Babin. His father, Johannes Bauer, seeks information
about him.

Jacob Gertehauer, Upper Milford Township, Bucks County
(now Lehigh County).

Tobias Weber, inn, half mile from Bethlehem.

Jost Henrich Sassaman, Maxatawny (Berks County).

Abraham Weidman, Cocalico Township, near Henry Zimmerman
(Lancaster County).

Daniel Preisz, Skippack, near Isaac Lein (Lane?)
(Montgomery County).

Henrich Staehli, Bern Township, on the Schuylkill (Berks
County).

Hansz Schantz, Conestoga (Lancaster County).

December 16, 1747

Johann Peter Schuhman arrived in this country seven years
ago, with his sister, Maria Catharina. The latter inquires
for him.

Isaac Klein, Salford Township (Montgomery County).

January 16, 1748

Herman Arndt, the old well digger, Falckner Swamp
(Montgomery County).

Joerg Zebitz, Saucon, six miles from Bethlehem.

John Doen, Bucks County, on Tohickon Creek.

Hansz Georg Weber, New Goshenhoppen.

Christian Steinman, two miles from Lancaster.

February 16, 1748

Simon Siron has removed from Plymouth Meeting House
(Montgomery County) to Philadelphia, on Second street, at the
Amsterdam Arms. He sells yarn and flax.

Johann Michel Weckesser, formerly magistrate of Korb,
Wurtemberg, arrived in Pennsylvania last autumn, and is going
abroad in May, but will return. He offers to carry letters.
He is now with Lorentz Riesz, stockingweaver, Germantown.

Matheus Walter, Goshenhoppen (Montgomery County).

Martin Schmitt, Old Goshenhoppen (Montgomery County).

February 16, 1748

Henrich Walter, locksmith, Lancaster.

March 16, 1748

William Fischer, Daniel Mausz, Bernhart Mausz, Tulpehocken (Berks County).

Jacob Kuntz, Johann Nickel Kuntz, Conestoga (Lancaster
County).

Jacob Schaack, weaver, from Lorraine, who arrived last
autumn, is asked to come to Jacob Keiter, Skippack (Montgomery County).

Peter Acker, Cocalico (Lancaster County).

Melcher Schneider, three miles from Lancaster, gave
security to Michel Baeyerle, Lancaster, to permit Antoni Ritz,
Baeyerle's indentured servant, to work for Schneider for wages.
Ritz ran away with a free youth, Antoni von der Burg, a saddler. Ritz is 19-20 years old.

Georg Frey, Peter Frey and their sister Maria arrived in
this country six years ago last autumn and were indentured in
Conestoga (Lancaster County). Their sister, Anna Margretha
Freyin, seeks them. Notify Jacob Weyermann, Hatfield Township,
Philadelphia County (now Montgomery).

Melcher Kolb, New Goshenhoppen.

Hansz Georg Welcker, New Goshenhoppen.

April 16, 1748

Hansz Rolland, six miles from Lancaster, in Leacock Township.

Benedictus Muentz, Falckner Swamp (Montgomery County).

Georg Schoener, Falckner Swamp (Montgomery County).

Daniel Meidinger, cooper, Lancaster.

Martin Waltz, joiner, Lancaster.

May 16, 1748

Juliana Catharina Stumpin served with Georg Hoehn, Tulpehocken (Berks County), then married and left. Her brother,
Herman Stump, seeks her. He is with Lenert Christel, Indianfield, at the source of Skippack Creek (Franconia Township,
Montgomery County).

Nicholas Fischer, near Macungie (Lehigh County), with
Adam Daeschler.

Christian Wagner, near Emanuel Zimmermann, Conestoga
(Lancaster County).

May 16, 1748

Jacob Schertz, Strasburg Township (Lancaster County).

Hansz Georg Voegele, Colebrookdale (Berks County).

Vallentin Nungesser, Old Goshenhoppen (Montgomery County).

June 16, 1748

Ludwig Sauermilch, Douglass, where Manatawny Creek joing the Schuylkill (Montgomery County).

July 16, 1748

Adam Wambold, "Taegli Township," wife, Anna Odillia.

Jacob Stauffer, on the West Branch (of Perkiomen Creek), in Falckner Swamp, near Mount Pleasant Furnace.

Johann Georg Bergmann, on the Ridge (Ridge avenue), Roxborough Township, Philadelphia County, near Andrew Robeson's mill, offers his plantation for sale.

Wendel Wittman, near Germantown.

Andreas Beyerle, Lancaster.

August 16, 1748

Jacob Fuchs, Weidenthal, above Oley (Berks County).

Jacob Buchwalter, Colebrookdale Township (Berks County).

September 16, 1748

Ludwig Botts, Bern Township (Berks County); wife, Christina.

Henrich Kreider, Cocalico Township (Lancaster County); wife, Elisabeth.

Christian Frick, Bern Township (Berks County).

October 1, 1748

Nicolaus Schmidt, from Bettenhausen, in the Palatinate.

Johannes Adam, from Labenheim, now in Anweil (New Jersey).

November 1, 1748

Nicolaus Schnaesz, Tulpehocken (Berks County), with Jacob Ledermann, seeks his brother Henrich.

Johannes Haenge, on Indian Creek (Franconia Township, Montgomery County), is going to Germany.

November 1, 1748

Christian Schneider, Goshenhoppen, at Mayberry's iron works.

Hansz Georg Welcker, New Goshenhoppen (Montgomery County), advertises that a stray mare is in possession of his son, on Geret in Haeven's (DeHaven) place.

Dietrich Welcker, Skippack (Montgomery County).

Lazarua Weidner, Oley (Berks County).

Herman Fischer, New Goshenhoppen.

December 1, 1748

Johann Michel Mayer, formerly of Graetzingen, is now in Pennsylvania.

Hansz Adam Bader, at Gottschalk's mill, Skippack (Montgomery County), seeks his brothers, Peter and Matheus, with whom he came to this country last year.

Jonas Koehler, on William Moore's plantation, Moyamensing, Philadelphia County.

Hansz Gerber, Quitapohilla, near the furnace (Lebanon County).

Abraham Reiff, Conestoga (Lancaster County).

Wilhelm Coerckes, Goshenhoppen (Montgomery County).

December 16, 1748

Johann Daniel Jacob, from Auerbach, near Zweybruecken, arrived in this country three years ago. This autumn his mother, Anna Maria Jacobin, arrived, and she seeks her son. She is with Johannes Berger, Reformed schoolmaster.

Ludwig Bickel, on Perkiomen Creek, near Pannebecker's mill (Montgomery County).

Johannes Hippel, on the Schuylkill, four miles from Trappe.

Moses Heymann, New Hanover (Montgomery County).

Georg Bast, Maxatawny (Berks County); wife, Dorothea.

Uli Huy, on the Schuylkill, near Seisemer Reit.

Georg Bachman, Saucon (Lehigh County).

Abraham Clementz, Skippack (Montgomery County).

Christophel Obel, Macungie (Lehigh County).

January 16, 1749

Henrich Demuth, smith, Lancaster, advertises that his servant, Johannes Weyand, 20 years old, ran away.

John Maecklevaein, Norrington (Montgomery County).

Michel Kerwer, Swatara; wife, Eva Magdalena.

Friedrich Fischer, living with his son between Philadelphia and Germantown.

February 16, 1749

Hansz Reiszner, Upper Saucon (Lehigh County).

April 16, 1749

Conrad Schweighausser, Philadelphia, Arch street, third house from Second street, next to Septimus Robinson, justice, sells scythes and peddlers' wares.

Joseph Fabian, 15 years old, has been indentured to a trade three times by his guardian, Georg Welcker, Goshenhoppen (Montgomery County), but he ran away each time.

Henrich Peter, dyer, Falckner Swamp, near Jan Neisz, Jacob Mayer, Waldoerffer and Philip Hahn (Montgomery County).

Jacob Eichholtz, landlord of the Plow inn, Lancaster.

May 16, 1749

Georg Buchhart, Falckner Swamp (Montgomery County).

Rudolph Herte, Falckner Swamp (Montgomery County).

June 1, 1749

Imanuel Schneider, with Christophel Obel, Macungie (Lehigh County), seeks his two sons, Hansz Henrich, 23 years old, and Philip, 25 years old.

Henrich Adam, Maxatawny (Berks County); wife, Maria.

Johann Gottschi, saddler, Germantown.

June 16, 1749

Jacob Bach, on the Schuylkill in Coventry Township (Chester County).

Jacob Schupp, shoemaker, Cocalico (Lancaster County).

July 16, 1749

Hansz Jacob Hiestand, west side of the Susquehanna River, on Little Codorus Creek, two miles from York.

July 16, 1749

Johannes Wolff, Goshenhoppen at Grafen mill (Montgomery County).

Theobold End, saddler, Germantown.

Martin Miller, Chestnut Hill (Philadelphia).

Isaac Krall, shoemaker, Skippack (Montgomery County).

August 1, 1749

Johannes Recher, born at Brattle, two miles above Basel, was indentured eleven years ago, along with his brother Friedrich and his sisters, Elisabeth and Margretha. He wishes to hear from them. He is now in Anweil (New Jersey), with Peter Rockenfelder.

August 16, 1749

Gottfried Liebgeb, Germantown, died from injuries die to falling from a wagon.

Johann Godfrey, Germantown, opposite the printing shop, in Georg Schmitt's house, sharpens scissors and knives.

Georg Doerr, Tulpehocken (Berks County), advertises that his servant, Frantz Ebler, 25-30 years old, ran away.

September 1, 1749

Mattheas Geiger, Salem County (New Jersey), seven miles from the glass house.

Michel Guckes seeks his brothers, Johannes and Henrich.

Andreas Spring, above Trappe, near the stone house.

September 16, 1749

Peter Koch, merchant, of Philadelphia, died on the 10th at his plantation, along Wissahickon Creek.

Peter Baer, Water street, near Market, Philadelphia, sells hardware.

Andreas Ziegler, Skippack (Montgomery County).

October 16, 1749

Alexander Forbes, Philadelphia, advertises that his German servant, Margaret Kleinin, 18 years old, ran away.

Hieronimus Weber, Skippack (Montgomery County), near Jacob Dettweiler.

Abraham Schreiner, Old Goshenhoppen, near Daniel Hiester (Sumneytown, Montgomery County).

October 16, 1749

Johann Conrad Lorschbach, near the stone church, Old Goshenhoppen (Montgomery County).

Georg Frey, Conestoga (Lancaster County), with Bastian Reyer, seeks his sister, Christina Margaretha Freyin, and his brother Peter, and also Maria Frantze Freyin.

Johannes Geschwind, near Willem Goergus, Goshenhoppen (Montgomery County), sells medicines.

Christopher Protzmann, dyer, Lancaster, with Abraham Mayer.

Johannes Eigender, on the Great Lehigh, five miles above Bethlehem, offers his plantation for sale.

Daniel Hill, between the Schuylkill and "Lane Creek".

Daniel Longenecker, on the Schuylkill.

Henrich Bamberger, Upper Salford Township (Montgomery County).

Georg Dennent, Whitemarsh (Montgomery County).

November 1, 1749

Georg Adam Weidner, Oley (Berks County), wants a workman for his tile and brick kilns.

Johann Trump and Ernst Hauszkiper, on the North Wales road.

Philip Misze seeks his step-brother, Paulus del Curand, who arrived in this country two years ago. Inquire of Conrad Weiser, at Tulpehocken (Berks County).

Casper Jansen, Upper Dublin, Springfield (Montgomery County).

Simon Muench, Bern Township, on the Northkill (Berks County).

Peter Seyler, near Trappe.

Conrad Geib, on Muddy Creek.

Christoffel Paust, Hanover Township, from Ober Sueltzen.

Samuel Hoch, Oley (Berks County).

Michel Seider, Saucon (Northampton County).

Carl Reyer, Falckner Swamp (Montgomery County).

Christian Fretz, on Deep Run, Perkasie (Bucks County).

Henrich Clemmer, Skippack (Montgomery County).

Wilhelm Werth, Perkasie, Bucks County.

November 1, 1749

Christian Eberhart, Falckner Swamp (Montgomery County).

November 16, 1749

Information is wanted about Gottfried Reichert, from Staeten, unterm Heuchelberg, who left there seven years ago.

Michel Brand, Falckner Swamp, near the Schuylkill (Montgomery County), advertises that his German servant, Georg Schreiner, ran away. He arrived in this country last autumn, from Hammen, near Worms, and is 22 years old.

Old Peter Wentz died in Methacton (Montgomery County).

Michael Hillegas died in Philadelphia.

Matheus Lentz, Plymouth (Montgomery County), on John Davis' land.

Simon Schmitt, Falckner Swamp, with Deringer (Montgomery County).

Peter Ganter, Lancaster.

December 1, 1749

Dewald Hussa, wheelwright, arrived in this country this year. His friend, Jacob Manny, Durham Township, (Bucks County) seeks him. Manny lives four miles from Durham Furnace.

Jacob Farni, near Hansz Zimmerman, wants Friedrich Rentz to call for his smithing tools.

Hacob Haart, unmarried, from Heppenheim, near Alzey, arrived in America a year ago. His brother-in-law, Henrich Landes, Perkasie (Bucks County), inquires for him.

Adam Forsch, Oley Hills (Berks County).

Peter Doerr, Macungie (Lehigh County).

Johann Remberg, Forks of the Delaware (Easton).

December 16, 1749

Jacob Bayerle offers to sell or rent two plantations, a new mill, with two pairs of stones, also oil and saw mills, on Conestoga Creek (Lancaster County).

Adam Klaempfer, Philadelphia, offers to sell or rent a plantation on Tohickon Creek (Bucks County), 33 miles from Philadelphia.

Hans Wolff Berlet, miller, arrived in this country seventeen years ago. His brothers, Johann Conrad, papermaker, and Paul, carpenter, have now arrived and seek their brother. Johann Conrad is at Oley (Berks County), with Mr. Womelsdorff.

December 16, 1749

Wilhelm Ermel, Skippack, on the Branch (of Perkiomen Creek, Montgomery County).

Sebastian Herreman, three miles from Trappe.

Jacob Schuhmacher, Skippack (Montgomery County).

January 16, 1750

Johann Jacob Hecker, Quitapahilla (Lebanon County), near Herman Ohrendorff, six years ago indentured his daughter, Carolina Charlotte, to Johann Conrad Ist. He wants to know her whereabouts.

Johann Kistler, from the "Berner Gebiet, von Boetzen," arrived this year and is with Abraham Herr, Conestoga (Lancaster County). He seeks his brother, Henrich Kistler, who arrived in this country twelve years ago.

Margretha Hoffsessin, who recently arrived in this country and is now at Oley with Antoni Jaeger, seeks her daughter, Maria Hoffsessin.

Christian Laubach, Saucon, offers his plantation for sale.

Andreas Weisz, Frederick (Montgomery County), offers his plantation for sale.

Henrich Frey, Skippack (Montgomery County), offers his fulling mill for sale.

Jacob Eckman, Old Goshenhoppen (Montgomery County).

Jacob Kurr, Hosensack (Lehigh County).

February 1, 1750

James Campbell offers a plantation for sale in Tinicum, Bucks County, in Streper's tract.

John Estborn (Eastburn), Norriton, Philadelphia County (now Montgomery), offers a plantation for sale in Durham Township, Bucks County, where Thomas Tad (Todd) lives.

Henrich Scheid, Macungie (Lehigh County).

Jacob Dast, smith, Skippack (Montgomery County), on Isaac Klein's place.

February 16, 1750

Thomas Blaer, Springfield, at Durham, near the furnace, Bucks County, offers a plantation for sale.

Michael Dithart, Saucon, six miles from Durham Furnace, advertises that his German servant, Jacob Hemmerle, a carpenter, ran away.

February 16, 1750

Philip Ziegler, Ridge Valley, Upper Salford (Montgomery County).

March 16, 1750

Heinrich Schellenberger, miller near Germantown, has taken the mill of the late Andrew Robeson, is operating it and lives there. (The mill was at the mouth of Wissahickon Creek).

Announcement is made of the sale of the property of the late Johannes Butzer, blacksmith, Germantown.

Peter Weller, Amith Township, on Manatawny Creek (Berks County), with Philip Boyer, came to America nine years ago, with his two sisters, one of whom married Johann Christ Schmitt. Her name is Anna Fry. The other sister is Eva Maria Wellerin.(sic) He seeks information about them.

Hansz Martin Gerig, Exeter County (sic), in the Schwartz-wald, three miles from Justice Buun (Boone), offers a plantation for rent (Berks County).

Johann Dietrich Bauman, Goshenhoppen, Marlborough Township (Montgomery County).

James Webb, Lancaster.

Jacob Klein, carpenter, Germantown.

Martin Meylin, Lampeter Township, Lancaster County.

April 16, 1750

Peter Spicker, Lancaster, near the court house, urges debtors to pay before the May fair. Payments may be made to him or to Dietrich Welcker, Skippack (Montgomery County), or Friedrich Marsteller, Methacton (Montgomery County). Spicker sells peddlers' wares.

Daniel Huber, for several years with Jacob Reiff, in Skippack (Montgomery County), recently left. His brother, Christian, in Conestoga (Lancaster County), seeks him.

Christian Fenstermacher, Market street, Philadelphia, near Joseph Gray's sign of the Conestoga Wagon.

The house and lot in Lancaster where Georg Gibson lives is for sale. An inn has been conducted there for several years.

Johann Conrad Berlet, papermaker journeyman; wife, Anna Maria, born Zollerin.

Johann Peter Schmitt, Cocalico Township, Lancaster County; wife; Elisabeth, a Hollander.

Velten Beckers, Conestoga (Lancaster County).

May 1, 1750

Abraham Reiber, of Sandhofen, and his wife, Anna Margretha, daughter of Hansz Jacob Reuther, of Ophau, arrived in Pennsylvania last autumn. They are at Hansz Bauer's house, Goshenhoppen (Montgomery County), and they seek Frantz Bero and his wife Susanna.

Philip Braun arrived in this country eleven years ago, with his father, Wendel Braun, and two sisters, Maria Chatarina and Susanna. He served in Raritan (New Jersey), with Herman Klein.

Johannes Baer, Leacock Township, Lancaster County, at Hantz Guten's place.

Edward Schmaut, Lancaster, offers 400 acres for sale over the Susquehanna on Bermudian Creek, near the Great Conewago; also houses and lots in Lancaster.

Catharina Eberhartin arrived in this country last autumn, with her daughters, Maria and Anna. She was separated from her daughters, and now seeks them.

Peter Federolf, Goshenhoppen, advertises that his German servant, Christoph Firschner, 25 years old, ran away.

May 16, 1750

Martin Joerger, Falckner Swamp (Montgomery County), advertises that his servant, Jacob Schotter, ran away.

Jacob Feree, Leacock Township, Lancaster County.

June 1, 1750

Johann Henrich Sickman, unmarried, born in Hanover, Lutheran, is confined in the Philadelphia prison because he owes 20 passage costs, etc. He offers himself to anyone; is capable of teaching; he taught school the past winter with Peter Reiff and Jacob Tribelbitz, at Oley (Berks County).

Martin Schroeter, with Johannes Schneider, Lancaster, indentured his four children last autumn, and wants to know what became of them. They are: daughters, Christina and Elisabeth; stepsons, Hansz Georg Wambach and Peter Wambach. He also seeks his brother-in-law, Johannes Anstert.

Barbara Zentzerin seeks her sister, Odillia Zentzerin. They and their brother, born in Sultz, in Lower Alsace, arrived in this country last autumn. Notify Georg Mueller, Tulpehocken (Berks County).

Relatives seek Maria Frantza Freyin, who was indentured to the wife of Friedrich Hob.

Matheus Reichert, Upper Goshenhoppen, near Mayberry's Furnace.

Friedrich Hertzog, Upper Salford, in Ridge Valley (Montgomery County).

June 1, 1750

William Wacoff, Heidelberg Township; wife, Barbara.

June 16, 1750

Anna Elisabeth, widow of Lorentz Loch, from Braunholder, Zweibruecken, arrived in this country last autumn and lives at North Wales (Gwynedd Township, Montgomery County), with Nicolaus Schmell. She seeks her brother, Johann Adam Schmell, from Cassel, who has been in America fourteen years.

Jacob Oberholtzer, Upper Salford, at Jacob Landes' mill (Montgomery County).

Georg Breckel, Earl Township (Lancaster County); wife, Juliana.

July 1, 1750

Jacob Wentz, Skippack, Worcester Township (Montgomery County).

Michel Jost, Bedminster Township (Bucks County), near Blaesz Bayer.

July 16, 1750

Andreas Weisz, Limert Township (Limerick Township ? Montgomery County); wife, Judith.

Johannes Schrack, Providence (Montgomery County); sign of the Three Crowns.

Bernhard Hubele, Lancaster.

Jacob Dettweiler, Franconia Township (Montgomery County).

August 1, 1750

Hansz Michel Kunsers, Sinking Springs, Tulpehocken (Berks County); wife, Anna Chatarina.

Peter Wentz, Methacton (Montgomery County).

Johannes Bleyer, Great Swamp (Bucks County), one mile from Swamp Mill.

Peter Becker, Providence Township, between Skippack and Perkiomen Creeks (Montgomery County), tailor.

Jost Doerr, Whitpain Township (Montgomery County).

August 18, 1750

Joseph Steinman, Conestoga Township (Lancaster County), advertises that his German servant, Andreas Fehl, 19 years old, ran away.

August 18, 1750

Hansz Peter Fischer and his wife, Maria Elisabeth Gasserin, who arrived in this country last autumn, seek the latter's brother, Peter Gasser, from Gunters-Hoffen, Alsace, who came here twelve years ago. Fischer and his wife are in Heidelberg Township, "an der Brunen Kehr," on Michel Schauer's place.

Henrich Lora, Falckner Swamp (Montgomery County), offers to rent a large tannery formerly operated by the late Johannes Beener.

Jacob Ofe, Peheck Township, Somerset County, East Jersey, advertises that his German servant, Melcher Calpen, or Calvin, 21 years old, ran away. He had previously served in Pennsylvania.

William Kentel, Limerick Township, above Trappe, Philadelphia County (now Montgomery), advertises that his Irish servant, Philip Harrison, ran away.

Jacob Stutzman, on the Schuylkill, near Martin Orner.

Christian Bernhart, Upper Salford, Ridge Valley (Montgomery County).

Diel Bauer, Falckner Swamp, on McCall's land (Montgomery County).

September 1, 1750

Ernst Sigmund Seydel, Oley (Berks County), gives notice that last year he became security for the payment of the passage costs of a Swiss named Daniel Schaeubeli, and eventually he had to pay these costs. Two small children of Schaeubeli were indentured. Schaeubeli had another son, 19 years old, who has coaxed away his younger brother from Seydel's service, pretending he was going to raise the money needed to free the lad. He has collected three times the sum required, and has bought a fiddle and a cow with the money.

David Luembeck, bookbinder, from Mannheim, Germany, now in Philadelphia with Mr. Keppele, expects to go to Germany for his family in the autumn.

Wilhelm Werth, Perkasie, Hilltown Township, Bucks County; wife, Elisabeth.

Christiana Pfauin, widow, from Sultz, Wurtemberg, last year indentured her son, Hansz Michel Pfau, to an Englishman, and she would like to know where he lives.

Jacob Vollmer, Tulpehocken (Berks County), offers a plantation for sale.

Johann Dietrich Ott, York, sharpens tools in Lancaster at court time.

Michel Fiseman, one mile from the Blue Mountains, on the Schuylkill.

Belten Kaerper, Allemangel, Bucks County (sic) (Albany Township, Berks County).

September 1, 1750

Peter Schwenk, Old Goshenhoppen, Upper Salford Township (Montgomery County).

Georg Bechtel, New Goshenhoppen, on the Branch (of Perkiomen Creek, Montgomery County).

Georg Joerger, Falckner Swamp (Montgomery County).

Johannes Steiner, Coventry Township, Chester County.

Peter Baal, Macungie (Lehigh County).

September 16, 1750

Christian Mueller, Tinicum, four miles from Durham Furnace (Bucks County), near Conrad Kister, offers a plantation for sale.

Arion Kerckhart, over the Susquehanna, near York, on Creutz Creek, arrived last autumn from Neu Hembspach. He seeks his "Vetter" (cousin or uncle), Velten Kerckhart, who came to this country seven years ago from Reuberem, on the Brem.

Philip Angel, Falckner Swamp (Montgomery County).

Nicolas Bob, Perkasie, Bedminster Township (Bucks County).

Jacob Ulm, Earl Township, Lancaster County.

October 1, 1750

Peter Steger, near Trappe, over the Schuylkill, near Kaiser's mill.

Johann Bosz, Bedminster Township, Bucks County.

Friedrich Hoehn, Heidelberg Township, Lancaster County (now Lebanon).

October 16, 1750

Henrich Christman, linenweaver, from a place two hours from Traarbach, "aus dem Claeninger Kirchspiel," arrived in this country eight or nine years ago, with his family. This year his sister, Maria Margaret, and her husband, Anthon Graeber, a smith, arrived in Conestoga, on Cocalico Creek (Lancaster County), where they are with Johann Nickel Zerrfasz, near the Ephrata Cloister, and they seek news of Henrich.

Thomas Speri arrived in this country twelve years ago. His brother, Nicklaus Speri, arrived this year, and he is in Long Swamp, near Maxatawny (Berks County), with Nicolaus Schwartz, and he seeks Thomas.

Abraham Bauman, servant with Hieronimus Mueller, Conestoga (Lancaster County).

October 16, 1750

Nicolaus Seitzinger, Tulpehocken (Berks County), on the
late Georg Graf's place, offers for rent a plantation the
house on which was heretofore an inn.

Henrich Eberle, on Swatara Creek (Lebanon or Dauphin
County).

Jacob Unterkoffner, near Norris' mill (Norristown).

Henry Funck, Perkasie (Bucks County).

November 1, 1750

Johann Georg Mueller arrived in this country several weeks
ago from Germany and has gone to Goshenhoppen.

John Jones, tanner, Germantown.

Adam Schmell, Falckner Swamp (Montgomery County).

Nicolaus Ickes, Limerick Township, above Trappe (Montgomery County).

November 16, 1750

Leonhart Gesell, Tulpehocken (Berks County), near Conrad
Weiser, inquires for Philip Jacob Reinlaender, tanner, who
formerly lived at Derckem on the Hart.

Georg Adam Weidner, three miles above Thomas Botts'
(Potts') furnace, on Manatawny Creek (Berks County), wants
tilemakers and limeburners.

Sigmund Baserman, Philadelphia, baker, adjoining M.
Hillegas, offers a house for rent.

Georg Shuffert, Long Swamp, near Maxatawny (Berks County).

Jacob Grueszinger, New Goshenhoppen, near Maybury's
furnace.

Peter Conrad, Falckner Swamp (Montgomery County).

December 16, 1750

Jacob Danner, a wheelwright's son from Schaffhausen, arrived in this country last year. His brother, Johann Georg,
arrived this year and seeks Jacob. Johann Georg is with
Christian Benner, in Franconia Township (Montgomery County).

Christopher Krausze, New Goshenhoppen, near Abraham
Mauer's mill, advertises that his filly disappeared. It came
from Gergorius Schultz, Macungie (Lehigh County).

Peter Schicker sells cutlery in Lancaster, adjoining
Caspar Schaffner.

Philip Drumm, Delaware Forks, on the Lehigh, offers land
for sale (Easton).

December 16, 1750

Adam Schausz, miller on Perkiomen Creek in Pawling's mill, offers to sell his mill in Bucks County, at the Forks of the Delaware.

Henrich Deringer, Hanover Township (Probably New Hanover Township, Montgomery County).

Johannes Martin, Goshenhoppen, Upper Hanover (Montgomery County).

Johannes Rothermel, Weidenthal, Upper Oley (Berks County).

Martin Dachebach, Falckner Swamp (Montgomery County).

Paul Schneider, Goshenhoppen.

Daniel Borneman, New Goshenhoppen.

Georg Schoener, Falckner Swamp (Montgomery County).

January 1, 1751

Gottfried Baumgaertner, Battleton Township, on Little Swatara Creek, Lancaster County; wife, Anna Catharina, daughter of Vallentin Kiefer.

Joseph Baernes, Harlem (Horsham?) Township, Philadelphia County, 17 miles from Philadelphia, on Deyer's road, offers a plantation for sale.

Georg Reichman, Tulpehocken (Berks County), with Christian Hoen.

Georg Eberhart, Tulpehocken (Berks County).

Johannes Schmitt, Bowman's lane, Germantown.

Carl Bensel, Germantown, sells medicine.

January 16, 1751

Johann Jacob Reil, Schwartzwald, near Oley (Berks County); wife, Maria Catharina.

Michael Streits, tanner, in the house formerly occupied by Bernhart Roser, Germantown.

February 1, 1751

Sebastian Moser, Upper Hanover, in McCall's Manor (Montgomery County).

Henrich Froelich, Rising Sun, between Philadelphia and Germantown, on Captain Gutman's place.

Vallentin Scherer, near Trappe.

February 16, 1751

Bernhart Dotterer and Georg Joerger, "Vormunder," (guardians, executors?) offer for rent the late Rudolph Marolf's mill, in Colebrookdale Township (Berks County).

Friedrich Bershold, Goshenhoppen; wife, Anna Maria Elisabeth, born Ehrin.

Jacob Wannemacher, Goshenhoppen.

March 1, 1751

Joseph Hart, Newtown, offers for sale a plantation in Upper Milford Township, Bucks County (now Lehigh), the former property of Nicolaus Walbert. Peter Walbert now lives there.

Johannes Lehn, over the Susquehanna, 12 miles from York, offers his place for sale.

Andreas Huck, merchant, Second street, Philadelphia, the third house below William Brenson.

Abraham Bauer, New Goshenhoppen.

Ulrich Scherer, on Saucon Creek.

March 16, 1751

Johann Bartholomae, Philadelphia County, offers to sell a plantation on which there formerly was an Indian town known as Mussicamicken.

Martin Dachenbach, Falckner Swamp, on McCall's land (now Douglass Township, Montgomery County).

Georg Schoener, Falckner Swamp (Montgomery County).

Michel Fabian, above the Delaware Forks (above Easton).

April 1, 1751

Georg Henrich Steinoehl, from Wurtemberg, a smith in Conestoga (Lancaster County), with Christian Weber, near Jacob Bayerle's mill, inquires for his brother-in-law, Gottfried Gruenzweisz, a woolcomber.

Georg Peter Funck, who arrived last autumn from Zweybruecken region and is serving in Germantown with John Jones, tanner, inquires for his cousin, Carl Glaser.

Peter Weidner, in the new town of Roadingtown, on the Schuylkill, wants a brickmaker.

Christophel Frantziscus, Lampeter Township, Lancaster County.

April 16, 1751

Herman Adam, starch and soap maker, Germantown, in Paul Krepner's house, next to Gottfried Lehman, the potter; he also bleaches linen cloth and yarn.

Sarah Mentenhall, administratrix, advertises a public sale of the house and land in York where George Mentenhall formerly lived, well known as an inn.

Johannes Handwerck, Frederick Township (Montgomery County), with Johannes Zieber.

Stephen Benezet died in Germantown on April 1.

May 1, 1751

Hansz Georg Bender, one mile from Frankford, at Point No-Point, on the Delaware (Philadelphia).

Christiana, widow of Henrich Haen, Lampeter Township, Lancaster County.

Georg Wambold, Rockhill Township, Bucks County.

May 16, 1751

Philip Hoch, on Oley road, two miles from Manatawny Creek, in Hanover Township (New Hanover Township, Montgomery County), offers a plantation for sale.

Peter Holtzaeder, Heidelberg Township, three miles from Conrad Weiser's on Tulpehocken Creek, at Johann Nickel's mill, offers a plantation for sale.

Margretha Duermgerm arrived in this country last autumn, with her mother and brother-in-law, Adam Fichs, and she now seeks them. She is at the Glass House.

Robert Jamison, Warwick Township, Bucks County, advertises that his German servant, Adam Layer, 45 years old, ran away.

Johannes Reiffschneider, Douglass Township, Falckner Swamp (Montgomery County).

Jacob Frey, near Perkasie; wife, Maria Elisabeth.

June 1, 1751

Georg Mueller, Lebanon, Hunterdon County, New Jersey, advertises that his German servant, Hansz Jacob Kaaby, 17 years old, ran away. He is reported to have been with Friedrich Eisen and Philip Schaut over the Susquehanna, and they then left for Carolina.

Johannes Keller, a smith, came to this country last autumn, and on the voyage borrowed five doubloons from Johannes Knoerr, who afterwards lived for a time in Philadelphia but is now dead. Keller is requested to send the money to Dorst Knoerr, Reading.

June 1, 1751

Jacob Haszler, who arrived in this country a year and a
half ago, inquires for his brother Bastian. Notify Hansz Zimmerman, Cocalico (Lancaster County).

Jacob Stausz and Nicolaus Lochman, of Germantown, lodged
with Antoni Ceiger, on Manatawny Creek, and while there their
horses disappeared.

June 16, 1751

Jacob Faner, near Dewald Scholas, over the Susquehanna, on
Conewago Creek (York County), seeks his brother, Hansz Georg.

Conrad Berlet, papermaker, of Oley (Berks County); wife,
Anna Maria, born Klasin.

Abraham Maeyer, between Lancaster and Christian Steinman's
mill.

Willem Speck, Oley (Berks County).

Jacob Arndt, Skippack (Montgomery County).

Frantz Rusz, Saucon.

July 16, 1751

Georg Dannehower, miller, at Shellenberger's mill, Germantown.

Mathias Gmaehlin, glazier, Methacton, Worcester Township
(Montgomery County).

Andreas Griminger, Methacton (Montgomery County), near
Matheus Ridenhauszen (Rittenhouse).

April 1, 1751

Maria Magdalena Heldtin two years ago indentured her daughter, Maria Chatarina, to Jacob Eschelman, a smith, two miles
from Lancaster, and she would like to hear from her.

Daniel Weiser, Oley (Berks County), offers a plantation for
sale.

Lenert Gerhart, Methacton, Norriton Township, Philadelphia
County (now Montgomery).

Johannes Naesz, Ridge Valley, Bucks County, Rockhill Township, near Peter Schneider.

Georg Oesterle, Skippack (Montgomery County).

Georg Mayer, Skippack (Montgomery County).

August 16, 1751

Marcus Hulings, Bucks County, near Durham Furnace, advertises that his German servant, Jacob Bender, 45 years old, and his wife ran away. The wife, Catharine, is 30 years old, and they have a child, Michel, 11 months old, who has club feet.

Johannes Boehm, book printer, Philadelphia, died at the end of last month.

Jacob Baer, Hatfield Township, near Montgomery, in Bucks County.

Nicolaus Angene, Perkasie, Bedminster Township (Bucks County).

Peter Drexler, Macungie (Lehigh County).

September 1, 1751

Johann Peter Saeyler, near Falckner Swamp (Montgomery County), near Henrich Deringer's who has been in this country 24 years, seeks his brother Felix, who came from Ruchheim two years ago.

Lightning struck Jacob Beutelman's house, Perkasie, and he was killed.

Sebastian Neff, Springfield, four miles from Germantown (Springfield Township, Montgomery County).

Johannes Bruner, New Goshenhoppen.

Jacob Mayer, Falckner Swamp (Montgomery County).

Christian Gut, Brecknock Township, Lancaster County.

Jacob Baum, Alsace, Berks County; wife, Susanna Margretha.

September 16, 1751

Philip Balthaser Craeszman, Amity Township (Berks County), 44 miles from Philadelphia and 14 miles from Reading, offers for sale a plantation on the road by the Swedes. The White Stag inn is part of the property. Marcus Hulings formerly lived there.

Simon Siron, Second street, Philadelphia, at the sign of the Amsterdam Arms, adjoining William Clemm, offers for sale a house and lot on Skippack road, next to Michel Klein's plantation.

Christian Loeser, Plymouth, one mile from Plymouth Meeting House (Montgomery County).

Samuel Mackel (McCall), living in Germantown and Philadelphia.

Christian Fischer, upper end of Germantown.

October 1, 1751

Johann Henrich Junghenn, unmarried, of Tinicum (Bucks County), expects to go to Germany. Commissions for him may be forwarded to Johannes Zacharias, tanner, Germantown.

Nicolaus Seitzinger, Tulpehocken (Berks County), gives notice that as his wife has died he is going to Germany.

Magdalena Haussmanin arrived in this country last year and indentured her children, but received no papers. Her sons are Daniel Loedy, 24 years old, and Hansz Loedy, 13 years old. The mother seeks information about them. She is with Hansz Adam Schneider, near Schnecker's mill, Conestoga (Lancaster County).

Johann Adam Dock, tailor, left Anweiler, near Landau, ten years ago. Her sister, Anna Margretha, with her second husband, Jacob Werth, arrived in this country two years ago, and she seeks her brother. She is at Trappe.

October 16, 1751

Daniel Hiester, tanner, Goshenhoppen (Montgomery County).

Rudolph Hoch, Hanover Township, saddler.

November 1, 1751

Herman Arndt arrived in this country 19 years ago from Hanau, with his three sons, Peter, Michel and Jacob, and a daughter, Anna Maria. His son Henrich, a stockingweaver, arrived this year, and he seeks the other members of the family. He is living near the Reformed Church in Philadelphia.

Gertraut Engelin, living with Nicolaus Kern, at the Blue Mountains, inquires for her brother, Johann Jacob Engel, who arrived in this country ten years ago from Mandel.

Jacob Haege (Hagy), papermaker, near Germantown, advertises that two of his servants ran away--Daniel Maeckardy and Johannes Lantzel, the latter a German 17 years old.

Christophel Rabin, Three Tuns inn, six miles outside Germantown, in Whitemarsh Township (Montgomery County), advertises that his German servant, Alexander Schuetz, ran away.

Ulrich Neff, born at Zeil, in Zurich Gebieth, is going to Switzerland. Commissions for him may be left in Germantown, with Georg Schmitt, in the late Bauman's house.

Augustin Neisser, clockmaker, at the lower end of Germantown.

November 16, 1751

Detrich Ramsauer, near Trappe, one mile from the Lutheran Church, offers a plantation for sale.

Vallentin Schales, near Rising Sun, between Philadelphia and Germantown, with Mr. Kirchhof.

November 16, 1751

Georg Miltenberger, Kensington, near Philadelphia.

Herman Lor, New Goshenhoppen.

December 16, 1751

Hansz Michel Beymueller, of Schoen-Eich, wrote to Germany five years ago urging his wife's relatives to come to America. Maria Chatarina Braunin, from Schoen-Eich, has arrived in this country and seeks Beymueller. She is with Matheus Kaiser, Germantown.

Johannes Steinman, Lancaster County, near Mr. Wright's ferry, in the Susquehanna, advertises that his German servant, Johannes Ritweiler, 16 years old, ran away. The boy's father is Michel Ritweiler, living in the Swamp.

Johann Christoph Ohle, furrier, upper end of Germantown, near Friedrich Hesser, the baker.

Peter Miller, bookseller, Germantown.

January 1, 1752

Hansz Georg Schneider, from Gilstein, in Herrnberger Amt, last spring in Germany loaned a sum of money to a neighbor, Christian Ruffer. They came to Pennsylvania on different ships. Schneider lives on the Ridge (Ridge avenue, Philadelphia), near Johannes Butterweck, near Germantown, and he seeks Ruffer.

Johann Jost Eigenbrod, living in Frederick County, Maryland, on Monocacy Creek, understands his sister, Sophia Elisabeth Eigenbrodin, arrived in this country last year, and he seeks information about her.

Henrich Riedt, Old Goshenhoppen (Montgomery County), offers to sell or rent a mill on Perkiomen Creek and 100 acres.

Johannes Schwing, Frederick Township (Montgomery County), offers a plantation for sale, one mile from Grafen mill.

January 16, 1752

Henrich Settler, Frederick Township, near Falckner Swamp (Montgomery County).

February 1, 1752

Johann Ludwig Spiesz, tailor, near Lancaster.

Conrad Reich, Shenandoah (Virginia).

Johann Georg Hoffman, with Henrich Schenck, Conestoga (Lancaster County).

Johann Henrich Weidman, care of Huber, Conestoga (Lancaster County).

February 1, 1752

Andreas Schaub, linenweaver, Conestoga (Lancaster County).

Johann Peter Rabensberger, Conestoga (Lancaster County).

Johannes and Christian Huber, Conestoga (Lancaster County).

Johannes Krausz, unmarried, tailor, with Jacob Hackman, Skippack (Montgomery County).

Hansz Georg Bergman, tailor, Roxborough (Philadelphia).

Johann Georg Schlicher, New Goshenhoppen.

Maria Agnesz Hoffmaennin, with Altdoerffer, three miles from Henrich Deringer.

Johann Henrich Hoffman, with Joh. Matheus Schmitt, Anweil (New Jersey).

Johann Adam Fuchs, with Christian Klein or Marinus Schmitt, Falckner Swamp (Montgomery County).

Johann Henrich Fuchs, Falckner Swamp (Montgomery County).

Christian Klein, carpenter, Falckner Swamp (Montgomery County).

Wilhelm Hoechstenbach, Raritan or Rahway (New Jersey).

Christoph Nagel, Falckner Swamp (Montgomery County).

Johann Georg Sauerbier, Oley (Berks County).

Johann Jacob Wetzel, Great Swamp (Bucks County).

Conrad Seibel, Skippack (Montgomery County).

Henrich Bachman, Saucon.

Casper Holtzhauer, New Goshenhoppen.

Abraham Drantsu, Goshenhoppen.

Johann Philip Wirthmann, Blue Mountains.

Abraham Landes, Perkasie.

Johann Jacob Hippel, Trappe.

Matheus Hollebach and Matheus Reichert offer for sale a plantation in Hanover Township, in Falckner Swamp, on the road from Philadelphia to Oley (Montgomery County), where the late Georg Schoener lived. The house has been an inn for many years.

Jacob Storck arrived last autumn from Alsace, from Ritters-Hofen, in the Hattner-Amt. His mother, Anna Maria Storckin, with her son Dewald and daughter Anna Maria, arrived this autumn and they are free of passage costs. They seek Jacob. They are with Johannes Kuhn, near the Reformed Church, Philadelphia.

February 1, 1752

Johann Gottschalck, Skippack, in Hatfield Township (Montgomery County), advertises that his apprentice, Jacob Knausz, 16 years old, ran away.

Sebastian Beisch, Durham road, seven miles below Durham Furnace (Bucks County), offers his plantation for sale.

Johann Nicolaus Kreszmann, a quarter mile from the upper end of Germantown, back of the Lutheran Church, offers his place for sale or rent.

March 1, 1752

Johann Friedrich Vigera, Arch street, Philadelphia, opposite the Academy, between Fourth and Fifth streets, sells books.

Johannes Mueller, from Knillingen, son of a gold refiner, arrived in America 16 years ago. This autumn his brother Andreas arrived and he seeks Johannes. Andreas is with Paul Koester, Skippack (Montgomery County).

Susanna Dusiusin, widow, formerly of Schoharie (New York), later of Germantown, is asked to communicate with Mr. Brunnholtz, Philadelphia.

April 1, 1752

Johannes Becker, Paradise Run, over the Susquehanna, three hours from York.

Johann Jost Zimmerman, over the Susquehanna, in Virginia, twelve hours from Bergstrasz.

Wilhelm Hoffman, over the Susquehanna, Paradise Township, York County.

Christian Freindel, Germantown.

Daniel Schneider came from Nassau-Siegischen two years ago. Two brothers, Caspar and Hansz Henrich, arrived last autumn and are living in Anweil (N.J.), near Peter Jung, together with their brother-in-law, Anton Stutt. Stutt also has news for Henrich Hartman, who arrived in America two years ago, from Nassau-Siegenischen.

Johannes Mack, Goshenhoppen, wants a smith.

Ludwig Steffen, Frederick County, Virginia, has land for sale.

Friedrich Schell, on Little Saucon Creek.

April 16, 1752

Johann Detier, Stockingweaver, lower Germantown, advertises that his servant, Zacharias Jordan, native born, 18 years old, ran away.

April 16, 1752

Johann Peter Klump, tailor, near the Reformed Church, Germantown; wife, Hanetta Amalia.

Joseph Hart, sheriff of Bucks County, advertises the sale of the grist mill and 200 acres in Heidelberg Township, belonging to Georg Croner, at Johannes Drechsler's, Macungie, on execution of Henrich Kepler and Johannes Hambrecht.

Henrich Mueller, from Switzerland, Zurich Gebiet, arrived in America eight years ago, with his daughters, Regely and Elisabeth, and they were separated. Elisabeth is with Peter Zimmerman, at Swamp, and will be free in the autumn of next year. She seeks news of her father and sister.

Daniel Womelsdorff, Oley (Berks County), advertises for a papermaker to operate his mill on shares.

Friedrich Erb, joiner, North Wales (Gwynedd, Montgomery County).

Christian Brechviel's widow, Swatara.

Christian Reidenbach, Weidenthal (Berks County).

Joh. Jacob Gertenhayer, Macungie (Lehigh County).

Philip Wentz, Old Goshenhoppen (Montgomery County).

May 1, 1752

Anna Maria Wolfelspergerin, born Heimbergerin, on the voyage to America placed her clothing in the custody of Philip Ernst Wagner, white nailsmith, from Wurtemberg, Mockmuhler Amt. She seeks information about him. She is with Christian Buechsler, Cocalico Township, one mile from Hansz Bucher (Lancaster County).

Johann Conrad Spiesz, Kreisz Creek.

May 16, 1752

Friedrich Eschbach and Johannes Hugel are going to Germany after the harvest. They will take letters if forwarded to Johannes Eschbach or Johannes Hugel, Falckner Swamp (Montgomery County).

Georg Voegele, Oley Hills (Berks County); wife Catharina.

June 1, 1752

Johann Michel Immel, Manheim Township, Lancaster County, advertises that his servant, Lenert Merckel, 40 years old, ran away. He has friends in Skippack (Montgomery County).

Friedrich Hertzog, Upper Salford, Ridge Valley (Montgomery County), offers to sell a mill and farm.

Philip Meth, Tulpehocken Township (Berks County); wife Anna Maria.

June 1, 1752

Anthony Neuhaus, merchant, Germantown, opposite Holtzappel.

June 16, 1752

The late Peter Koch's plantation at Chestnut Hill (above Germantown), next to Wigart Miller, is for sale, with an adjacent paper mill, several houses and 200 acres.

Leonhart von Rufft, Colebrookdale Township (Berks County), with John Potts.

Hansz Gnaege, Bethel Township (Berks County), advertises that he bought 250 acres from Michael Theisz, Tulpehocken, and gave him bonds, but a disagreement ensued and he will not pay the bonds.

James Lennox, over the Susquehanna, on Beaver Creek, thirteen miles from York, northwest toward Carlisle, on the Great road, offers a plantation at public sale.

Gottfried Reichert, from Staedten unterm Heuchelberg, has heard that his father, Martin Reichert, has arrived in America and wishes to hear from him.

Georg Becker, Kensington (Philadelphia); wife, Elisabeth.

Michel Fischer, Alsace (Berks County); wife, Anna Margretha.

July 1, 1752

Georg Joerger and Bernhart Dotterer, Executors, offer for sale a mill in Colebrookdale (Berks County), two miles from Potts' iron works, where the late Rudolph Marolff lived.

Johannes Landes, Colebrookdale, near John Potts (Berks County).

Henry Schreffler, oil mill, near Germantown.

July 16, 1752

Henry Schellenberger and Rudolph Sorber, executors, offer for sale the mill of the late Casper Meyer, near Germantown.

Johann Schutzmann was shot and killed last Wednesday in Bern Township (Berks County), by Michael Renner, who mistook Schutzmann for a deer at a salt lick.

August 16, 1752

Anna Longstreth, Warminster Township, Bucks County, advertises that her German servant, Eva Maria Naegelin, 33 years old, ran away.

Cornelius Bogert, innkeeper, Raritan (N.J.), advertises that his German servant, Henrich Theodorus Tettman, ran away.

August 16, 1752

Johannes Martin, five miles above Trappe, over the Schuyl-kill, near Simon Schunck (Chester County), is going to Germany for the autumn fair. Commissions for him may be left with Johannes Utzman, Lancaster, or Jacob Kern, Reading.

Peter Reinhart, Old Goshenhoppen, on Perkiomen Creek (Montgomery County).

Georg Weisel, Perkasie, on the Branch (of Perkiomen Creek), Rockhill Township (Bucks County).

Leonhart Reber, on the Andoloni, in Wentzler Township (Windsor Township, Berks County?).

Hansz Martin Gehrig, Exeter, Berks County.

September 16, 1752

Jacob Graf, Second street, Philadelphia, mason, advertises that his German servant, Leonhart Sommer, 23 years old, ran away.

Jacob Craffert (Crawford) has rented a fulling mill on Wissahickon Creek from William Rittenhouse. It was built by Mathias Englis.

Anna Barbara Braeunischoltzerin, Great Swamp, near Michel Eberhart, came to America with her son, Hansz Adam Braeuni-scholtz. The son was indentured to a German named Jacob Frey, who cannot now be found, and the mother seeks information about him.

Peter Eberhart, on Neshaminy Creek, in Hetfort (Hatfield?) Township (Montgomery County), bought Friedrich Gotz's plan-tation and gave bonds, which are now in dispute.

Jacob Ziegenfusz, Rockhill Township, Bucks County.

Peter Knecht, Lower Saucon (Northampton County).

October 1, 1752

Philip Henrich Hauptman, Allemangel (Albany Township, Berks County), in the Blue Mountains.

Johannes Willems, Oley (Berks County).

Elias Heszle, Goshenhoppen.

Abraham Hiestand, Great Swamp, Bucks County, offers his plantation for sale.

Christian Rincker, Lower Saucon Township, Northampton County.

Dietrich Ramsauer, New Providence, near Trappe, offers for sale the plantation where he now lives.

October 16, 1752

Johannes Zacharias, tanner, administrator of the late Johannes Grasz (Grace), tanner, Germantown.

Conrad Schweitzer, Chestnut Hill (above Germantown), one mile from Conrad Bartsch, near Johannes Schaeffer.

David Sutter, upper end of Germantown.

Georg Oesterle, Skippack, Franconia Township, Philadelphia County (now Montgomery), on the Branch of Perkiomen Creek, offers a plantation for sale.

Moritz Lorentz, Colebrookdale, on the Catholic pastor's place. (Bally, Berks County).

Philip Ziegler, Upper Salford Township, Philadelphia County (now Montgomery).

November 1, 1752

Johannes Birckelbach, on Cocalico Creek (Lancaster County).

Conrad Frick, upper end of Germantown.

Johann Peter Herpel, Oley (Berks County).

Jacob Wetzel, New Goshenhoppen.

Jacob Henrich Hoffman, Tulpehocken (Berks County).

Andreas Wind, Great Swamp (Bucks County).

Johannes Feit, Blue Mountains.

Johann Caspar Repp, Maxatawny (Berks County).

Maria Johanna Benderin, widow, arrived in America five years ago, with three daughters, Maria Margretha, Apollonia and Christina. The daughters have served their time, and Maria, who is with Henrich Zimmerman, Conestoga (Lancaster County), seeks her mother.

Johannes Eckroth, Allemangel (Albany Township), Berks County, in the Blue Mountains.

Vallentin Vogd, Falckner Swamp (Montgomery County), near Henrich Deringer.

Johannes Graeszman, Rockhill Township (Bucks County), on the Branch of Perkiomen Creek.

Simon Geres, Springfield (Township, Montgomery County), on North Wales road (now Bethlehem pike).

Christopher Yaeckel, New Goshenhoppen.

Hansz Habbecker, Warwick.

November 16, 1752

Henrich Weisz, Great Swamp, bought 160 acres from Hansz Baer, unmarried, on the Northkill, in the Blue Mountains. Now there is a dispute about the deed.

John Maeckledery, Whitpain Township, Philadelphia County (now Montgomery).

Jacob Bildman, from Bietigheim, five miles from Stuttgart, is going to Germany. Commissions for him may be left with Michel Ege, Philadelphia. Jacob Bildman seeks his brother, Christoph Samuel, a smith, who has been in America two years.

Stephen Reppert, Oley Hills (Berks County), between Loescher's and Mayberry furnaces.

Michel Seider, Saucon.

Casper Dorst, Heidelberg Township.

Jeremias Baer, Bern Township (Berks County).

December 1, 1752

Georg Adam Weidner, on Manatawny Creek, three miles above Potts' furnace (Berks County), wants a limeburner and brick and tile maker.

Peter Schmitt, on Little Swatara Creek, advertises that his German servant, Johanna Busch, ran away.

Johannes David Albrecht, stockingweaver, arrived in America last year and left his wife, who was in confinement, with friends. Now he cannot be found. Information about him may be sent to Peter Schneider, Rockhill Township, Bucks County.

Jacob Rindy, New Goshenhoppen.

December 16, 1752

Henrich Schaaf, living with Christophel Heumacher, on the Little Lehigh, "in der Schmaltzgasz," had his brother come to America this year, and he finds in the Philadelphia mayor's book that the brother, Friedrich Schaaf, was indentured to Johannes Bauman, whose place of residence is not given. Henrich Schaaf seeks information about Bauman.

Simon Haasz, tailor, Hosensack (Lehigh County).

Joh. Georg Kop, Blue Mountains.

Anna Maria Soffina, Falckner Swamp (Montgomery County).

Peter Binckhart, over the Lehigh.

Adam Hillegass, Goshenhoppen (Montgomery County).

Jacob Koch, near Trappe.

Wilhelm Kassel, New Goshenhoppen.

38   GERMAN SETTLERS OF PENNSYLVANIA

April 1, 1753

Alexander Zartman, Warwick Township, Lancaster County, advertises that two of his servants ran away--Michael Fahner, 24 years old, and his wife, both Wurtembergers.

Johannes Pampus, school teacher in Anweil (N.J.), seeks Johannes Flender and Johann Jacob Trumbach, from Nassau Siegenischen. Inform Peter Jung or Wilhelm Kaesz, Anweil.

Ulrich Gaebi, one mile from Mayberry's furnace (Green Lane, Montgomery County).

David Schaeffer, Second street, Philadelphia, where Christian Schneider formerly lived.

Johannes Wildanger, Bedminster Township, on Tohickon Creek (Bucks County).

Wilhelm Jung, adjoining Michael Ege, Philadelphia.

Jacob Eigner, Macungie (Lehigh County).

May 16, 1753

Johannes Eigender, Egypt, Northampton County (now Lehigh County).

Jacob Mechling and Samuel Mechling offer for sale the plantation of their father, the late Jacob Mechling, in Colebrookdale Township, Berks County, near Thomas Potts' furnace.

Henrich Rosenberger, near Skippack Creek in Franconia Township (Montgomery County), advertises that his German servant, Maria Magdalena Wernerin, 24 years old, ran away.

Henrich Klein, Quitapahilla, Lebanon Township, Lancaster County (now Lebanon County), advertises that his German servant, Johannes Scherer, 40 years old, ran away.

Catharina Gehlerin, 22 years old, was indentured off the ship last autumn. Her parents seek her.

Henrich Brunner, joiner, Upper Saucon (Lehigh County).

Johann Roeszner, Upper Saucon, Northampton County (now Lehigh).

Philip Lau and Christian Lau, brothers, Manchester Township, York County, advertise that their German servant, Jacob Dinninger, ran away. He is a miller and was born in Neustadt an den Linden.

Christopher Heumacher, Macungie (Lehigh County).

Daniel Lefever, Lampeter Township, Lancaster County, advertises that his German servant, Johannes Haasz, 18 years old, ran away.

Simon Reichert arrived in America last autumn and is with Vallentin Jung, Upper Saucon (Lehigh County). He understands his daughter, Christina Reichertin, is in service in Conestoga (Lancaster County), and he wants to hear from her.

May 16, 1753

Adam Bach, Quitopahilla, Lebanon Township, Lancaster County (Now Lebanon County).

Widow Maebry (Mayberry), New Hanover Township (Montgomery County), offers a plantation for sale, formerly the property of Philip Kaercher. Information may be had from Bernhart Iserloh, on Pennypack Creek, at the stone bridge (Philadelphia).

Simon Schneider, near Georg Graf, Lancaster.

August 1, 1753

Theobald End, saddler, offers a house for sale at the lower end of Germantown, the former residence of Bernhart Roser, baker.

October 16, 1753

Juliana Fellenzerin, of Creutzenach, came to America ten years ago and was with Jacob Bauman, Germantown. She married a tailor named Wolff, and they went to the Blue Mountains. Her brother, Johannes Feltzer, arrived last year, and awaits news about her at Bastian Neff's--Schuh Bastel--at the Crown tavern, outside Germantown.

Peter Werle has resumed business as landlord of the Red Ox inn, at the lower end of Germantown, his license having been renewed.

Johannes Baumann, dealer in Rifles and guns, Germantown.

Januray 16, 1754

Johannes Schnell, Stone Arabia (New York), warns the public against his son-in-law, Johannes Werning, formerly pastor in New York, who is believed to have gone to Maryland or Virginia.

Friedrich Steiner, Coventry Township, Chester County; wife, Depy (Deborah).

Johannes Holtz, Race street, Philadelphia, adjoining John Roots, advertises a plantation for rent on Ridge road, between Germantown and the Schuylkill.

Georg Steinruck, New Hanover, on the Manor Land (McCall's Manor, now Douglass Township, Montgomery County).

Georg Hoffman, Egypt, on the Jordan (Lehigh County), advertises that his German servant, Jacob Werth, 40 years old, ran away.

Georg Leydy, Skippack, offers a plantation for sale in Northampton County, four miles from Easton, near Johannes Roth's. Information may be had from Nicolaus Baest or Henrich Arndt, near the place.

Vallentin Marter, from Guentzenheim, now with Martin Fritz, Manatawny, at the White Horse, with the Swedes (Berks County), will be free in the spring; he seeks Michel Oberle.

January 16, 1754

Andreas Schmitt, Falckner Swamp (Montgomery County), advertises that his German servant, Susanna Elzertin, ran away. She is from the Isenburg region.

Hartwig Arndt, Canajoharie, New York, advertises that his German servant, Johann Wendel Beylstein, ran away. He is a tailor, 21 years old.

Michael Fischer, Alsace Township (Berks County); wife, Anna Margretha.

Daniel Schweitzer, Coventry Township, Chester County.

Matheus Schlauch, Lancaster.

February 1, 1754

Erhart Gloesz, smith, near Lancaster, on the road past Peter Eby's mill, has information that Henrich Knoblauch has arrived in America with an important letter for him, and he urges Knoblauch to forward the letter.

Martin Schroeder's stepson, Peter Wannebach, is in service with Michael Drachel, on the Great Lehigh. He seeks information about his parents.

Johannes Hochman, Oley Hills (Berks County), near Jacob Schmitt.

Herman Muehlheim, Morris County, New Jersey.

Georg Joerger, New Hanover Township (Montgomery County).

Georg Grund, Weissenberg Township (Lehigh County).

February 16, 1754

Rosina Dorothea Rostin, born Kauffmaennin, from Waldenburg aus dem Hohenlohischen, arrived at Petepsco November 12, 1753, on the ship of Captain Rattray, and was sold at vendue. She has a brother-in-law in Conestoga (Lancaster County), named Spahr, a wheelwright, and a sister, Maria Catharina, and she seeks information about them, which may be sent to John Jansen, merchant, Annapolis (Maryland).

Walter McCool offers for sale his plantation of more than 200 acres in Rockhill Township, Bucks County, at Pleasant Spring Creek, adjoining lands of Johannes Funck and Adam Dauny.

Martin Schneider, thoroughly trained watchmaker, born in Nurnberg, and Johann End, clockmaker, trained here, have formed a partnership to sell old and new clocks and repair clocks and watches, in Germantown, with Theobold End, saddler.

Johann Georg Schneider opens an apothecary shop in the German style on Race street, near Second, Philadelphia.

Jacob Steiger (Styer), Methacton (Montgomery County), adminstrator of the estate of his brother, Stephanus Steiger.

February 16, 1754

Caspar Heiszer, North Wales road, near the Bell inn, gave
security for his brother Peter, unmarried, and seeks information about him.

March 16, 1754

Johannes Geschwind, medical doctor, Goshenhoppen (Montgomery County), next to Dietrich Bauman and Friedrich Hillegass.

Henrich Wolff, Alsace Township, Berks County, advertises
that his Dutch servant, Henrich Kuhlmueller, 37 years old, ran
away.

Gottfried Langenbein, Limerick Township, Philadelphia
County (now Montgomery).

Nicolaus Reckser, Hereford Township, Berks County.

Michael Schwab, York, offers a plantation for sale.

April 1, 1754

Leonhart Abel, Chestnut-Haycock Township, Bucks County,
above Tohickon Creek, advertises that his German servant, Peter
Winckler, ran away, taking along his wife, Anna Maria, and their
2-year-old child.

Johann Phillipp Drietsch, from the Darmstadt region, arrived in America 12 months ago, with his son, Johann Jacob. The
son is in Anweil (N.J.), with Justus Gansz, and seeks his
father.

Friedrich Becker, Exeter Township, Berks County, advertises that his servant, Johannes Hertun, ran away.

Jonas Koehler, innkeeper, outside Philadelphia, died.

June 16, 1754

Jost Pfannekucken gives notice that those who bought goods
at the vendue of the property of the late Christoffel Trube,
Hilltown Township, Bucks County, should make payment.

Catharina Hackerin, indentured a year and a half ago, is
sought by her father, Johannes Hacker, Tulpehocken (Berks
County), with Conrad Fellebaum.

Henrich Pannebecker died recently, aged 81 years. Many
books had been borrowed from him. Those who have these books
are asked to return them to Peter Pannebecker or Cornelius
Theiszen.

Georg Etter, wheelwright, in the White Oak Land, Rapho
Township, Lancaster County, seeks his son Christian, who was
indentured in Philadelphia several years ago to Wilhelm Mueller,
in the Jerseys.

June 16, 1754

Adam Wittman, Reading, offers for sale a grist mill on Muddy Creek, eight miles from Reading.

Christian Wagemann, Vincent Township, Chester County; wife, Elisabeth, born Leibgebin.

Ernst Juncken, Third street, Philadelphia, near Anton Armbruster.

Michel Graether, Reading, advertises that his German servant, Martin Klemm, ran away.

Conrad Kramer, Bensel's lane, Germantown.

Andreas Hertz, Salisbury Township, Lancaster County.

July 16, 1754

His widow continues the business of the late Johannes Zacharias, tanner, Germantown.

Johannes Busch, near Peter Schmitt, on Little Swatara Creek.

Johann Albrecht Hackenmueller, windlassmaker, Second street, Philadelphia, near Lenert Melcher.

Stephen Onjon advertises that two German servants ran away from his furnace on Gunpowder River, Maryland--Nicolaus Gaerdner, 35 years old, and Conrad Haenz, 23 years old.

Johannes Hiestand, five miles from Lancaster toward the Susquehanna.

Vallentin Schalles removes his board yard in Philadelphia from Adam Andreas' wharf to Michel Hillegas' wharf.

Christopher Zimmer, Lebanon Township, Lancaster County (now Lebanon County), offers his plantation for sale.

David Davis, Charlestown, Chester County, advertises that his German servant, Johann Adam Herner, 22 years old, ran away.

Eberhart Martin, soapboiler, Reading.

Leonard Froelich, Bensel's lane, Germantown.

Christoph Schneider, Anweil (New Jersey).

August 1, 1754

Jacob Reinier, merchant, arrived from Switzerland with medicines last autumn, and they are for sale in Reading in Peter Haas' house, on the Market Place.

Martin Kirschner, Bern Township, Berks County, advertises that his servant ran away--Anna Margretha Muellerin, born Bambergerin, 34 years old.

August 1, 1754

Philip Boehm, Whitpain Township, Philadelphia County (now Montgomery), advertises his plantation of 100 acres for sale.

Friedrich Becker, Second street, Philadelphia, near Daniel Mackenet, coppersmith.

Adam Wissenant, Heidelberg Township, Berks County.

Lorentz Rothermel, Blue Mountains, four miles above Messillemer mill, advertises that his German servant, Jacob Brandt, 19 years old, ran away.

Dilman Kolb the younger, Perkiomen and Skippack Township (now Skippack Township, Montgomery County).

David Daeschler, Market street, Philadelphia, dealer in paint and hardware.

Friedrich Stein, Lancaster, advertises that his German servant, Philip Andreas Pitzler, ran away. He is a saddler, 28 years old.

William Maeckenait, Upper Freehold, Monmouth County (New Jersey), advertises that his servant, Balthes Speckholtz, 25 years old, ran away.

Joseph Williams, Merion Township, on Lancaster road (Lower Merion Township, Montgomery County), near the Hart tavern, advertises that his German servant, Friedrich Wandel, 19 years old, ran away.

Jacob Rauw, Allemangel, Hill Township (Albany Township, Berks County).

Michel Huber, Upper Hanover Township (Montgomery County).

Johannes Schwind, Easton.

September 1, 1754

Georg Martin Wagner, Rockhill Township, Bucks County, advertises that his brother Johannes, a victim of epilepsy, has wandered away.

Ulrich Eckler, York Township, offers to sell his plantation of 311 acres, eight miles from York, on Creutz Creek, Apply to Henrich Lebart, miller, Creutz Creek.

Peter Schertz, Bart Township, Lancaster County, advertises that his German servant, Efrosina (Eva Rosina) Barbara Groszin, 35 years old, ran away.

Anthony Taeschler, Market street, Philadelphia, opposite the prison, sells saddler ware.

Johannes Graf, Frederick Township, Old Goshenhoppen (Montgomery County).

Paulus Gorner, locksmith, Lancaster, near the prison, in the old locksmith's shop.

September 1, 1754

   Johannes Neuer, Allemangel (Albany Township, Berks County).

   Peter Holl, Great Swamp, Bucks County.

November 16, 1754

   Henrich Weitzel, Hatfield Township, Philadelphia County (now Montgomery), living on Jan Henrich's place, arrived in this country three years ago with his brother Dietrich. They were separated, and Henrich now seeks Dietrich.

   Jacob Mueller, "in Maidenhaet," with Johannes Enerson, inquires for his sister, Rosina Muellerin, who arrived in this country five years ago from Undinge, Amt Anrach, Wurtemberg.

   Isaac Meyer and Jacob Rubeley, Conestoga Township, Lancaster County, advertise that two servants ran away--Jacob Huber, German, 25 years old, and Johannes Bragon, 25 years old, formerly of Mount Holly, New Jersey.

   Jacob Lang, near Hereford Township, Oley Hills (Berks County).

   Daniel Hamm, Oley Hills, Berks County, near Hereford Township.

   Tobias Joerger, Douglass Township, McCall's Land (Montgomery County).

   Johannes Niebel, on Pennypack Creek, Lower Dublin Township, Philadelphia County.

   Georg Mueller, Lebanon Township, Hunterdon County, New Jersey; wife, Christina.

   Samuel Speicher, Hempfield Township, four miles from Lancaster in Manheim Township.

   Jacob Brubacher, two miles from Lancaster in Manheim Township.

   Balser Laar, Lower Saucon Township, Northampton County.

   Adam Gottwold, Skippack (Montgomery County).

   Adam-Liebegut, Falckner Swamp (Montgomery County).

   Jacob Pfeiffer, three miles from Lancaster.

   Elias Hessle, Lower Saucon (Northampton County).

   Michel Huber, Upper Hanover (Montgomery County).

December 1, 1754

   Bernhart Roser, two miles from Germantown, in Bristol Township, on York road, conducts the tannery formerly operated by his son-in-law, Krafft Richstein.

   Johannes Meyer, butcher, near James Delaplaine, Germantown.

December 1, 1754

Johannes Schimel, Falckner Swamp (Montgomery County), advertises that his German servant, Friedrich Hess, a toolsmith, ran away.

Johann Wilhelm Gebhard, shoemaker, arrived in this country three years ago. His parents arrived this year, and they seek their son. Notify Pastor Handschuh, Germantown.

Nicolaus Frantz, Upper Saucon, Northampton County (now Lehigh).

Johannes Frantz, Cocalico Township, Lancaster County.

Lorentz Croy, Maxatawny (Berks County).

Jacob Hetzler, Tulpehocken (Berks County).

December 16, 1754

Johannes Herpel, Trappe, New Providence Township, Philadelphia County (now Montgomery), advertises that his German servant, Bernhard Zimmermann, 17 years old, ran away.

Daniel Meyberg, a smith, arrived in this country 18 years ago. His brother, Friedrich Meyberg, arrived this autumn, having passed through the East Indies and Holland, and he seeks his brother. Friedrich is at Deep Run, Perkasie (Bucks County), with Abraham Schwartz.

Lorentz Spindler, tailor, Lancaster County, near Hantz Ulrich Huber and Jacob Huber, seeks his brother, Philip David Spindler, who arrived in this country in 1752. He is a sievemaker from Halle.

Ulrich Krafftberger arrived in this country two years ago. His sister, Anna Barbara Krafftbergerin, with Conrad Schwartz, Lancaster, inquires for her brother.

January 1, 1755

Johannes Kresz, on the Great Lehigh at Egypt (Lehigh County), hatmaker; wife, Catharina, widow of Friedrich Eberhart.

Adam Krames, Upper Milford Township, Northampton County (now Lehigh).

Simon Henrich Hoecker, at Cocalico Mill (Lancaster County).

Christopher Weber, Swedes ford, over the Schuylkill (Montgomery County).

Henrich Denig, Skippack (Montgomery County), near Isaac Klein.

Henrich Kollicker, on the Swatara.

Johann Michel Jost, one mile from Blaesz Bayer.

January 16, 1755

Ulrich Hagemann, called the Hussar, died suddenly in Germantown the last day of 1754, in his 84th year. He had no children.

Matheus Schaeuffele, Old Goshenhoppen (Montgomery County), took over the plantation of his father-in-law, Ludwig Lehmann, and gave his brother-in-law, Jacob Keller, a bond for £100. He has now returned the plantation to Lehmann, and issues warning against payment on the bond.

Nicholas Kressmann, Philadelphia, near the Lutheran Church, has a plantation for sale near Germantown.

Peter Hahn, formerly of Northampton County, has left his home, and Christian Heidel has attached his property. The creditors are to meet in Christoph Wagner's house, Lower Saucon.

Anthony Eckel, Easton, has left his home, and Johann Fricker has attached his property. The creditors are to meet at Peter Ketlin's, Easton.

Moses Herman, Reading, dealer in dry goods and groceries.

February 1, 1755

Philip Schrack, near Trappe, New Providence Township (Montgomery County), early in 1752 permitted his servant, Margreta Haaszin, to seek a new master or pay him £12, 10s, whereupon she disappeared.

Johann Guenter, West Chester, above New York, advertises that his German servant, David Laetscher, a tailor, ran away.

Adam Herman moved out of Pennsylvania owing debts. Georg Welcher attached £15, 12s of Herman's inheritance. Creditors are asked to appear at the house of Henry Antes, Philadelphia County.

Ludwig Lauman, Lancaster, near the court house, sells books and other merchandise.

Johannes Bohn and Georg Heyl, shoemaker, at the glass house.

Johannes Bauszen, Upper Salford Township (Montgomery County).

Johannes Mansz, Allemangel (Albany Township, Berks County).

Johannes Heill, Falckner Swamp (Montgomery County).

Velten Alt, Falckner Swamp (Montgomery County).

Baltzer Fueller, Frederick Township (Montgomery County).

Johannes Mueller, Heidelberg Township.

Nicolaus Maesz and Henrich Maesz have disappeared, and Christian Huegel has attached their property. Creditors are to appear at Christian Huegel's house, Lower Saucon, Northampton County.

February 1, 1755

Christian Schenck, Conestoga, on Pequea Creek (Lancaster County), advertises that his German servant, Adam Weber, 16 years old, ran away. He arrived in this country last autumn.

Georg Ruth, tailor, Whitemarsh (Montgomery County), on Tulpehocken road, next to Mr. Kittler's great house, offers his plantation for sale.

Henrich Neff, Manor Township, five miles from Lancaster.

Henrich Dier, Oley Hills, Berks County.

March 1, 1755

Martin Beck, dyer, upper end of Germantown, at Peter Leibert's, the turner, second house below Anthony Gilbert, landlord of the Crown inn.

Christophel Jacobi, Bettelhausen (Beggarstown, at the upper end of Germantown), merchant.

Georg Gaertner went to Germany last year and has returned through Virginia, Maryland and Philadelphia, and is now at Tulpehocken with Conrad Weiser. He has a stockingweaving frame for Adam Edelman, unmarried, stockingweaver.

Johann Schaub, from Zanszingen or Basel, arrived in this country with his brother Martin. Both were indentured and were separated. Johann is with Moses Peters, in Montgomery Township (Montgomery County), and he seeks Martin.

Philip Weiler, a mason, three of whose fingers on the left hand are missing, arrived in this country in 1753 and was sold to a German in New Jersey. His parents, living near Ephrata, inquire for him.

Peter Jung, Nockamixon Township, Bucks County, advertises that his German servant, William Conrad, ran away.

Philip Engert, Upper Dublin Township (Montgomery County), above Farmar's mill.

Georg Doerr, Heidelberg Township, Berks County.

Matheus Drenckel, Alsace Township, Berks County.

Mathias Sieal, Lancaster, adjoining Widow Walterin.

March 16, 1755

Samuel Bossert, Colebrookdale, near Oley (Berks County), offers a plantation for sale.

Georg Honig, Lancaster, expects to remove elsewhere.

April 1, 1755

Johann Wilhelm Esch, from Runckelischen Land, arrived in America a year and a half ago. His brother Henrich arrived last autumn, and is serving with Georg Schmitt, opposite the printer, in Germantown. He seeks his brother.

Anton Petri, from Breitschit, Nassau Dillenburg, arrived in America last autumn, and he seeks his "Vetter" (cousin or uncle), named Petri, who has been in America 40 years and is said to be a justice in a region named "zum Korb".

Johannes Wilmuenster, Carlstadt (Charlestown, Chester County?).

Samuel Corrent, at Dietrich Welcker's iron works.

Pastor Wiszler, Egypt (Lehigh County).

Pastor Waldschmitt, on Cocalico Creek (Lancaster County).

Joh. Henrich Kester, Blue Mountains.

Henrich Gruber, Tulpehocken (Berks County).

Peter Muth, on Tulpehocken road.

Joh. Henrich Rohrbach, Alsace (Berks County).

April 16, 1755

Samuel Flower and Benedict Bartholomae advertise that three German servants ran away from Reading Furnace, Chester County: A wheelwright named Jennewein, Christian Fismeyer, 22 years old, and Andreas Golden, 20 years old.

Benjamin Merjon, Towamencin Township, Philadelphia County (now Montgomery), offers for sale a plantation on Bethlehem road, 25 miles from Philadelphia.

Henrich Scheuer, Alsace Township, Berks County; wife, Apollonia.

Carl Witz, Falckner Swamp (Montgomery County).

May 1, 1755

Johannes Light, Dutch pastor at New Brunswick, N.J., advertises that his German servant, Anna Maria Aldin, indentured for four years on February 15, 1754, received permission from him to seek another master, whereupon she disappeared.

Matheus Klaen arrived in America last autumn from Rexingen, Nassau, and indentured two boys--Hansz Michael Klaen, 14 years old, and Andreas Klaen, 12 years old. Mattheus Klaen was sick at the time and received no indenture papers nor does he know the names of the masters. He died and his widow seeks her sons. Information may be sent to David Schaefer, Philadelphia.

Friedrich Wambold, Skippack, Towamencin Township (Montgomery County).

May 1, 1755

Wennert Blecher, tanner, near Dr. Rieger, Lancaster.

William Edmonds, store, Bethlehem.

May 16, 1755

Jacob Treibelbitz, Weidenthal (Willowdale), between
Maxatawny and Oley (Berks County).

Abraham Schreiner, Rockhill Township, Bucks County, on the
Branch (of Perkiomen Creek), advertises that his German servant,
Anna Maria Seibertin, ran away.

Michael Leonhart, three miles from Skippack Creek, in Jacob
Umstat's mill (Montgomery County).

Ludwich Falckenstein, near Philadelphia, at the lower
ferry.

Johann Henrich Otto, Tulpehocken (Berks County), weaver.

Michel Schaefer, Tulpehocken (Berks County).

Johannes Sowasch, Oley Hills, Berks County.

June 1, 1755

Jacob Bickel, Tulpehocken (Berks County), near Mathias
Naffziger, last autumn indentured a 12-year-old boy, Johannes
Bickel. The name of the master in the indenture paper is
illegible; it looks like Johannes Hach or Hay. Information a-
bout him is desired.

Ernst Sigmund Seydel, Alsace, Berks County, advertises that
his German servant, Barbara Maszerin, ran away. She is a native
of Wurtemberg.

Johann Adam Bohl, with Andreas Wind, Upper Saucon (Lehigh
County).

Henrich Faber, smith, near Andreas Wind.

Anton Semich, a hunter, Falckner Swamp (Montgomery County).

Henrich Riedt, Old Goshenhoppen (Montgomery County), offers
a plantation and a new mill for sale.

Bernhart Gilbert, Indianfield, near Skippack, near Georg
Groeszman (Franconia Township, Montgomery County).

Christoffel Wagner, innkeeper, Saucon.

Martin Weidmann, Cocalico, four miles from Ephrata, on
Middle Creek (Lancaster County).

June 16, 1755

Matthae Raey, Abington, Philadelphia County (now Montgomery), near Pletcher's mill, advertises that his German servant, Nicolaus Schandler, ran away. He is a weaver, 17-18 years
old.

Jacob Mohr, Salisbury Township, Northampton County (now
Lehigh), advertises that a servant, Georg Goetz, 31 years old,
ran away, taking with him his wife, 45 years old.

Jacob Rummen, Upper Dublin Township, eight miles from
Germantown, near Farmar's mill (Montgomery County).

Rudi Sauter, Donegal Township, on the Susquehanna, advertises that his German servant, Friedrich Schwartz, 14 years old,
ran away.

Henrich Wolff, three miles from Reading, in Alsace Township, advertises that his Low German servant, Henrich Gumilder,
36 years old, ran away.

Wilhelm Albert, Tulpehocken (Berks County).

July 1, 1755

Stephen Bernhart, Maidencreek Township, Berks County, advertises that his German servant, Conrad Wolff, 20 years old,
ran away.

Michel Baertges, tanner, Philadelphia, near the sugar
house.

Thomas Daermer, shoemaker, Philadelphia, advertises that
his German apprentice, Henrich Dietzel, 21 years old, ran away.

Johannes Schneider, New Hanover (Montgomery County), advertises that his German servant, Magdalena Hartmaennin, ran
away. She is a native of Wurtemberg.

Rudi Brobaeck, Horseshoe road, nine miles from Lancaster.

Johannes Heckitswiller, landlord of the Red Lion inn, King
street, Lancaster.

Jacob Weber, Amity Township (Berks County), ten miles from
Reading, on Tulpehocken road, offers a plantation for sale.

July 16, 1755

Joseph Kauffmann, merchant, Second street, Philadelphia.

Friedrich Eschbach, Falckner Swamp, Philadelphia County
(now Montgomery), offers a plantation for sale.

Jacob Teischer, miller, Richmond Township, Berks County,
advertises that his German servant, Marcus Neidaeser, a stockingweaver, ran away.

James Barclay, Harington, Bucks County, advertises that
his Scotch servant, Neil MacFall, 18 years old, ran away.

July 16, 1755

John Dschill, West Jersey, near Haddonfield, Gloucester
County (New Jersey), advertises that his German servant, Tobias
Mueck, 22 years old, ran away.

Johann Georg Beck, Second street, Philadelphia.

Christopher Schupert, Whitemarsh Township, one mile from
Spring Mill (Montgomery County).

August 1, 1755

Henricus Wenig, Skippack (Montgomery County).

Isaac Kaey, Haddonfield, Gloucester County, New Jersey,
advertises that his German servant, Hansz Zeller, ran away. He
is a miller, 33 years old.

Samuel Sansom, Philadelphia, advertises that his servant,
Charlotte Maria Conradin, ran away. She is a native of Hanover,
22 years old and had served seven months.

William Bradford, Philadelphia, advertises that his German servant, Maria Charlotte Hamannin, 20 years old, ran away.

Philip Boehm, Whitpain Township (Montgomery County), offers
good rum and molasses for sale cheap.
            (This was the Rev. John Philip Boehm, noted
            Reformed pastor).

Nicolaus Hasselbach, papermaker at the former Koch mill,
on Wissahickon Creek, three miles from Germantown, offers to
hire out his servant, Wilhelm Stroud, 20 years old, who is ac-
customed to farm work.

Alexander Calley, Whitemarsh (Montgomery County), advertises that his Irish servant, Daniel Grant, 20 years old, ran
away.

Jack Alliod, a joiner, Oley (Berks County), near Nicolaus
Lesher, arrived in this country two years ago, and his daughter, Charlotte Alliod, 22 years old, was indentured. He seeks
her.

Friedrich Bayer, Macungie (Lehigh County).

Johann Neisz, Franconia Township, near Henrich Funck (Montgomery County).

August 16, 1755

Michel Helfferig, Macungie Township (Lehigh County).

September 1, 1755

Peter Pa-nebecker, Skippack (Montgomery County), has built
a fulling mill, which is in charge of an experienced fuller,
William Nenny.

September 16, 1755

Georg Carl, over the Schuylkill, near Potts' iron works, advertises that his German servant, Jacob Meisel, 20 years old, ran away.

Adam Schwarnbach, seven miles from Reading.

Johannes Graeff, Goshenhoppen, Philadelphia County (now Montgomery), advertises that his German servant, Conrad Beiler, ran away.

Henrich Hambrecht, Whiteland Township, Chester County, 25 miles from Philadelphia, on Conestoga road, advertises a plantation for sale.

October 1, 1755

Matheus Henrich, Skippack, Towamencin Township (Montgomery County), advertises a saw mill and 60 acres for sale.

Jacob Sutz, Tulpehocken, Heidelberg Township, near Paul Legel, seeks his brothers, Andreas and Johannes.

Johannes Reifschneider, Amity Township, Berks County, advertises that his German servant, Johann Henrie Bentzel, 20 years old, ran away.

Georg Kaestner, Whitpain (Montgomery County), advertises that his German servant, Catharina Petersin, 22 years old, ran away.

Dewald Diel, Rising Sun, between Philadelphia and Germantown.

October 16, 1755

Peter Edelmann, on the Altilane, near Christoph Kuhn, formerly of Fuerstenguischen, near Eberbach, or Heidelberg, seeks his brother-in-law, Johannes Adam Schaefer.

Joseph Ney, Cocalico Township, two miles from Dr. Bucher (Lancaster County), advertises that his servant, Abraham Holtzhauer, ran away.

Johannes Clements, Salford Township, Philadelphia County (now Montgomery).

Samuel Senger, on the Swatara Creek, Lancaster County, three miles from Justice Gilbreth.

Hansz Georg Baechtel, on the West Branch (of Perkiomen Creek).

Herman Fischer, Upper Hanover Township (Montgomery County).

Henrich Ress, Hatfield Township (Montgomery County).

November 1, 1755

Jost Vollert, near Bethlehem, advertises that his German servant, Catharina Barbara Schwimmerin, ran away. She is 25 years old and came from Grosz Ingersheim.

Andreas Kauffmann, two miles from Lancaster, near Steinman's mill.

Theil Neisz, Skippack, one mile below Jacob Wentz (Montgomery County).

Johannes Wurmann, Bedmister Township, on Tohickon Creek, Bucks County.

Jacob Riedt, Tulpehocken (Berks County), at the iron works.

Georg Adam Baumann, Exeter, Berks County, two miles from Christian Gehrig.

Johannes Stauffer, Lancaster County, near Jacob Huber's furnace.

Georg Hermany, Linnert Township, Northampton County (Lynn Township ? Lehigh County).

Frantz Noll, Little Conewago, York County, advertises that his horse was taken on the road by Sebastian May, who formerly taught school in Lancaster County at Mr. Doerr's. He offers £3 reward for the return of the horse.

Isaac Levan the younger, one-quarter mile from Reading, on the Schuylkill.

Antoni Fischer, Maxatawny, Berks County.

Georg Riedt, over the Blue Mountains.

Christian Henerich, Oley Hills (Berks County).

December 1, 1755

Jan Jansen, Salford Township, near Gabriel Schuler (Montgomery County).

Johann Caspar Dorst, Heidelberg Township, Berks County; wife, Barbara.

Philip Kleinert, Weisenberg, above Macungie (Lehigh County).

Johann Henrich Krausz, tinsmith, Second street, Philadelphia.

December 16, 1755

Reimer Land and Bodo Otto, doctors of medicine, arrived last October from Germany, and are practicing medicine at the house of Henrich Hoffecker, Front street, Philadelphia, near Benjamin Shoemaker.

December 16, 1755

Martin Neuszle, Donegal Township, Lancaster County.

Erhart Mueller, Falckner Swamp (Montgomery County).

January 16, 1756

Johannes Drechsler, Macungie (Lehigh County), offers an inn, dwelling and land for sale.

Carl Essig, Whitemarsh Township (Montgomery County), near Spring Mill, on James Stout's place.

Michel Dreydel, Manheim Township, Lancaster County, on Michel Gerber's place.

Mathew Potter, on William Logan's plantation, near Germantown, advertises that his English servant, Edward Fiely, ran away.

Jacob Christler, tailor, Philadelphia, advertises that his German servant, Conrad Spendel, 17 years old, ran away.

February 1, 1756

Johann Georg Schneider, German apothecary, at the sign of the silver bullet, Race street, near Second, Philadelphia.

Christian Hoffert, Whitpain Township (Montgomery County), 18 miles from Philadelphia, offers part of his plantation for sale.

Henrich Fretter, Philadelphia, opposite William Master's mill.

Jacob Schiede, on William Master's land, near Philadelphia.

Georg Gaeriner, Tulpehocken (Berks County).

Nicolaus Cerfas, Cocalico Township, Lancaster County.

February 16, 1756

Reimer Land and Bodo Otto, medical doctors, announce that the former will continue to practice in Philadelphia and the latter will locate in Germantown, in Cornelius Engel's house.

Michael Dieter, Springfield Township, Bucks County, six miles from Durham Furnace.

Georg Fritz, Amity Township, (Berks County), one mile from the forge on Thomas Potts' land.

Jacob Sorber, on William Rittenhouse's land, near Germantown.

Abraham Im-Ober-steg, merchant, Lancaster.

Ulrich Sauberlich, Whitehall (Lehigh County).

March 1, 1756

Jonas Moehlig, Raritan, New Germantown, New Jersey, gives notice that he will ride post between that region and Philadelphia.

Anna Margretha Braunin a year and a half ago indentured a boy off the ship, but received no papers. She seeks the master. The boy's name was Hansz Adam Braun.

Johannes Bender, Berwick Township, Lancaster County (?).

Adam Sontag, Tulpehocken (Berks County).

April 1, 1756

Martin Buchner, German schoolmaster at Anweil, New Jersey, arrived at Philadelphia in the autumn of 1753. Part of his passage costs being due, he gave up as security a chest containing his household goods and books. The chest was placed in Michel Ege's stable. Buchner paid the sum due the following summer to Daniel Benezet, and had the chest sent to Anweil. When the chest was examined it was found that it had been opened and eleven books were missing, about half the number of books in the chest. He believes someone borrowed the books to read them, and he requests their return.

Plantation for sale in Heidelberg Township, Berks County, on Cacoosing Creek, including a grist mill and saw mill and two houses, where Martin Linck and Adam Schoeck live, and also an adjoining place where Christopher Oechslen lives.

Christian Ewy, Warwick Township, Lancaster County, on Cocalico Creek, three miles from Jacob Huber.

Henrich Graff, smith, Tulpehocken (Berks County).

May 16, 1756

Johannes Wilhelm Wiegand began April 9, 1755, to teach the free school in Philadelphia, Ƶ25 to Ƶ30 a year being promised him. He taught one year, 60 children being enrolled. He received from the paymaster in Philadelphia Ƶ5, and from Mr. Schlatter no better comfort ("keinen bessern Trost") Therefore the free school is ended.
          (This refers to the unsuccessful school system proposed under English auspices for the Germans).

Twenty residents of Amity Township (Berks County), on Tulpehocken road, at the new store, have built a school house, and a teacher is wanted. Apply to Daniel Ludwig or Hansz Dieter Greiner.

Johann Adam Nicodemus, born at Medenbach, Nassau Dilleburg, and now living near Lancaster, is asked to apply to Johann Caspar Lapp, pastor at Anweil (New Jersey), with regard to his son, who has been freed from a harsh master, Georg Trimmer, of Anweil.

Philip Faust, Bern Township (Berks County), advertises that his servant, Hansz Adam Ebbler, 16 years old, ran away.

May 16, 1756

Jacob Albert, Bethel Township, Lancaster County, on Little Swatara Creek.

Christophel Jordan, Upper Saucon (Lehigh County).

Friedrich Emerich, Bristol Township, two miles from Germantown.

Johannes Grim, Bern Township (Berks County), 12 miles above Reading.

Joseph Steffen, Macungie (Lehigh County), advertises that his servant, Ludwig Hartmann, ran away.

Henrich Kuehn, Salisbury Township, Northampton County (now Lehigh).

Joseph Habecker, Manor Township, Lancaster County.

June 1, 1756

Hansz Michel Seitz arrived in this country six years ago last autumn. His son of the same name was indentured. The son is asked to notify the parents of his whereabouts. They are with Mordecai Thomson, Ridley Township, Chester County (now Delaware).

Conrad Staenger, Rockhill Township, Bucks County.

Philip Jacob Jung, on John Wister's place, Germantown.

June 16, 1756

Moritz Zincke, from Lauterberg, Hanover, came to America three years ago. His brother-in-law, Bodo Otto, in Germantown, wants to know where he is.

Nicolaus Arnold, Maxatawny (Berks County), near Jacob Levan, arrived in this country two years ago last autumn, with his brother Philip, and was indentured for three years. Nicolaus seeks news of Philip.

Henrich Stettler, New Hanover (Montgomery County).

Michel Becker, Kensington, near Philadelphia.

July 1, 1756

Adam Guusz, baker, Second street, Philadelphia, advertises that his German servant, Jean Georq Lofferend, 13-14 years old, ran away.

Conrad Jung, Conestoga road, at the Blue Ball (Lancaster County), advertises that his servant, Adam Grund, 45 years old, ran away. Grund's son is in service on the Great Swatara Creek.

Michael Hoffman, Skippack, near Wilhelm Tennes' place (Montgomery County).

July 1, 1756

Abraham Jaeckel (Yeakel), Upper Hanover Township, Philadelphia County (now Montgomery).

August 16, 1756

Rollin Harris, Amity Township, Manatawny (Berks County),
on Andreas Leicken's place.

Friedrich Fender, merchant, late of Germantown.

Georg Roth, Cocalico Township, Lancaster County.

August 21, 1756

Philip Schweigert, Earl Township, three miles from Ephrata
(Lancaster County).

Johannes Wenger, New Hanover, where Manatawny Creek flows
into the Schuylkill (Montgomery County).

September 4, 1756

Benjamin Lancaster, Whitemarsh Township (Montgomery
County), offers a plantation for sale in Bedminster Township,
Bucks County.

Andreas Keppler, New Hanover Township, Philadelphia County
(now Montgomery), advertises that his German servant, Anna Lint-
zin, ran away.

Maetheus Schaeffer, Macungie (Lehigh County); wife, Maria
Christina.

Henrich Hauptmann, Oley (Berks County), near Johannes Lora.

Georg Kistler, Allemangel (Albany Township, Berks County).

Andreas Lauck and wife, Germantown.

John Jones, Esq., justice of the peace, Germantown.

Hansz Weiss, on William Master's place (Philadelphia).

Jacob Fischer, Tulpehocken Township, Berks County.

September 16, 1756

Georg Schaefer, Bowman's lane, Germantown.

October 2, 1756

Jacob Emmerig, Bethel Township, Berks County.

Jacob Ulmer, Upper Merion Township (Montgomery County).

Casper Haen, Heidelberg Township.

October 16, 1756

Jacob Kopp, Hanover Township, two miles from the Schuylkill (New Hanover Township ? Montgomery County).

Johannes Joder the younger, Manatawny, Berks County; wife, Sara.

Jacob Nusz, Upper Salford (Montgomery County).

Georg Reuther, Goshenhoppen.

Jacob Frauecker, two miles below Nazareth.

Johannes Schaefer, Lancaster County, one and a half miles from Ephrata.

Peter Haasz, Macungie Township (Lehigh County).

October 30, 1756

Friedrich Schmidt, Rockhill Township, Bucks County, near Peter Schneider.

Maria Bachmaennin, Upper Saucon Township, Northampton County (now Lehigh).

Carl Schull, Lindau Township, Allemangel (Lynn Township ? Lehigh County).

November 13, 1756

Peter Leibert, upper end of Germantown, the second house below Antoni Gilbert, Crown landlord, at the sign of the Bible and Spinning Wheel, advertises that as Christopher Sauer the younger no longer rebinds old books, he will bind both new and old books.

Georg Koeling several years ago indentured his stepdaughter, Anna Maria Pfarin, to an Englishman in Bucks County. She is free this year and she may find her mother and stepfather in the Oley Hills, near Conrad Preisz (Berks County).

Georg Stoesz, Philadelphia, at the lower ferry in the Schuylkill.

Peter Lang and Johannes Lang, neighbors in Maxatawny (Berks County).

Henrich Wetstein, Maxatawny (Berks County).

Friedrich Beiteman, Falckner Swamp (Montgomery County).

Johann Gottfried Mueller, Skippack (Montgomery County).

Hansz Henrich Weber, on the Susquehannah.

Elias Specht, Falckner Swamp (Montgomery County).

Christian Stauffer, Lower Salford, on Skippack Creek (Montgomery County).

November 13, 1756

Abraham Mayer, one mile from Lancaster.

Jacob Moritz, "Berghiller Township, near Macungie".

November 27, 1756

Johannes Seybold, Cresheim, outside Germantown, on Samuel Davis' place.

Henrich Schnaebele, Leacock Townhip, Lancaster County.

Lorentz Bausum, Tulpehocken (Berks County).

Jacob Wuest, Paradise Township, York County.

December 11, 1756

Johannes Bast, Maxatawny, one mile from Daniel Levan, Berks County.

Michael Grosz, Lancaster.

December 25, 1756

Peter Treszler, New Goshenhoppen; wife, Margretha Weberin.

James Hammer, on the Schuylkill, four miles above Trappe, New Providence Township (now Upper Providence Township, Montgomery County), advertises that his German servant, Valentin Pentzinger, ran away. He is 38 years old and arrived in this country four weeks ago.

Rudolph Hoch, above Oley, at Willowdale (Berks County), advertises that his German boy, Georg Geisz, 15 years old, ran away.

Georg Michel Wolff, Earl Township, Lancaster County, one and a half miles from Georg Henckel, innkeeper, on Conestoga Creek.

Jacob Hettler, Reading; wife, Sibilla.

January 8, 1757

Henrich Jacob, Warwick Township, Lancaster County, near Henrich Voltz, two miles from Michel Mayer.

Friedrich Reitz, Whitehall Township (Lehigh County), on Feather Creek.

Valentin Voigt, born in Sultzfeld, one hour from Saxe Meiningen, it is believed is living ten miles from Philadelphia. Relatives in Sultzfeld wish to communicate with him with regard to the death of his step-brother, Johann Mattheus Voigt. Send word to Friedrich Otto, Bethlehem.

Dietrich Schaff, Lancaster.

January 22, 1757

John Piu (Pugh), Upper Saucon (Lehigh County); wife, Maria.

Adam Schuler, Upper Milford Township, Northampton County (now Lehigh), near David Guessi.

Martin Hausser, one mile from Lancaster, on Jacob Mayer's place.

Johannes Hencke, Upper Milford, Northampton County (now Lehigh).

February 5, 1757

John Johns, one mile below Bethlehem, on the Lehigh River, offers a plantation of 500 acres for rent.

Pool Balljet, Whitehall Township (Lehigh County).

February 19, 1757

Jacob Franck, late glazier in Lancaster, and his wife are both dead. Their friends, brothers and sisters, viz: Christoffel Franck, Henrich Franck, Andreas Franck, Anna Maria Franckin, Maria Gertraut Muellerin, Michel Mueller and Christian Mueller, are asked to apply to the executors for their inheritance. Friedrich Dambach, Johannes Eberman, Krafft Roeser, executors.

Michael Buerge (Bergey), Indian Creek (Montgomery County).

Johann Grothausz offers to sell a plantation three miles above Germantown, in Springfield (Montgomery County), whereon there has been a tile kiln for a long time; situated on the Great road to Germantown.

Adam Dummel, Macungie Township, Northampton County (now Lehigh); wife, Catharina.

March 5, 1757

Reiner Land, doctor and operator, Front street, opposite the Red Lion, Philadelphia, will remove from Philadelphia on June 15.

Conrad Coter, Hilltown Township, Perkasie, Bucks County, offers a plantation for sale.

Georg Overbeck, Bucks County, four miles from Durham Furnace, advertises that a servant, Johannes Schmitt, ran away.

Michael Schick, near Hansz Fretz, Bedminster Township, (Bucks County), seeks his sister, Margaretha Schickin, who arrived in this country two years ago last autumn.

Methusalem Iwans (Evans), Upper Dublin (Montgomery County), seven miles from Germantown.

March 10, 1757

Ludwig Sengeisen, Race street, Philadelphia, near the
Lutheran Church.

Georg Bergstraeszer, constable of Rockhill Township, Bucks
County, has arrested an unmarried German, Henrich Gilbert, as
a runaway.

Michel Koebel, Forks of the Delaware (vicinity of Easton).

Abraham Levan, Exeter Township, Berks County.

Jacob Levan, Maxatawny (Berks County).

Bernhart Straub, Salisbury Township (Lehigh County).

April 2, 1757

Anna Obertin, widow, Upper Milford Township, Northampton
County (now Lehigh), gives notice of the disappearance of her
son, Abraham Obert.

Georg Doerr, Heidelberg Township; son-in-law, Isaac
Boetzel.

Baltzer Hess, Williamstown Township (Williams Township,
Northampton County).

April 16, 1757

Johannes Rentz, baker and innkeeper, Ebenezer, South
Carolina (Georgia?), is informed his brother, Johann Georg
Rentz, from Weihl, in Schoenenbuch, arrived in Pennsylvania five
years ago and seeks information about Johannes.

Jacob Lang, Willings Township, below Easton (Williams
Township, Northampton County).

Johannes Cortel, near Abraham Herr, Manor Township, Lancaster County.

Jacob Danner, Long Swamp, Berks County.

April 30, 1757

Mathusalem Evans, Upper Dublin Township (Montgomery County),
offers a plantation for sale, one mile from Samuel Morris' mill,
in Whitemarsh, and thirteen miles from Philadelphia, comprising
100 acres, on Wissahickon Creek.

Dewald Becker enlisted in the King's army and took away
with him the papers of his and Adam Wagner's land. Wagner
bought the land from Andreas Buschung, in Derry Township, Lancaster County. He serves warning against any purchase of the
land from Becker.

Johann Peter Reinhard, Upper Saucon Township, Northampton
County (now Lehigh).

GERMAN SETTLERS OF PENNSYLVANIA

62

May 14, 1757

Peter Hittel, Upper Milford Township, Northampton County (now Lehigh), seeks Johannes Linn, whose wife is named Maria Margretha.

Philip Schilling, Skippack Township (Montgomery County), one mile from Peter Pfannebecker.

Baltzer Jaeger, Linn Township, Northampton County (Lynn Township, Lehigh County).

Anna Eva Gaertnerin, above the old oil mill, Germantown.

Friedrich Stahl, Berks County; wife, Susanna.

May 29, 1757

Balthaser Roser, tanner, executor of Wilhelm Hoffman, late smith, Germantown.

Alexander Forster, on Little Conestoga Creek, nine miles this side of Ephrata, will ride the post from Philadelphia and Germantown to that region.

Marx Hohnecker, two miles below Philadelphia in Passyunk Township, advertises that his German servant, Christina Meschelin, ran away. She is 30-40 years old and of the Romish faith.

Jacob Bender, Heidelberg Township, Northampton County, at the Blue Mountains (now Lehigh).

John Mitchell, Whitemarsh Township, Philadelphia County (now Montgomery).

Jacob Vollmer, Tulpehocken (Berks County), wants a tile-maker.

Philip Roschan, Oley Hills, on Beaver Creek (Berks County).

June 11, 1757

Peter Schaeffer, Rockhill Township, near Tohickon Creek (Bucks County), offers a grist mill and 120 acres for sale.

Joseph Gasz, Cocalico Township, Lancaster County.

June 25, 1757

Caspar Hausser, serving in Skippack (Montgomery County) with Georg Weidner, seeks information about his brothers, Johannes and Christoph, his sisters, Regina and Barbara, and his mother, Barbara, who are in this country.

Joh. Hilarius Becker, school teacher in lower Germantown.

Daniel Sold, Whitehall Township, Northampton County (now Lehigh).

June 25, 1757

Adam Mensch, Cohansey, Cumberland County (New Jersey),
inquires for his brother, Johann Nickel Mensch, who arrived in
this country four years ago from Deimberg, "aus dem Crumbacher
Amt," He is 28 years old and probably is indentured.

Johann Georg Best, from Nurnberg, serving with James
Horner, Allen Township, nine miles from Bethlehem, inquires for
his mother, Christina Bestin, and her five children, who arrived at Philadelphia in 1754.

Philip Lehning, Ruscombmanor (Berks County); wife, Catharina.

Matthias Schmutzer, Lebanon Township (Lebanon County);
wife Regina Zwerin.

Peter Gottschall, Hempfield Township, five miles from Lancaster.

Friedrich Rauschenberger, Lehigh Township, Northampton
County, two miles from Gnadenthal, in the Forks of the Delaware.

July 9, 1757

Georg Schmitt, outside Germantown, near William Allen, Esq.
(Mount Airy, Philadelphia).

Peter Brunholtz, former preacher in Philadelphia, died
July 7 and was buried today.

William Falck, on Isaac Norris' place, at Three-Mile Run,
between Philadelphia and Germantown.

Georg Mayer, two miles above Trappe.

Johann Leonhart Heiszer, Macungie (Lehigh County).

July 23, 1757

Johannes Schimmel, Falckner Swamp (Montgomery County);
wife, Magdalena.

Jacob Stauffer, miller, Warwick Township, Lancaster
County, near Huber's iron works.

Hansz Greber, York; wife, Anna Maria

Philip Haymann, Friedensthal.

Johann Laumann, Martic Township, Lancaster County.

Henrich Grimm, Frankford, Philadelphia County.

August 5, 1757

Philip Wentz, Worcester Township, Skippack (Montgomery
County), offers for rent a tile kiln, dwelling and land.

August 5, 1757

Jacob Walter was in Colebrookdale a year ago, with his father, Adam Walter, who pretends to be a surgeon, and his brother-in-law, Johan Cappler. All left that place. They are asked to notify Georg Ritter, at that place, or David Schultz, Goshenhoppen (Montgomery County).

Georg Neisz, Falckner Swamp, Frederick Township (Montgomery County), advertises that his German tanner apprentice, Philip Glaeser, 17-18 years old, ran away.

Nicolaus Henrich, on Captain Harrison's place, three miles from Philadelphia, on Ridge road.

Henrich Heist, Goshenhoppen (Montgomery County), on Johann Dieter Bauman's place.

August 20, 1757

William Althousz, Falckner Swamp, Philadelphia County (now Montgomery), two miles from Jost Pfannekuchen, advertises that his German servant, Christophel Barel, 18 years old, ran away.

Henrich Hartmann, Philadelphia, unmarried, miller is in prison for a debt of £17, 10s. He is willing to serve anyone who will pay the debt.

Georg Kriebel, Lower Salford Township, on Skippack Creek (Montgomery County).

Michel Rein, Earl Township, on Mill Creek, Lancaster County.

Abraham Orszenbacher, Indianfield (Franconia Township, Montgomery County).

September 3, 1757

Georg Ewy left his home in Bethel Township, Northampton County, and Diel Bower has taken possession of his property. Those having claims may present them at Johannes Lefeber's, Forks Township.

Johannes Weber, Limerick Township, on Perkiomen Creek (Montgomery County), three miles from Trappe, near Pawling's mill, on Hieronymus Haaien's place.

September 17, 1757

Peter Pannenbecker, Skippack Township, on Perkiomen Creek (Montgomery County).

Jacob Franck, Falckner Swamp (Montgomery County), on the late Martin Buetting's place.

Christoph Hoffman, Lower Salford (Montgomery County), one mile from Gabriel Schuler.

Abraham Brubacher, Lancaster County, Cocalico Township, near Martin Weidmann.

September 17, 1757

Michael Rentzler, Bern Township (Berks County).

Georg Dollinger, Oley (Berks County); wife, Margretha.

Georg Kehl, Tulpehocken Township (Berks County).

October 1, 1757

Jacob Richter, on the Ridge, four miles from Andrew Robeson's mill (Ridge avenue, Philadelphia).

David Baringer, bookseller, Easton.

Hansz Wenger, Cocalico (Lancaster County).

October 15, 1757

Ludwig Weisz, surveyor, Race street, between Second and Third, Philadelphia.

Georg Clausz, one mile from Bethlehem, on Burnside's place.

Adam Ulrich, Oley Hills (Berks County).

Michael Lang, Oley Hills (Berks County).

Thomas Bennphilip, Oley Hills (Berks County).

October 29, 1757

Johann Georg Hoffmann, a smith, arrived in this country five years ago from Nassau-Dillburg. His brother, Johann Jacob, a wheelwright, arrived four years ago, and he seeks Johann Georg. Johann Jacob is in Allemangel, Linn Township, with Philip Moser (Lynn Township, Lehigh County).

Johann Gottlieb Schloweisz is sought by his sister Catharina Ehlerin, from Kleebrun, Wurtemberg, who lately lived in Luneburg, near Halifax, and has now come to Philadelphia. She is now in her second marriage, with Mr. Hirschmann, of Luneburg. In Philadelphia she is staying with Johann Georg Schneider, apothecary, Race street.

Andreas Weckesser, landlord of the King of Prussia inn, Germantown.

Michael Spiegel, Macungie Township, Northampton County (now Lehigh), offers a mill and plantation for sale.

Conrad Schultz, late doctor in Flourtown, six miles above Germantown (Montgomery County). Barbara Schultzin, executrix, offers his real estate and personal property for sale.

Henrich Rohn, Bethlehem Township; wife, Regina, daughter of Peter Hartman.

Christian Gehman, Hereford Township, Berks County, near Peter Federolf.

October 29, 1757

Philip Oblinger, Quitopahilla, near Peter Kucher (Lebanon County).

Jacob Zimmerman, on Mr. Plumstead's place, Whitehall Township, on Cedar Creek (Lehigh County).

Johannes Sechler, Allemangel on the Andelany, one mile from Justice Eberth.

Johannes Schorp, Reading.

Johannes Sauter, Coventry Township, Chester County.

Johannes Steiner, "Innton Township".

Martin Bechtel, "Hanover Township, Berks County".

George Bechtel, Hereford Township, Berks County.

Daniel Gillman, Frankford (Philadelphia).

November 12, 1757

Johannes Ickes, smith, Limerick Township, Philadelphia County (now Montgomery), advertises that his German apprentice, Andreas Krohm, ran away. He comes from Hanover, and is 17 years old.

Valentin Noll, Limerick Township (Montgomery County).

Georg Friedrich Bayer, cutler and sharpener, Philadelphia, Water street, between Market and "Drd" street, at the second lantern.

Jost Wiegand, New Goshenhoppen, one mile from Hansz Meyer's mill.

Lenert Raeber, Windsor Township, Berks County, 13 miles from Reading.

Abraham Reiff, Lancaster County, one mile from Ebi's mill.

David Billman, Allemangel (Albany Township, Berks County).

Carl Reyer, Providence Township, near Trappe.

November 26, 1757

Georg Graomeling, from Sennfeld, near Adelsheim, arrived at Philadelphia five years ago. His brother Jacob came in another ship, arriving in Maryland. Georg, who lives in Skippack (Montgomery County), at Welcker's mill, seeks information about Jacob.

Johann Henrich Falcke, Heidelberg Township; wife, Anna Martha.

Michel Krausz, Greenwich Township, near Maxatawny (Berks County).

November 26, 1757

Andreas Knoedler, Heidelberg Township, Northampton County (now Lehigh).

Rudolph Dotterer, Oley (Berks County); wife, Margretha.

Jacob Schirardi, Maxatawny, Berks County.

Jacob Bachmann, Long Swamp, Berks County.

December 10, 1757

Thomas Foerstner, born near Nurnberg, arrived in America twelve years ago, with his brother Georg. Georg was indentured, and Thomas seeks information about him. Thomas is with Johannes Georger (Geiger?), Falckner Swamp (Montgomery County), one mile from Johannes Schneider.

Andreas Breckel, furrier, Third street, near Market, Philadelphia.

Adam Dietz, Blue Mountains; wife, Sibella Dorothea.

Michel Koeppel, Lebanon Township (Lebanon County).

Philip Odenweller, Williams Township, Lower Saucon (Northampton County).

December 24, 1757

Isaac Williams, New Britain Township, Bucks County, offers a plantation for sale on the Great road from Butler's mill (Chalfont) to the North Wales Meeting House (Gwynedd).

Patrick Carr, Moreland Township, Philadelphia County, one mile from Fletcher's mill.

Johann Conrad Menges, Upper Milford Township, Northampton County (now Lehigh), with his brother-in-law, Nazius, one and a half miles from Abraham Meyer, of New Goshenhoppen, seeks his brother, Johann Georg Menges, who arrived in America eight years ago. The latter was born at Hebstel, Grafschaft Fuerstenau, and is a tailor.

January 21, 1758

Georg Adam Weidner, Colebrookdale Township, Berks County, advertises that his German servant, Johann Henrich Unckelbach, a tilemaker, ran away.

Jacob Stahly, Chestnut Hill, Philadelphia, "Riedmacher".

Peter Volck, Oley Hills (Berks County); wife, Catharina Barbara.

Isaac Rausch, dyer, upper end of Germantown.

Wendel Lautermilch, Heidelberg Township, Lancaster County (now Lebanon).

January 21, 1758

Jacob Kadermann, Tulpehocken, Berks County.

Hansz Henrich Mayer, from Pinckel, Switzerland, arrived in America fourteen years ago, and is in Greenwich Township, near Maxatawny, Berks County. He seeks his brother Anton, who arrived four years ago.

Johannes Kantz, Upper Salford (Montgomery County), "auf des Tauben Plantasche"--on the deaf man's plantation--a half mile from the late Jacob Nusz's place.

Johannes Rudolph, a half mile from Philadelphia on the younger Anthony Morris' place.

John Davis, New Britain Township, Bucks County, near Butler's mill, offers for sale the inn where Thomas Nixon lived.

Conrad Strudt arrived in Pennsylvania four years ago from Rothebach, two hours from Hanau, with his wife Maria, and as they could not pay for their passage they wanted to enter service together. After waiting six weeks without being able to make such arrangements, they sold their clothes to allay their hunger, and finally were indentured separately. The wife has served four years in Williamstown (Wilmington?) in Christiana Hundred, with Joseph Muddert. She will be free in October and she seeks her husband.

February 4, 1758

Johannes Stapp, Whitpain Township, Philadelphia County (now Montgomery), 18 miles from Philadelphia, near Philip Boehm's place.

Philip Hartmann, Oley (Berks County), three years ago took into his service Anna Eva, born Frauenfelderin, from Litzelbach, near Neukirchen, Amt Lichtenberg, Hesse Darmstadt. Information is sought about her mother's sister, Catharine, who married Johann Jacob Goetz in Pennsylvania.

Giszbert Gilbert, Limerick Township, Philadelphia County (now Montgomery).

Georg Gernant, Bern Township, Berks County.

Henrich Happel, Plainfield Township, Northampton County.

February 18, 1758

Isaac Theisen, Upper Dublin, Philadelphia County (now Montgomery), advertises that his German servant, Anna Maria Meyerin, 23 years old, ran away.

Michel Wilhelm, Ruscombmanor Township, Berks County.

Abraham Schwartz, Franconia Township, Philadelphia County (now Montgomery).

March 4, 1758

Johann Hammer, maltmaker, Cresheim, Germantown, Philadelphia County (now Mount Airy).

Michael Omensetter, miller, Cresheim, Germantown (now
Mount Airy).

Conrad Weidner, Cresheim, near W. Allen's summer house
(Mount Airy, Philadelphia).

Isaac Rausch, dyer, upper end of Germantown, near the
Lutheran Church, advertises that his father, Nicholas is dead,
but the widow and son will continue the business.

Georg Philip Fuhrman and Juliana Fuhrmanin arrived in this
country twenty years ago from Muehlbach, on the Necker, near
Ober-Mimpffen, between Heilbrun and Heidelberg. Their sister,
Catharina Fuhrmanin, came three years later, and information
about her is desired. Juliana is the wife of Johann Georg
Baszel, Saucon, two miles from Michel Bischoff.

Georg Berckemeyer arrived in this country three years ago
last autumn, with his sister, Anna Gertraut Berckemeyerin, from
the Maesenheim region. Georg is serving with Melchior Baser,
in Macungie (Lehigh County). He will be free in the autumn, and
he seeks information as to his sister.

March 18, 1758

Christian Hoerner, Limerick Township, Philadelphia County
(now Montgomery), one mile from Pawling's mill.

Wilhelm Spatz, Heidelberg Township, Berks County; wife
Anna Elisabeth.

Henrich Gelto, New Britain Township, Bucks County.

April 1, 1758

Friedrich Ocks (Ax), Germantown, notifies Valentin Klein
that Christiana Haaszin is dead.

Alexander Mack, Chestnut Hill (Philadelphia).

Peter Eret, Colebrookdale, Berks County.

Thomas Blackledge, Lower Milford Township (Lehigh County).

Jacob Herb, Colebrookdale Township, Berks County.

David Jag, Falckner Swamp (Montgomery County).

April 15, 1758

Maria Klingmaennin served with Jacob Rorer, 9-10 miles
from Lancaster, and then with Jonas Nold, Hempfield Township,
seven miles from Lancaster. She died there, and information is
sought about her relatives.

April 15, 1758

Germantown tavern, sign of the White Horse, formerly Bernhart Roszer's, for sale; apply to Theobald End, saddler.

Henrich Brennerman, Skippack, Towamencin Township (Montgomery County).

Daniel Roemmig, Lower Saucon, Northampton County.

May 13, 1758

Thomas Paul, mason, of Maryland, sought work in Philadelphia. His wife, Maria, having heard nothing from him for three months, seeks information about him, or else who will be compelled to indenture their children.

Robert Jones, Worcester Township, Philadelphia County (now Montgomery), near Skippack Creek.

Michel Daeni, Pikeland Township, Chester County, advertises that his German servant, Johann Gottlieb Weisz, ran away.

Henrich Schneider, Springfield Township, six miles above Germantown (Montgomery County).

Michel Kuuser, Dublin Township, Philadelphia County, near Joseph Waacker.

May 27, 1758

Jacob Schelly, Great Swamp, Lower Milford Township.

June 10, 1758

Tract of 1000 acres near Tohickon Creek, Bedminster Township, Bucks County, for sale. It is occupied by Christoph Grumann, Godfrid Gruber, Valentin Philip, Adam Stein, Hartmann Tettermann and Conrad Wittmann.

Peter Krebs, his wife Magdalena and their family arrived at Philadelphia five years ago last autumn. Their daughter, Anna Maria, was indentured in Lancaster to English people, who removed to Charlestown, Maryland, and then to Williamsburg, Virginia. Maria was freed and is now in Baltimore, with Samuel Hook, and she seeks her mother.

Jacob Beyerle, opposite King of Prussia inn, Germantown.

Christian Busz, Great Swamp, Bucks County.

Jacob Maag, Red Lion inn, Second street, Philadelphia.

Nicolaus Moritz, Reading.

June 24, 1758

Reimer Land, doctor of medicine and chirurgus, has left Philadelphia and is now at Falckner Swamp (Montgomery County), living in the house of the Jew Moses Heyman.

June 24, 1758

Stoffel Frantz, Cocalico Township, Lancaster County; wife, Magdalena.

Casper Egli, Cocalico Township, Lancaster County, four miles from Ephrata.

Johannes Martin, Upper Dublin Township (Montgomery County).

Jacob Ludwig, eight miles from Lancaster.

Johannes Bayer, Heidelberg Township, Berks County.

Peter Fischer, Falckner Swamp (Montgomery County).

Michel Drachsel, on the Great Lehigh, with Paul Balljet.

July 8, 1758

Meyer Josephson, formerly occupying Moses Heyman's store, Reading, has opened a new store in Steinmetz's house, at the Market Place, Reading.

Johannes Klein, New York, advertises that his German boy, Thomas Jewens, ran away. The boy has a brother about 10 years old in Philadelphia and friends in Lancaster.

Peter Reither, Cecil County, Maryland, on Bohemia Manor, near the church.

Bastian Krausz, Salisbury Township, Northampton County (now Lehigh).

Henrich Roeder, Forks of the Delaware, two miles from Nazareth.

Jacob Rebold, stockingweaver, Germantown.

Jacob Fischer, Chestnut Hill (Philadelphia).

Peter Kucher, on the Quittapohilla (Lebanon County).

Georg Lesch, Heidelberg (Lehigh County).

Andrew Eisenhart, Macungie (Lehigh County).

Peter Roedler, Long Swamp, Berks County.

Willem Theisen, Skippack (Montgomery County).

July 22, 1758

Michael Schaffner, at John Van Daren's, in the former mill of Andrew Robeson (at the mouth of Wissahickon Creek, Philadelphia).

August 19, 1758

Anna Maria, widow of Wilhelm Hoffman, the smith, offers to lease his smith shop, on the main street, Germantown.

Jacob Ruppert, plantation, two miles outside Germantown, near Michael Mueller.

Michael Horlacher, New Goshenhoppen.

Jacob Clementz, Towamencin Township (Montgomery County); wife, Margretha.

Peter Baszler, Whitehall Township, Northampton County (now Lehigh), near Adam Daeschler, on the Great Lehigh.

Peter Hoffmann, Salisbury Township, Northampton County (now Lehigh), on the Little Lehigh.

Johannes Maurer, Great Swamp, Bucks County, near Michel Horlacher.

Andreas Beck, Skippack (Montgomery County), near Bernhart Rap.

September 2, 1758

Daniel Levan, Maxatawyn (Berks County), advertises that his German servant, Carl Matheus, 17 years old, ran away.

Henrich Damberger, near Farmar's mill (Whitemarsh Township, Montgomery County).

Johannes Nicklas, Whitehall Township, Northampton County (now Lehigh), near Cedar Creek.

Hansz Zug and his neighbor, Christian Forrer, Oley (Berks County).

Henrich Hering, Great Swamp, on Tohickon Creek (Bucks County).

Georg Kolb, Chestnut Hill (Philadelphia).

Conrad Frick, Germantown.

Peter Zimmerman, Cocalico, Lancaster County.

September 16, 1758

Nickel Baeringer, Oley Hills (Berks County); wife, Catharina.

Leonhart Reber, Windsor Township, thirteen miles above Reading, on the Schuylkill.

September 30, 1758

Michel Oerter, from Ober Otterbach, in Gutenberger Amt, has a brother Georg, who came to America seven years ago, of whom he seeks information. Address, Dietrich Welcker's iron works.

September 30, 1758

Johannes Theobald, born in Habspeyer, Oberamt Lantern, Chur
Pfaltz, arrived in America in 1752, and his sister, Catharina
Theobaldin, arrived the same year. She was married on the voyage. Their brother Caspar arrived fifteen years ago. Johannes,
who lives in Lancaster County, three miles from Ephrata, seeks
information about his relatives.

Hanickel Kuntz, Salisbury, Northampton County (now Lehigh).

October 14, 1758

Margretha Koellerin, widow, arrived in America eight years
ago from the Zurich region. Her brother, Hansz Ulrich Wuensch,
Conestoga, Manor Township (Lancaster County), with John Ross,
seeks her.

Adam Ernst, Tinitum Township, on Tohickon Creek, Bucks
County.

Lorentz Hautz, Bethel Township, Berks County, near Fort
Henry.

Peter Linn, Lower Milford, Bucks County; wife, Margretha.

Nicolaus Jost, near Reading.

October 28, 1758

Anna Margretha Eckhardtin, widow, several years ago indentured her 12-year-old-son, Gottfried Eckhardt, to Valentin
Muckle, a German merchant in Bucks County. Both disappeared,
and she seeks information about them.

Stephanus Katler and his wife Magdalena came to Philadelphia nine years ago. Their son Peter went to the Raritan
region (New Jersey), 50-60 miles from Philadelphia, and was with
some Dutch people there. The father died. Information about
Peter is sought by his brother Michel, who is with Michel
Schenck, one mile from Lancaster.

Conrad Detterer, Indianfield, Franconia Township (Montgomery County).

Simon Burckhard, Warwick Township, Lancaster County; wife,
Catharina; father-in-law, Adam Brandt, of Quitopahilla (Lebanon
County).

Jacob Kopp, Hanover Township, Falckner Swamp, near the
Schuylkill (New Hanover Township, Montgomery County).

Rudy Bossert, "on the Antolany," Greenwich Township, Berks
County.

November 11, 1758

Leon Nathan, Reading, Penn street, adjoining Peter Haasz,
merchant.

November 11, 1758

Lorentz Hippel, Vincent Township, on the Schuylkill (Chester County).

Christian Brennerman, Towamencin Township (Montgomery County).

Peter Kreutzer, Tulpehocken Township, Berks County.

Joseph Mauntz, Heidelberg Township, Berks County.

Georg Bader, Maxatawny (Berks County).

Jacob Rieth, Tulpehocken, Berks County).

November 25, 1758

Henrich Frey, smith, on Indian Creek, Franconia Township, Philadelphia County (now Montgomery), offers a plantation for sale.

Jelias Rosenberger, Hatfield Township, Philadelphia County (now Montgomery).

Nicolaus Handwerck, Heidelberg Township, Northampton County (now Lehigh).

Johannes Nicolaus Straszer, Albany Township, Berks County.

Moses Binder, Falckner Swamp (Montgomery County).

Andreas Ohl, Goshenhoppen (Montgomery County).

Peter Klein, Long Swamp, Berks County.

Arnold Eberhard, Whitehall Township, on the Lehigh.

December 9, 1758

Conrad Jung, landlord of the Blue Ball inn, Second street, Philadelphia, offers for sale a house equipped for an inn on the Lancaster road, 19 miles from Philadelphia, the sign of the Blue Ball.

Conrad Schmidt, Alsace Township, Berks County, three miles from Reading, wants workers for his tile kiln.

Philip Geissinger, Upper Saucon Township, Northampton County (now Lehigh), advertises that Abraham Spenenberger, who entered his employ for one year on July 24, fled on July 30.

Nicolaus Nickom, Hereford Township, Berks County.

Michel Rodger, Oley Township, Berks County.

Georg Mueller, Windsor Township, Berks County, near Benjamin Kaeplin, on the Schuylkill.

Lenert Keplinger, Windsor Township, Berks County.

December 23, 1758

Johann Conrad Schmidt, near Philadelphia; wife, Maria Rosina.

Arnold Billig, Albany Township, Berks County; wife, Sophia.

Nicolaus Mayer, Macungie, Northampton County (now Lehigh).

Johannes Mellinger, on Cocalico Creek, near Ephrata.

Georg Schreiber, upper Germantown.

January 5, 1759

Adam Schmitt, 14 years old, a servant, was arrested and is in the Easton prison. He is believed to have run away from Christian Rothermel.

Jost Pfannekuchen, Franconia Township, Philadelphia County (now Montgomery), offers a plantation for sale in Hilltown Township, Bucks County, the former property of the late Christofel Drubi.

David Hebbenheimer, living two miles from Easton with Stoffel Buettenbinder, arrived in America eight years ago, and he seeks information about his father's brother, who came to America several years earlier.

Anna Margretha Hessin, who is in the service of James Wilson, Derry Township, Lancaster County (now Dauphin), 25 miles from Lancaster, seeks information about her sister, who married Bastian Geringer; her brothers, Henrich Hess and Johannes Hess, and her sister, Anna Hessin.

Nicolaus Henrich, Northern Liberties of Philadelphia, on Ridge road, on Captain Harris place, three miles from Philadelphia.

January 19, 1759

Gottlieb David Ettlin, Derry Township, Lancaster County (now Dauphin).

February 2, 1759

Johannes Schweitzer, Germantown, sergeant in Captain Diefe's (Davis?) company, offers a reward for the capture of a runaway soldier.

Maria Iserlohin, living with Henrich Schmitt the younger, New Goshenhoppen, urges payment by those who owe her for medicines.

Jacob Friedrich Ochsenreuter has been with the soldiers for 18 months; his wife, Anna Christina, is missing.

Johannes Lescher, Oley (Berks County), offers a plantation for rent.

Jacob Dilier, near Philadelphia; wife, Helena.

February 2, 1759

Rudolph Lang, Oxford Township, Philadelphia County.

Ulrich Fischer, Moettlingen.

February 16, 1759

Peter Baszler, Whitehall Township, on the Great Lehigh (Lehigh County).

Melcher Hartrampff, Quini Township, Philadelphia County (Gwynedd Township ? Montgomery County).

March 2, 1759

Henrich Schneider, from the Dillenburg region, arrived at New York five years ago and is now with Sebastian Graf, one mile from Lancaster. He seeks his mother, Elisabeth Schneiderin, and his sisters, Catharina and Anna Maria, who came to Philadelphia a year after his arrival.

Gottlieb Gander, from Lomersheim, Wurtemberg, linen weaver, arrived in America six years ago and is now in Frederick, Maryland. He seeks information about his brothers, Augustinius and Christian, who came to America four years ago.

Ludwig Schellbasz, from Rohre, Darmstadt region, miller, living nine miles from Frederick, Maryland, seeks information about one of his sisters who came to America. He left three sisters in Germany, and does not know which of them came to America. Notify Conrad Grosch, Frederick, Md.

Frantz Brostmann, Tulpehocken Township, Berks County, near Peter Spicker.

Friedrich Marr, on Peter Bruecker's land, Cocalico Township, Lancaster County.

Jacob Kaercher, "Secklermeister," Market street, Philadelphia.

March 16, 1759

Henrich Kellso, New Britain Township, Bucks County, offers a plantation for sale.

Nathaniel Thomas, one mile from Germantown, offers a place for sale at the forks of the road at Chestnut Hill. Jacob Galiede lives near by. Joseph Muddere is at Barth's mill.

Johann Feigel, New Goshenhoppen, with Henrich Heist.

Conrad Weber, Bristol Township, a mile from Germantown.

Hansz Adam Schwenk, Albany Township, Berks County.

Johannes Joder, Oley, Berks County.

John Huber, Hempfield Township, Lancaster County.

March 30, 1759

Richard Langer, Oley Hills (Berks County), near Johannes Loescher's furnace.

Philip Fischhorn, on Little Swatara Creek.

Johannes Weickert, Oley, Berks County.

April 13, 1759

Nicolaus Salede, Tulpehocken Township, Berks County, seeks information about his brother-in-law, Henrich Hess, from Heichlem, who was in service in New York. Salede is from Bergzabern.

Michael Muhlberger, Chestnut Hill, Philadelphia County, advertises that Johannes Holland, born in Hanover, ran away from him.

Johannes Riest, Germantown, advertises that his apprentice, Christian Mayer, 14 years old, ran away.

Wilhelm Frick has opened an apothecary shop in Reading in Wilhelm Hottenstein's house.

Georg Bender, Franconis Township, Philadelphia County (now Montgomery).

Michel Rischel, Macungie, on the Little Lehigh (Lehigh County).

Gottfried Rohrer, Tulpehocken Township, Berks County.

Ulrich Spiesz, Bethel Township, Berks County.

Christel Glemmer, Springfield Township, Bucks County.

Feit Rab, Tulpehocken Township, Lancaster County (sic).

April 17, 1759

Jacob Denig, Lower Salford Township, Philadelphia County (now Montgomery); wife, Anna Maria.

Adam Lat, Greenwich Township, Berks County.

May 11, 1759

Jacob Levi and Bernet Jacob, in company, on Muehlbach road, five miles from Conrad Weiser's inn and one mile from Saltzgeber and two miles from Tulpehocken, in Lancaster County, merchants. No business is transacted on Saturday or Sunday because they are Jews.

Samuel Fockel, sicklesmith, formerly on Maxatawny road, in Long Swamp, between Peter Federolff's and Peter Metz's, has removed and now lives a full mile on the side toward Bethlehem on old Jacob Coller's place.

Anna Maria Linck, with Joseph Flegel, Chestnut Hill, Philadelphia County, inquires for her sister, Frony Pfeifferin.

78   GERMAN SETTLERS OF PENNSYLVANIA

May 11, 1759

   Michel Wohlfahrt, Tulpehocken Township, Berks County.

   David Guessi, Upper Milford Township, Northampton County
(now Lehigh).

   Henrich Gesander, Quitopahilla (Lebanon County), one mile
from Stoeffel Zimmer's mill.

   Georg Lindenmuth, Bern Township, Berks County.

   Matthes Loszer, Bethel Township, Lancaster County (now
Lebanon).

May 25, 1759

   Gottlieb Fischer, care of Johannes Herr's mill, Lampeter
Township, Lancaster County, six miles from Lancaster, who arrived in America nine years ago, seeks his brother, Matthes.

   Magdalena Maeres, sister of William Levering, Roxborough
Township, Philadelphia County, was crushed so that she became
crippled, five years ago, by Henrich Summer, and she walks on
two crutches. The court held Summer in bonds of ₤40, but he
has disappeared and changed his name to Henrich Singer. His
wife is named Maria, and he has a son Joseph.

   Johannes Gottwald, at Justus Schmitt's, near Germantown.

   Nicolaus Schaeffer, Tulpehocken Township, Berks County.

   Johannes Bob, Tulpehocken Township, Lancaster County (sic);
wife, Elisabeth.

   Joseph Schmitt, on Skippack road, near Gerret Dehaven's
mill, on Skippack Creek (Montgomery County).

   Gottfried Schmelcher, Kensington, by the windmill, near
Philadelphia.

   Johannes Schaeffer, Lynn Township (Lehigh County).

   Richard Graham, Rockhill Township, Bucks County, near
Samuel Dien's inn, offers a plantation for sale.

June 5, 1759

   Benjamin Nathan, who recently arrived in America, has
opened a store in Heidelberg, Lancaster County, in the stone
house built by Philip Erpff.

   Johann Georg Kuhn, Montgomery Township (Montgomery County),
near the meeting house (Gwynedd), seeks information about Martin
Kuhn, son of his brother, Georg Martin Kuhn.

   Simon Dreisbach, in Germantown, with Baltes Roeser, offers
for sale a plantation of 200 acres in Lehigh Township, Northampton County, near Joost Dreisbach's mill.

   Peter Spicker, Tulpehocken (Berks County), store.

June 5, 1759

Nicolaus Holteman, Lower Salford (Montgomery County).

June 22, 1759

Johannes Schaeffer, on Peter Hoenen's place, Heidelberg Township, Berks County.

Jacob Mueller, Wensen Township (Windsor?), Berks County; wife, Maria.

Nicolaus Emrich, Allemangel (Albany Township, Berks County), near Willem Schneider, inquires for his two sons, and one daughter. The older son, Valentin, is married; the other son, Friedrich, is single.

Peter Schneider, Frankford road, Kensington, Philadelphia County.

Johann Bayle, Plumstead Township, Bucks County.

Jacob Huweler, Tulpehocken (Berks County).

July 6, 1759

David Levi, New Goshenhoppen, on Philip Riedt's place (Montgomery County), advertises that formerly he was in partnership with Moses Heymann but now he conducts the shop himself.

Christopher Mueller, Lower Saucon, Northampton County.

Joh. Jacob Beehr, on the Plains (Hatfield Township, Montgomery County).

Conrad Klein, mason, on the Schuylkill.

Georg Wegele, Lower Salford Township (Montgomery County); wife, Anna Margaretta.

Michael Moll, Upper Hanover Township (Montgomery County).

July 20, 1759

Richard Hardley advertises that at the time of the August court he will open a store in Reading in the house where John Schmitt lived.

Johannes Umensetter, Oley, Berks County, in Hansz Joder's mill.

Michael Schnerr, Whitehall Township (Lehigh County), on Cedar Creek; wife, Margretha.

Peter Merckel, Mesillum, Berks County.

August 3, 1759

Valentin Kuemmel, on Pequea Creek, seven miles from Lancaster and one mile from Henrich Schlenck.

August 17, 1759

Johann Lentz, who arrived in America five years ago, seeks his three daughters and one son. Notify Johannes Pfister, Northampton Township, Bucks County.

Nicolaus Neiser, Philadelphia; wife, Barbara.

August 31, 1759

Kilian Gaugler, Old Goshenhoppen, Upper Salford Township (Montgomery County).

Peter Anspach, Tulpehocken Township, Berks County.

Levi Budd, Philadelphia, advertises that Christoffel Spring, a German tailor, ran away. He is 40 years old, and speaks French, German and English.

Georg Mueller, Richland Township, Bucks County; wife, Maria Elisabeth.

Jacob Schaeff, Alsace Township, Berks County.

Philip Heist, Hanover Township, near Abraham Mayer's mill (Lebanon or Dauphin County).

September 14, 1759

Bernhard Mayer, Falckner Swamp (Montgomery County); wife, Anna Maria.

Nicolaus Keim, Reading, wants to employ a turner.

September 28, 1759

Johannes Benninghof, Philadelphia, care of Valentin Schales or Johannes Beiszler, merchants, has information of an inheritance for Elisabeth Sophia Siebenbergin, spinster, born in Hattingen, in dem Clerischen, near Wesel. She was expected to come to America with a High German family to visit her brother, but did not come. Her brothers in America and Holland seek her.

Johann Eberhard Bens, Ringwood, Hunterdon County, New Jersey, seeks information about his step-brother, Christian Friedrich Desan, who served with an English smith five miles from White Horse inn, on Lancaster road.

Peter Raszber, Skippack (Montgomery County), with Georg Doelp, is going to Germany.

Valentin Stober, Lancaster County, advertises that his brother Martin, 28 years old, disappeared in August, 1758.

Daniel Hoch, Weidenthal (Willowdale), Richmond Township, Berks County.

Samuel Hoch, Oley, Berks County.

Johannes Roth, New Goshenhoppen, on Buettinger's place.

September 28, 1759

Georg Losch, powdermaker, near Germantown.

October 12, 1759

Johann Lehman, Germantown, offers for rent the house and pottery shop of his late father, Godfried Lehman.

Georg Baszel is now living in Chester County. He formerly lived in Upper Saucon (Lehigh County).

Michael Christ, Kensington, one mile from Philadelphia.

Johannes Romig, with Valentin Kuehle, Rockhill Township, Bucks County, who comes from Neustadt, an der groszen Linden, seeks his three brothers, Georg Michel, Georg and Christian, who have been in 'America for many years. Notify Adam Wittman, Reading.

Philip Walter, Macungie, on the Little Lehigh (Lehigh County).

Isaac Kauffman, Warwick Township, Lancaster County; wife, Christina.

Friedrich Stump, Heidelberg Township, Lancaster County, merchant. He transacts business on Saturday.

Jacob Beltz, Limerick Township, Philadelphia County (now Montgomery).

Johannes Zerbe, Heidelberg Township, Berks County.

October 26, 1759

Ulrich Gruber, Upper Hanover Township, Philadelphia County (now Montgomery).

Jacob Dattelmann, New Goshenhoppen, Upper Hanover Township (Montgomery County).

Valentin Kratz, Upper Salford Township (Montgomery County).

Martin Weszner, formerly of Exeter, Berks County; wife, Barbara.

Michael Schmitt, Chestnut Hill, Philadelphia County.

Georg Henrich Joseph, Rockhill Township, Bucks County.

Peter Dick, Bethlehem Township, Northampton County.

Johannes Weisz, Germantown road, near Philadelphia.

Joost Leech, Oley (Berks County).

November 9, 1759

Anna Dorothea Kluntzin, with Georg Mueller, Maxatawny (Berks County), who arrived in America seven years ago, seeks her brother, Conrad Kluntz.

Abraham Rener, New York, by the fresh water, seeks his brother, Christoffel Rener, who has been in America for six years and would inform him his father, mother, brother and sister are all well.

Michel Ganter, Windsor Township, Berks County; wife, Anna Maria.

Nicolaus Jansen, Whitpain Township, on Skippack road, Philadelphia County (now Montgomery).

Johannes Schnook, Lebanon Township, Lancaster County (now Lebanon County).

Bastian Mueller, several miles from Germantown.

Georg Imler, Paradise Township, York County.

Johannes Haberacker, Alsace, two miles from Reading.

Dewald Kuntz, Macungie Township (Lehigh County).

Henrich Hartmann, Rockhill Township, Bucks County.

November 23, 1759

Anna Nicolain, who served for two years with David Muma, Hempfield Township (Lancaster County), left last May to visit her sister and failed to return.

Martin Roery, Whitehall Township, Northampton County (now Lehigh).

Johannes Motzer, Lower Oley, in the hills (Berks County).

Georg Weyand, Upper Salford Township (Montgomery County).

Johannes Loescher, Oley (Berks County).

Johannes Bauman, near Ephrata.

December 7, 1759

Adam Simon Kuhn, Lancaster, has reopened his apothecary shop in Reading, near Adam Wittman. After opening the shop some years ago it had to be closed at times for lack of a competent attendant. The shop is now in charge of Daniel Adam Kurrer, a partner in the business. Adam Simon Kuhn continues to conduct his apothecary shop in Lancaster.

Martin Walborn, Heidelberg Township, Lancaster County (now Lebanon), one mile from Mr. Spicker.

Johannes Klein, on Israel Pemberton's plantation, near the lower ferry, Philadelphia.

December 7, 1759

Adolph Pannebecker, Limerick Township (Montgomery County).

Lorentz Hippel, on the Schuylkill, Vincent Township, Chester County.

Jacob Ziegenfusz, Rockland Township, Berks County, on Dietrich Schaeffer's place.

Johannes Mertz, Long Swamp, Berks County.

February 15, 1760

Sophia Dorothea Elisabetha Rorichin, New York, with Mr. Gebel, seeks her father, Ninges Rorich; her mother, Anengle; her brother, Friedrich Rorich, and her sister, Juliana Rorichin.

Johannes Ewald, Amity Township, Berks County, on Manatawny Creek, advertises that his German servant boy, Joerg Kauffmann, 16 years old, ran away.

Dorothea Ackerin, with Henrich Schenck, eight miles from Lancaster, came to America five years ago with her sister, Anna Catharina Ackerin, about whom she now seeks information.

Henrich Schaup, Rockhill Township, Bucks County, near Samuel Dien.

Ludwig Kipffel, four miles from York, on Codorus Creek.

Georg Bayer, Tulpehocken Township, Berks County.

Daniel Roemig, Bedminster Township, Bucks County.

February 29, 1760

Martin Schuck, Hempfield Township, Lancaster County; wife, Anna Maria.

Henrich Dilbon, Richmond Township, Berks County, on Mesilemer Creek.

Martin Kummerling, Bethel Township, Lancaster County (now Lebanon).

Gottfried Roehrer, Tulpehocken Township, Berks County.

March 28, 1760

Willem Jung, Kingsessing Township, Philadelphia County, one-half mile from the lower ferry in the Schuylkill.

Jacob Schrack, New Providence Township, Trappe, wants to employ a locksmith apprentice.

Henrich Wagner, Bethel Township, Lancaster County (now Lebanon).

Jacob Frie, between Philadelphia and Frankford; wife, Barbara.

March 28, 1760

Jacob Berger, potter's apprentice, Lancaster, with Henrich Hottenstein.

Conrad Wahneschmitt, Maxatawny, Berks County.

April 24, 1760

Johannes Albrecht and his wife Margretha, York Township, over the Susquehanna, had a son Jacob, who was indentured with English people in the Welsh Township, Philadelphia County (Lower Merion or Gwynedd Township, Montgomery County). The father is dead and the mother seeks information about her son.

Adam Klein, Williams Township, near Easton; wife, Elisabeth.

Jacob Losch and Ulrich Merckel, one mile from Germantown.

May 23, 1760

Johann Christophel Henszy, single, died while with Conrad Jacobi, Salisbury Township (Lehigh County), two miles from Bethlehem.

Simon Ritter came to America ten years ago with his cousin, Johannes Gach, who entered into service in New Jersey. Simon Ritter, who is now with Ludwig Laumann, Lancaster, seeks information about Gach.

Inquiry is made for Georg Bischoff, alias Dichan Albrecht, from Alsace, who lived in Whitemarsh Township, Philadelphia County (now Montgomery), up to the end of 1759.

Adam Kurtz, Limerick Township, Philadelphia County (now Montgomery).

Jacob Oberholtzer, Franconia Township (Montgomery County).

Rudy Kittinger, in Dirck Keyser's lane, Germantown.

Johannes Reiszer, Upper Saucon Township (Lehigh County).

Conrad Trunckler, on Durham Furnace land one mile from the furnace and one mile from Jacob Gucker, in Upper Saucon Township (Lehigh County).

Adam Willauer, Upper Milford Township, Northampton County (now Lehigh).

Christian Herman, Earl Township, Lancaster County.

June 6, 1760

Adolph Meyer, doctor and chirurgeon, has removed from Gabriel Schuler's, where he had lived for several years, to Methacton (now Fairview Village, Montgomery County), on the Reading road, next to the plantation of Christian G'melin, and near Rudolph Bunner.

June 6, 1760

Otmar Schnebely, Bethel Township, Lancaster County (now Lebanon).

Catharina Beringer and her daughter Catharina, care of Ludwig Stein, Lancaster, who came to America seven years ago, with another daughter, Ursula, seek information about Ursula. They came from Heilbrun.

Johannes Klockner, Allemangel, near Velten Probst (Albany Township, Berks County).

Johannes Arnold, Tulpehocken Township, Berks County.

Henrich Strehm, Lancaster County, on Cocalico Creek, one-quarter mile from Ephrata, near Abraham Schonauer, came to America five years and six months ago, with his brother, Henrich Adam, and he seeks information about the latter.

August 11, 1760

Adam Schaerer, North Wales, Philadelphia County Gwynedd Township, Montgomery County).

Abraham Fuellman, on Christian Miller's place, Lebanon Township, Lancaster County (now Lebanon).

Georg Emmert, Bethel Township, Berks County.

Jacob Knob, Cocalico Township, Lancaster County.

Christian Rayer, Manheim Township, Lancaster County.

Tobias Bickel, Tulpehocken Township, Berks County.

Andreas Berger, Frederick, Maryland; wife, Philippina.

Johann Eberhart Hartmann, serving with David Auen, Upper Saucon Township, Northampton County (now Lehigh), seeks information about his father, Friedrich Hartmann, his four brothers, Friedrich Johann Paulus, Gottlieb Friedrich, Joh. Philip and Wilhelm, and his sister, Rosina, all of whom arrived in America seven years ago.

Christian Ohrendorf, Heidelberg Township, Lancaster County (now Lebanon).

Bastian Seibert, Philadelphia, at the old sugar house, seeks his brother, Johannes Seibert, born unter Altertheim, bey Werthheim am Mayn, who arrived in America in 1751.

Johannes Kuhn and Barbara Kunhin, New York, opposite the High School, seek information about their daughter, Anna Maria, whom they have not seen for thirteen years.

Philip Reiner, Providence Township, Philadelphia County (now Montgomery).

Benjamin Nathan and his brother Lyon, of Reading, have opened a store in their house in Heidelberg, Lancaster County (now Lebanon).

August 11, 1760

Samuel Summine, Springfield Township, Bucks County.

Ludwig Benner, Rockhill Township, Bucks County.

January 2, 1761

Conrad Bauer, Reading, advertises that his German servant, Wilhelm Knorr, ran away. He is 18 years old and formerly served with the Pennsylvania soldiers.

Johann Martin Hoffman opens a store in Lancaster on King street, next to Widow Walter, dyer.

Peter Bieler, Great Swamp, Lower Milford Township, Bucks County.

Theobald Bieber, Richmond Township, Berks County.

Dr. Urban Kriebele has arrived at Philadelphia and is living in "Erdstrasze," with Mr. Knerr.

Ludwig Fillinger, Amity Township, Berks County; wife, Catharina.

Henrich Schopp, Heidelberg Township (Lebanon County).

Samuel Secker, Whitehall Township, Northampton County (now Lehigh).

Christel Hundsberger, Franconia Township, Philadelphia County (now Montgomery).

Ludwig Uber, butcher, Fourth street, between Race and Vine, Philadelphia.

Caspar Holtzhauer, Upper Milford Township, Northampton County (now Lehigh).

Johannes Weber, Hanover Township, Lancaster County (now Lebanon).

Melchior Scholtze, Upper Hanover Township (Montgomery County).

Henrich Finck, Coventry Township, Chester County.

Jacob Franciscus, Alsace Township, Berks County.

Henrich Fryer, Falckner Swamp (Montgomery County).

Jacob Graff, Cocalico Township, Lancaster County.

February 13, 1761

Conrad Acker, Limerick Township, near Johann Koplin, justice (Montgomery County).

Conrad Reiff, Oley (Berks County).

February 13, 1761

Peter Arnold, Sommer Bergen (Summer Hill?), Berks County.

Land of the Pennsylvania Land Company is advertised for sale, and names of occupants are given as follows:

Roxborough Township, Philadelphia County, 179 acres on Ridge road--Thomas Davis.

New Providence (Montgomery County), on the Schuylkill and Perkiomen Creek, 4000 acres--John Edwards, Thomas Francis, Thomas Rositer, Peter and James Skien, Thomas Gahagen, John Taney, Nathan Daevy, Arnold Fox, Samuel Bell and others.

Limerick Township (Montgomery County), 708 acres--James Hoven, Edward Bolten, John Jordan, Herman Stall.

Makefield Township, Bucks County, 4000 acres--Joseph Tomlinson, James Cross, William Lee, Jonathan Copper, Thomas and Samuel Merrick, Israel Doane, William Keith, William and Thomas Schmitt, James and William Dellon, Henrich Becker, Samuel and James McNair.

Lampeter and Manheim Townships, Lancaster County, 2500 acres--John Krick, David Crawford, Andreas Bersinger, James Patterson, Johann Rohrer, Christian Stoever, Widow McFilly, Joost Moser, ---- Rudischall and others.

Strasburg Township, on a branch of Pequea Creek, Lancaster County, 1874 acres--Matthes, Daniel and Henrich Schleyermacher, Robert Schmitt, John Huston, William Weit, Isaac Taylor and others.

Tinicum Township, Bucks County, 7500 acres, extending five miles along the Delaware River--David Neumann, Robert James, Nicolaus Pattison, Widow Marshall, Elisabeth and James Bayly, Johan Fretz, Dielman Kolb, Robert Stewart, Johan Kelly, James Kennedy, Henrich McIntire, James Wallace, Henrich Neuton and others.

Martin Rast began riding post January 19 between Reading and Philadelphia by horse. Beginning April 6 he will use a wagon, leaving Reading on Monday and arriving in Philadelphia on Tuesday evening, and leaving Philadelphia Friday and arriving in Reading Saturday evening. Weekly trips will be made until December 1, and thereafter every fourteen days.

Johan Martin Kirschmann, Maidencreek Township, Berks County, from the Wurtemberg domain of the Palatinate Duke in Weiler, seeks information about his mother, Catharina Kirschmannin, his two brothers-in-law, Christian and Friedrich Schwartz, and his two sisters, Maria and Catharina Kirschmannin.

Jonas Vogt, Bethel Township, Lancaster County (now Lebanon).

Andreas Hertz, Salisbury Township, Northampton County (now Lehigh), on the Little Lehigh.

Georg Schneider, one mile from the lower ferry in the Schuylkill and four miles from Philadelphia.

February 13, 1761

Johan Koplin, Limerick Township (Montgomery County), gives notice of the death of Jacob Nagel, single, in Limerick Township.

Philip Walter, Macungie, on the Little Lehigh (Lehigh County).

Friedrich Kobel, miller, Heidelberg Township, Berks County.

Bernhard Jacob, storekeeper, on the Muehlback (Mill Creek).

Adam Johe, Easton.

Jacob Roth, Oley (Berks County).

Matthes Miller, Springfield Township, Bucks County.

March 27, 1761

Peter Bernthaler, Northern Liberties of Philadelphia, on Germantown road, near Johannes Stellwagen, between Front and Second streets, sells kettles and does smith work.

Johann Mayer, butcher, Germantown.

Friedrich Bickin, Merion Township, Philadelphia County (Lower Merion Township, Montgomery County), advertises that his servant, Jacob Bueck, 18 years old, ran away.

Richard Hartle, Reading, adjoining Conrad Bauer, is selling out the contents of his store.

Jacob Hollinger, Lancaster, adjoining the Lutheran Church, has begun the dyeing business.

Samuel Moechling, Upper Milford Township, Northampton County (now Lehigh), advertises that two years ago his servant, Joh. Adam Beissel, 17 years old, ran away. He formerly worked with his father, Peter Beissel, at Durham Furnace.

Georg Keller, Philadelphia, Arch street, sign of the black eagle, buys linen rags.

Anna Mayerin, living near Middletown, New Jersey, born in Switzerland, in Winckel, Zuricher Gebieth, seeks her brother, Hansz Conrad Mayer, who came to America 27 years ago. Notify Jacob Rittenhouse, Germantown, or Abraham Mayer, New Goshenhoppen.

Christian Darck, a native of Hanover, who formerly lived in Franconia Township (Montgomery County), left there last February with his wife, two daughters and two sons.

Stephan Kurtz, Bern Township, Berks County.

Melcher Baer, Macungie (Lehigh County).

Adam Walborn, Bethel Township, Berks County.

March 27, 1761

Rudolph Mayer, Bethel Township, Berks County.

April 24, 1761

Georg Lachler, "Riedtmacher," formerly of Germantown, known as the Catholic weaver, is now on Market street, near Sixth, Philadelphia.

Jacob Maag, one mile from Germantown.

David Henderson, lawyer, Reading.

Johann Christ Henn, Heidelberg Township, Berks County.

Peter Bener, Rockhill Township, Bucks County.

Nicolaus Schwingel, Heidelberg Township, Berks County.

May 22, 1761

David Rittman and his wife, Maria Elisabeth, born Weissin, seek the latter's sister, Maria Catharina, born Weissin, from Langen Candel, bey Lindau. Her husband is Frantz Grosz, a weaver, who has a brother-in-law near Lancaster, Stoffel Geiger. David Rittman and his wife arrived at New York in 1755, and are in New York with Adam von dem Berg.

Andreas Beyer, Methacton, Worcester Township (Montgomery County), advertises that his German servant, Johannes Becker, 18 years old, ran away.

Conrad Schuetz, papermaker, Merion Township (Lower Merion Township, Montgomery County).

Henrich Meyer, on the Muehlbach (Mill Creek), Heidelberg Township, Lancaster County (now Lebanon).

Michel Bauermann, Weisenberg Township, Northampton County (now Lehigh).

Dorst Pfuester, Reading, advertises that his apprentice, Vincentz Schwitzgabel, ran away.

Johann Georg Werner, Bristol Township, Philadelphia County); wife, Margreth.

Paul and Philip Hartmann seek their brother, Gottlieb Friedrich, who was indentured eight years ago at Raritan, New Jersey. Notify Matthes Reichert, Falckner Swamp (Montgomery County).

Ludwig Gutbrod, Codorus, York County; wife, Elisabeth.

Ludwig Buetting, Germantown.

Daniel Ostwald, Lynn Township (Lehigh County).

Jacob Risser, Bern Township, Berks County.

Jacob Hartzel, Salisbury Township (Lehigh County).

May 22, 1761

Jacob Vogelsang, Rapho Township, Lancaster County.

Emig Reyer, Cocalico Township, Lancaster County.

Willem Henrich Hag, Maxatawny (Berks County).

Jacob Treibelbitz, Richmond Township, Berks County.

June 5, 1761

Mayer Josephsen, Berks County, has removed his store to the house adjoining that which he formerly occupied.

Caspar Foegel, New Goshenhoppen; wife, Anna Catharina.

Johannes Danckel, Macungie (Lehigh County).

Michel Hefli, Richmond Township, Berks County, one mile from Musillemer mill.

The widow of Michel Dieter, Springfield Township, Bucks County.

Johann Joerg Loosz, Bern Township, Berks County.

Hannes Germann, Rapho Township, Lancaster County.

Friedrich Spiegel, Macungie (Lehigh County).

June 19, 1761

James Delbert, smith, Germantown, opposite Simon Siron, merchant, advertises that his apprentice, William Oldemus, ran away.

Henrich Pannebecker, fuller, formerly on Perkiomen Creek, is now in Upper Salford Township (Montgomery County), one mile from Johannes Clement's mill, where he continues the fulling business.

Georg Christoph Reinhold, bookbinder, Second street, Philadelphia, opposite David Schaeffer, at the sign of the Bible.

John Miller, Plymouth Township (Montgomery County).

Henrich Mock, Warwick Township, Lancaster County.

Henrich Baumann, Lebanon Township, Lancaster County (now Lebanon County).

Philip Lehrer, Northern Liberties Township, Philadelphia County.

Martin Kersteter, Hanover Township, Lancaster County (now Lebanon or Dauphin).

Jacob Mellinger, Cocalico Township, Lancaster County.

Joseph Siegfried, Maxatawny Township, Berks County.

June 19, 1761

Johannes Stoetzel, Oley Township, Berks County.

Bernhard Gilbert, Franconia Township (Montgomery County), on Joost Pfannekuchen's place.

Martin Hoffman, Rockhill Township, Bucks County.

July 3, 1761

Jacob Schmidt, care of Antony Jaeger, Oley (Berks County), near the new furnace, who arrived in America six years ago, from Langenbramig, seeks his brother, Johan Adam, a clothmaker, who arrived seven years ago.

Eva Rosina Barbara Groszin, with Johann Stauffer, Warwick Township, Lancaster County, seeks her father, Leopold Valentin Grosz, a mason, and her brother, Johan Friedrich Grosz.

Conrad Krob, Whitehall Township, on the Great Lehigh (Lehigh County), advertises that his German servant, Matthes Matz, 16 years old, ran away.

Valentin Hagner, Market street, Philadelphia, advertises that his German apprentice, Johann Schumacher, ran away. He was born in America and is 16 years old.

Joachim Braeutigam, Colebrookdale Township, Berks County, at the old Potts furnace, inquires for his two children, whom his wife, Margaretha Elisabeth, took away with her four years ago. One, aged 7, is named Jedel; the other, aged 5, Dorothea Elisabeth.

David Vetter, Anweil, New Jersey.

Joh. Peter Schubman, on the Schuylkill.

Monsieur Frick, Lancaster, student in chirurgy.

Jacob Weltmer, linen weaver, Heidelberg.

Jacob Eister, Oley (Berks County); son, George.

Reinhart Miller, store, in Michel Reisz's old place, on Little Swatara Creek, Bethel Township (Lebanon County).

Isaac Levan the younger, Reading, buys hides and sells leather.

Christian Herr, Lampeter Township, Lancaster County.

Matthes Beszhor, Hanover Township, Lancaster County (now Lebanon or Dauphin). Also Jacob Beszor.

Johannes Kloos, Alsace Township, Berks County.

July 17, 1761

Israel Robeson, Robeson Township, Berks County, advertises that his native-born servant, William Allen, ran away.

July 17, 1761

Jacob Doerr, Falckner Swamp (Montgomery County).

Roland Jung, New Hanover Township (Montgomery County).

Peter Weiser, saddler, Reading.

July 31, 1761

Johann Wilhelm Hoffman, at the corner opposite Daniel Etter, Race street, Philadelphia, has established a sugar house, in association with John Cornman.

Matthes Sittler, Queen street, Lancaster, has begun business as a coppersmith.

Christian Fuchs, Donegal Township, Lancaster County.

Conrad Doll, born in the Palatinate near Landau, is going abroad. Commissions for him may be sent to Friedrich Doll, Hickorytown (Plymouth Township, Montgomery County).

Joachim Nagel, Douglass Township, Berks County.

Friedrich Winter, Tulpehocken Township, Berks County.

David Pfautz, carpenter, Lancaster; wife, Anna Barbara.

Georg Schlayer, New Goshenhoppen, at Johann Mack's mill, seeks his brother Henrich, who arrived in America nine years ago.

Johann Diel Wentz, Derry Township, Lancaster County (now Dauphin).

Johann Lebmann, Rapho Township, Lancaster County.

Jacob Kopp, Hanover Township, Philadelphia County (New Hanover ? Upper Hanover ? Montgomery County).

August 14, 1761

Andreas Schmitt, New Hanover Township (Montgomery County).

Peter Klein, Macungie (Lehigh County).

Peter Sume, Tulpehocken, Heidelberg Township, Lancaster County (now Lebanon or Dauphin).

Philip Jengwein, Lancaster Township, Lancaster County.

Gisbert Gilbert, Limerick Township (Montgomery County).

Philip Henrich Scholl, Lower Saucon Township, Northampton County.

Solomon Gruemely, Skippack Township (Montgomery County) near Pannebecker's mill.

Jacob Stamm, Albany Township, Berks County.

August 14, 1761

Adam Luetz, Northern Liberties of Philadelphia, two miles from Germantown.

August 28, 1761

Johannes and Elisabeth Bell, upper Germantown, opposite the Lutheran Church, third house above Jacob Genssel, at the sign of the combmaker, sell Catharina Diemer's salve.

Jacob Rincker, Chestnut Hill, Philadelphia County.

Jacob Strieby, Macungie (Lehigh County); wife, Eva.

Georg Happel, Flourtown (Montgomery County).

Michael Bischoff, Milford Township, Bucks County.

Johann Georg Weisz, schoolmaster, Heidelberg, Berks County.

Johann Georg Heist, Saucon.

Michael Kratz, New Goshenhoppen, with Robert Thomas.

Hannes Linde, Cocalico, Lancaster County, on Abraham Brubaker's land, near Martin Weidman.

September 11, 1761

Jacob Baertsch, Market street, Philadelphia, general store, sign of the Lamb.

Ulrich Hartmann, Worcester Township (Montgomery County), will hold a vendue, as he is going to Zweibruecken, Germany.

Jacob Bartsch, one mile from Philadelphia, on the late William Master's land.

Baltzer Feitz, Skippack Township (Montgomery County), near Diedrich Welcker's mill.

Jacob Gery, New Goshenhoppen, a half mile from Abraham Mayer's mill.

Isaac Lehmann, Lampeter Township, Lancaster County.

Peter Gruenewald, Richmond Township, Berks County.

Lorentz Hoffschaar, at the Tulpehocken iron works.

Jacob Traeusch, Heidelberg Township (Lebanon County).

September 25, 1761

David Mueller, apprentice of Casimer Missimer, New Hanover Township (Montgomery County), was arrested and held as a royal prisoner, but he escaped and fled. He is a tanner, 20 years old, and his parents live near Ephrata. Notify Justice Enoch Davies, Limerick Township (Montgomery County). Signed by Georg Juerger, constable, New Hanover.

September 25, 1761

Moses Heyman has removed his store from Second street to Market street, Philadelphia, adjoining the Indian King inn.

Johannes Scheidt, Alsace Township, Berks County; wife, Maria Eva.

Jacob Gensel, Germantown.

Wendel Ruehner, New Goshenhoppen.

Jacob Beiler, Oley (Berks County), near Samuel Hoch.

Willem Henrich Haag, Maxatawny, Berks County.

Walter Borck, Amity Township, Berks County.

Georg Helffrich, Upper Milford Township (Lehigh County).

Abraham Kassel, Rapho Township, Lancaster County.

Johannes Baer, Cocalico Township, Lancaster County.

October 2, 1761

David Ungerbieler, Bristol Township, two miles from Germantown, opposite Johannes Roeser.

Johannes Baumann, next door to the Mennonite Meeting House, Germantown, sells maps and books.

Michel Biegel, Quitopahilla (Lebanon County), seeks information about his aunt, Agnes, who married Henrich Bittel.

Baltes Lapp, Whitpain Township (Montgomery County), one-quarter mile from Boehm's Reformed Church.

Johann Martin Truckenmiller, Race street, corner of Third, Philadelphia, sells rum, wine, tea, coffee, etc.

Jacob Frick, one mile from Manatawny Creek, on the Great road.

October 7, 1761

Joost Wieand, New Goshenhoppen, born in Fresheim, in the Palatinate, and Adam Hellwig, Long Swamp, Berks County, born in Alzey, in the Palatinate von Kriegsfeld, four hours from Creutzenach, are preparing to go to Germany.

Jacob Boehm, German artist, Philadelphia, in Queen Ann alley, with Frantz Seener, German tailor, and opposite the Rossmuehle (horse mill) of Nicolaus Bargards, is ready to undertake any art work.

Johannes Schweighausen, Philadelphia, has removed his store to the house where Moses Herman formerly lived, the third house below Race street (sic).

Johann Martin Schuler, York Township, York County; wife, Elisabeth.

October 7, 1761

Johann Caspar Fitting, Elizabeth Township, Lancaster County.

Johannes Ferbe, miller at Peter Schauben's mill, Brecknock Township, Lancaster County.

Benjamin Rosenberger, Hatfield Township (Montgomery County).

Eleanor Kelly, Hilltown, Bucks County.

Conrad Grosch, Frederick, Maryland.

Jacob Bercki, Bern Township, Berks County.

Henrich Grimm, Maxatawny Township, Berks County.

Jacob Vollmer, Tulpehocken Township, Berks County.

October 23, 1761

John Boone and James Boone, tanners, Exeter Township, Berks County.

Nicolaus Hennicke, Lebanon, rides post between Lebanon and Lancaster.

Michel Schwob, York.

Philip Dresher, Long Swamp, Berks County.

Georg Gangwer, Easton.

Conrad Schweitzer and Johann Becker, Philadelphia, have rented the board wharf of Thomas Mayer, next to Salter's wharf.

Andreas Weimar, Albany County, seeks his brother Jacob, born at Hoffen, in Alsace, near Weissenburg, who came to America nine years ago. Notify Peter Paris, Philadelphia, at the corner house at Moravian alley on Second street.

Johann Ziemer, on James Meniesen's place, on Little Swatara Creek, Bethel Township (Lebanon County).

Georg Kelchner, Richmond Township, Berks County.

Christel Bamberger, Warwick Township, Lancaster County.

Andreas Drestner, Macungie (Lehigh County).

Ludwig Gaucker, Hereford Township, Berks County, near Mayburry's furnace.

Baltes Umpenbauer, Bern Township, Berks County, on the Northkill.

November 6, 1761

Jacob Nagele, lower Germantown, sells shoemaker's rosin and turpentine.

November 6, 1761

Anna Erbin, with Nicolaus Erb's wife, Quitopahilla (Lebanon County).

Margaretha Fretzin, New York, with Michael Kaeyser, by the fresh water, seeks her son, Burkhard Fretz, who has been in America six or seven years.

Friedrich Beppler, Heidelberg Town, born in Amt alten Hossel von Eidengesatz.

Simon Keppler, smith, Falckner Swamp (Montgomery County), a half mile from the old furnace in Little Oley--a Wurtemberger.

Alexander Diebendoerffer, Lower Milford Township, Bucks County.

Johann Michel Redelmoser, near Lancaster.

Johannes Mayer, shoemaker, near Ephrata.

Gottlieb Strohecker, Reading.

Johannes Schorb, Heidelberg Township, Berks County.

Nicolaus Jaeger, Oley (Berks County), advertises that his German servant, Christoffel von Ernst, 40 years old, ran away.

Hansz Martin Herder, Egypt Township (Lehigh County), three miles from Baal, on the Jordan.

Christian Cassel, Salisbury Township, on the Little Lehigh (Lehigh County).

Sebastian Horn, Springfield Township, Bucks County.

Rudy Bossert, on the Antelane.

Georg Leibegut, Whitehall Township (Lehigh County).

Peter Stoeckel, Whitehall Township (Lehigh County).

November 20, 1761

Hansz Adam Neidig, Brecknock Township, Lancaster County, seeks his brother-in-law, Joseph and Henrich Fichtner, who have been in America ten years. Their sister Dorothea is concerned about them.

Valentin Schales has removed his store and inn to a location on Second street nearer Market, between Vine and Race, Philadelphia.

Nicolaus Schneider, New Providence (Montgomery County).

Andreas Knoedler, Heidelberg Township (Lehigh County).

Georg Kribel, Towamencin Township (Montgomery County).

Joseph Zewitz, Upper Milford Township (Lehigh County).

December 18, 1761

Johann Nickel Walbert, Upper Milford Township (Lehigh County).

Friedrich Gotz, Skippack, Lower Salford Township (Montgomery County).

Johannes Haalman, Worcester Township, near Jacob Wentz (Montgomery County).

Lyon Nathan has returned to Reading and conducts his store in the house where Mayer Josephson formerly lived.

Jacob Graesel, Allemangel, Lynn Township (Lehigh County), seeks his brother Philip, who has been in America seven years.

Michel Klein, Reading, near Velten Coerper, sells snuff.

Hansz Frantz, Brecknock Township, Lancaster County.

Johann Teany, New Providence (Montgomery County).

Jacob Vogel, Macungie (Lehigh County).

Bernhard Schaertle, Bern Township, Berks County.

Andreas Krausz, Quitopahilla (Lebanon County), sells drugs.

Samuel Haupt, Upper Dublin, eight miles from Farmar's mill (Montgomery County), is going to Germany in January. He is at home in Creutzenach, in the Palatinate.

Frantz Schalter, with Dietrich Beutelmann, Alsace Township, Berks County.

January 29, 1762

Abraham Taylor, who is going to England, offers for sale his 70-acre plantation in Berks County, on Swatara Creek, occupied by Christoph Weiser; also another of 130 acres, occupied by Georg Seller, and an adjoining tract of 100 acres, occupied by heirs of the late Georg Bleystein.

Johannes Walter, Pikeland Township (Chester County), on the Great road, adjoining Squire Moore.

Johannes Roth, shoemaker, near Smithfield, Byberry Township, Philadelphia County.

Jacob Graethman, Whitehall Township (Lehigh County).

Johannes Unverzagt, gunsmith, Germantown.

Henry Lukens, Chestnut Hill, Philadelphia County.

Daniel Huhn, Bristol Township, Philadelphia County.

Jacob Eberle, Cocalico Township, Lancaster County.

Henrich Adami, Bucks County, near Georg Oberbeck.

January 29, 1762

Michel Musselman, Milford Township, Bucks County.

Georg Weidner, North Wales (Gwynedd Township, Montgomery County), one mile from the meeting house, where John Jones formerly lived.

Johannes Artzt, Heidelberg Township, Berks County.

Andreas Crossan, on Israel Pemberton's plantation, Kensington, Philadelphia County.

Matthes Willson and Jacob Heald, on Israel Pemberton's plantation, Kensington, Philadelphia County.

Henrich Addington, on Israel Pemberton's plantation at the Forks of the Brandywine.

Georg Moser, Northern Liberties of Philadelphia, gives notice that his father-in-law, Peter Schuh, is dead.

Jacob Zienet, Monocacy, Maryland. He was in Pittsburgh in 1759-61.

Gottfried Daubenbauer, Adamstown, Lancaster.

Moses Peters, Montgomery Township (Montgomery County) offers for sale the place adjoining his own, where Garret Peters lived.

Henrich von der Schleisz, Upper Salford Township (Montgomery County), offers for sale his farm of 180 acres, with a grist mill on Perkiomen Creek.

Johann Gellnitz, Lebanon Township (Lebanon County); wife, Elisabeth.

Nicolaus Brosius, beyond the Blue Mountains.

April 9, 1762

Herman Gerlach, stockingweaver, Cresheim (Mount Airy, Philadelphia).

Johann Bausz will be at his old place in Colebrookdale Township (Berks County), with Henrich Engel, to collect debts.

Valentin Bayer, Old Goshenhoppen (Montgomery County), on the Branch (of Perkiomen Creek), wants a tyler.

Henrich Hess, Berks County, near Johannes Loescher's furnace.

Benjamin Nathan, Lancaster County, and Lion Nathan, Reading, have terminated their partnership. Each now conducts a store.

Johannes Bausz has removed from Colebrookdale (Berks County), to Methacton (Worcester Township, Montgomery County), to the place where Rudolph Bonner conducted a tavern for a long time, and he will continue the tavern.

April 9, 1762

Jacob Krischer, Lancaster, seeks news of his sisters from Alzey--Sophia Krischerin, Mariamel Krischerin and Maria Lieberin.

Johannes Kleyenr, Cumru Township, Berks County; wife, Barbara.

Johannes Schwedener, Greenwich Township, Berks County.

Adam Zollman, Greenwich Township, Berks County.

Michel Bosch, at Captain Flower's furnace.

Hansz Adam Schmidt, Greenwich Township, Berks County.

Nicolaus Kern, Towamencin Township, Northampton County.

Peter Gerhard, at the Branch (of Perkiomen Creek), Franconia Township (Montgomery County).

Henrich Menge, Philadelphia, at Poole's bridge, is going to Freiburg, Frankfort and Butschbach, Germany.

Johann Georg Nattler, Bern Township, Berks County.

Christoffel Wittmer, Heidelberg.

Paulus and Valentin Wentz, Goshenhoppen (Montgomery County).

Johann Michel Kilian, near Lancaster.

Christian and Hans Adam Eva, Lancaster County.

Jacob Gaininger, Tulpehocken (Berks County).

Samuel Lefeber, Salisbury Township, Lancaster County.

Peter Schuhmann, Pikeland Township, Chester County, on French Creek.

Georg Blanck, Rockhill Township, Bucks County.

Valentin Eckert, Alsace Township, Berks County.

Casper Schnaebely, Bethel Township, Berks County.

Isaac Scharret, Macungie (Lehigh County).

WOCHENTLICHER PENNSYLVANISCHER STAATSBOTE

Published in Philadelphia by Heinrich Miller.

March 30, 1767

Jacob Wagner, cooper, has established a shop in the yard of Jacob Dietrich, tobacco spinner, corner Clifton or Shoemaker alley, between Arch and Race streets, Philadelphia.

May 25, 1767

Inquiry for Johannes Plarr, baker, from Alsace, who ten years ago conducted a bakery and mill eight miles from Philadelphia.

Martin Toman, born in Niederdorf, in Loedlichen Canton Basel, Switzerland, who formerly lived in Heidelberg, Lancaster County, and then at Chestnut Hill, Philadelphia County, is going to Europe.

Joh. Michel Baecker, school teacher, Tulpehocken (Berks County).

Joh. Henrich Kuntze, Frederick, Maryland.

Susanna Thomas, Earl Township, Lancaster County.

Johann Ruebenweller, New York; from Zeppenfeld.

Johann Engel, potter master, New York.

March 29, 1768

Anna Maria Beisserin, living with her son-in-law, Philip Alberti, Arch street, Philadelphia, where Johannes Beisser lived, is going abroad. Alberti makes tinware.

Josephum Antonium Santerini left Mannheim, Germany, 27 years ago for Philadelphia.

Johann Jacob Wetzel, Great Swamp (Bucks County).

Urban Eschenbrenner, on the Ridge (Ridge avenue), near Philadelphia.

Peter Hasenclever, New York, advertises that his indentured German lackey, Alexander Burckhard, ran away. He speaks German and French.

Andreas Fischer, on William Bell's place, near Frankford, Philadelphia County.

December 19, 1769

Michel Kuemmerly, Tyrone Township, York County (now Perry), seeks his brother, Hans Kuemmerly, born in Schleydorf, Wurtemberg, who came to America fifteen years ago. Their father died on the voyage and their mother soon after arriving at Philadelphia. Address, in care of William Walker, storekeeper in Tyrone Township.

May 22, 1770

Maria Barbara Koeblin, care of Thomas Clime, a Quaker, at Pequea, advertises that her daughter, aged 18 years, left the Little Brandywine last Christmas for Lancaster to enter service, and nothing has since been heard of her.

Melchior Stecher, Forks Township, Northampton County, three miles from Nazareth.

Peter Roth, Kensington, Philadelphia County.

Christian Weicks, Exeter Township, Berks County.

June 5, 1770

William Kerlin, on the Brandywine at Chadd's ford.

June 12, 1770

Dietrich Beyerle, care of Dietrich Taub, shoemaker, Second street, near Vine, Philadelphia, born in Langen Kandel, in Zweibrueckischen, near Landau, is going abroad.

Joh. Henrich Oberlander, beer brewer, Philadelphia.

Philip Matthes, smith servant, Lebanon Township (Lebanon County).

Joh. Adam Bausch, Middletown Township, Chester County (now Delaware County).

Joh. Bernh. Schuhman, Broad Bay, New England.

Philip Albrecht Mueller, Mecklenburg Township, on the cold Water, North Carolina.

Joh. Henrich Frey, Lebanon Township (Lebanon County).

Nicolaus Daumenlang, Frederick, Maryland.

Tobias Horein and Peter Wedel, Maryland, near Conegetschick.

Joh. Friedrich Riehl, Frederick, Md.

Carl Friedrich Siebert, butcher, Oley, Berks County.

Susanna Stoehrin, servant with Thomas Leavesley, a half hour from Germantown (Roxborough Township, Philadelphia County).

June 12, 1770

Jacob Beyer, Eyster Township, im Schwartzwald.

Jacob Lorch, from Druchtelfingen, Wurtemberg.

Andreas Roller, from Estelbrunn, Wurtemberg.

Hans Georg Kirn, from Groszen Astbach, Wurtemberg.

Christoph Mohr, York.

June 19, 1770

Friedrich Becker, Salisbury Township, Lancaster County.

June 26, 1770

Bernhard Lawersweiler, inn, Second street, Philadelphia, in the house where the late William Clempfer lived.

July 3, 1770

James Nevell's inn, the Rainbow, Northern Liberties of Philadelphia.

David Brisch, Exeter Township, Berks County.

Conrad Weber, Germantown.

July 24, 1770

Andreas Boszhart, shoemaker, Second street, Philadelphia, advertises that his apprentice, Jacob Peter, 19 years old, ran away.

Peter Hallom, Lancaster, advertises that his German servant, Martin Braun, 23-24 years old, ran away.

Lenert Lebo, Exeter Township, Berks County.

July 31, 1770

Georg Hoeppler, shoemaker, Providence Township (Montgomery County), advertises that his English apprentice, George Hutchinson, 16 years old, ran away.

Philip Crist, Paradise Township, York County, seven miles from York.

August 7, 1770

Johann Leonhard Zemsch, son of Wilhelm Friedrich Zemsch, former citizen and master needlemaker of Rotenburg, ob der Tauber, Frankischen Kreis (Franconia), left home in 1752 for the third time as a journeyman in the needle craft, going with his cousin, Jung, a needlemaker from Marggraflichen Boodischen

August 7, 1770

Residenz Stadt Durlach, and the Jung family. On the Stedman ship they went to New England and landed with Benjamin Shoemaker, merchant, in Philadelphia. Zemsch was indentured for his passage costs to an Irish miller, and his relatives heard nothing further about him. Information about Zemsch may be sent to the Rev. Mr. Muhlenberg.

August 14, 1770

Henrich Diebenberger, gunsmith, has removed from Second street to Market street, Philadelphia, the second house from the Black Bear inn.

Daniel MacFarland, Mount Holly, N. J., advertises that his German servant, Martin Lang, 38 years old, ran away.

Adam Eckart, dealer in windmills, Market street, Philadelphia, second house from Fifth.

Henrich Mueller, Vincent Township, Chester County; wife, Anna Maria.

September 18, 1770

Johannes Jung, on French Creek, Chester County, near Sebastian Kiely's inn, advertises that his German servant, Johann Nickel Huber, ran away.

Johannes Zeller, dealer in salt, Race street, corner of Third, Philadelphia.

Stephen Riegler, on Mrs. Master's place, near the Governor's mill, Philadelphia County.

Richard Wister advertises that his German servant, Adam Coopas, 18-19 years old, ran away from the Glass House, Salem County, New Jersey.

Jacob Seitz, Strasburg Township, Lancaster County.

Christoph Windhauer, on Muddy Creek.

October 2, 1770

Johann Berend, from Lisbon, carpenter and instrument maker, south side of Race street, between Third street and Moravian alley, Philadelphia, makes musical instruments.

October 9, 1770

Catharina Retterin, care of Georg Eyerich, near Yellow Springs, Pikeland Township, Chester County, came to America sixteen years ago with her father, Melchior Retter, now dead, her mother, Eva, her eldest sister, Anna Maria, her second sister, Margaretha, and her third sister, Magdalena. These three sisters were indentured in Philadelphia, and Catharina was indentured to Lorenz Hippel, in the country ("in dem Busch"). She seeks news of her family.

October 9, 1770

Peter Schott, Lower Milford Township, Bucks County, in the Great Swamp.

October 23, 1770

Johann Gilbert, doctor and chirurgus, has removed from Market street to Race street, opposite the Green Tree inn, between Second and Third, Philadelphia.

Johann Jacob Muehle, Conestoga Township, Lancaster County, advertises that his Irish servant ran away. He is 18-20 years old, and his name has been forgotten.

Elias Davison, Antrim Township, Cumberland County, advertises that his servant, Thomas Jones, ran away. He was born in Wales, and is 21 years old.

Andreas Schaefter, baker, Vine street, Philadelphia.

Bernhard Franck, Earl Township, Lancaster County.

October 30, 1770

Robert Armstrong, Fort Halifax, Upper Paxton Township, Lancaster County (now Dauphin), advertises that his Irish servant, James MacKinsey, ran away. He is 27 years old and arrived at New York seven years ago.

Dorothea Elisabeth Weberin, Germantown, on Christoph Meng's place, advertises a weaving frame for sale.

Christian Lehman, scrivener in Germantown for many years, has removed to Philadelphia, at the northwest corner house of Mr. Druckenmiller, between Race and Third streets. He is a surveyor, and he also sells nursery stock.

November 6, 1770

Johannes Andreas Messerschmidt advertises that his indentured boy, Johannes Kerner, 20 years old, ran away with an apprentice named Wolskiels, 17 years old, whose father lives in Lancaster and his grandfather in Ephrata.

January 1, 1771

Dieterich Ries has removed his inn from Fourth street, Philadelphia, adjoining the Academy, to Second street, near Arch, adjoining Michael Hillegass', where Jacob Ehrenzeller lived. The latter has removed to Ries' former place.

The government of the city of Durlach seeks information about Georg Eyszenlohr, son of a clergyman in Durlach, who came to America several years ago, and also about Gottlieb Weyda, who left Durlach sixteen years ago for the second time, with his sister, going to Pennsylvania. Later Weyda was with Johannes Jaeger, innkeeper in Oley, and he was thereabouts in recent times. Notify Johann Roman, storekeeper, Market street, Philadelphia.

January 8, 1771

Carl Stark, Encobus, Palatine County, New Jersey, with Ander Anderson, seeks information about his brother, Johann. The brothers were born in Messersbacher Hof, bey Rogehausen, in the Palatinate, and came to America six years ago in different ships.

January 15, 1771

Margaretha Dorothea Haermannin, from Betsdorf, Alsace, arrived in Philadelphia September 30, 1770. She later married Jacob Paulus, a tailor. She seeks information about her brother, Philip Henrich Haermann, a tailor, who came to America six or seven years ago. Notify Metzner, German apothecary, Philadelphia.

Georg Grotz, pantsmaker, Fourth street, second house from the Academy toward Market street, Philadelphia, sells sickles, scythes, etc.

Daniel Kahn, born in Canton Zurich and living in Lancaster, has returned from a journey abroad and advertises that Daniel Dschantz, of Niederwichtracht, Zurich Gebiet, seeks information about the Vies family, who came to America about 35 years ago, and especially Nicolaus Viesz, for whom there is a legacy from Elisabeth Dschantz and Magdalena Jung.

January 22, 1771

Friedrich Vogel, inn, Third street, near Arch, Philadelphia, next to Peter Miller, and diagonally opposite the Presbyterian Church, in the new house of Martin Kreuder.

April 2, 1771

Widow Ottin, bookbinder, has removed to a new place on Second street, Philadelphia, opposite Mr. Schweighauser, at the sign of the Golden Ball, third house from Mr. Kidd.

Thomas Hatton, scrivener, Falls of Schuylkill (Philadelphia).

Georg Schlosser, tanner, Second street, Philadelphia.

April 16, 1771

Henrich Bernhold, dealer in Herbs, Second street, Philadelphia, second door above the English church and opposite William Whitedread's inn.

Jacob Naegele, dealer in turpentine and cordial burner, Second street, Philadelphia, four doors from Vine and opposite Georg Schlosser.

April 23, 1771

Paul Zantzinger, Lancaster, continues the business of the late Michael Grosz, in the same house.

April 30, 1771

Peter Dishong, Schuylkill Mill, at the lower ferry, Philadelphia.

Daniel Kinport, Conestoga Township, Lancaster County, advertises that his servant, Johannes Winszly, ran away.

May 7, 1771

Johann Wilhelm Kalls, Reformed clergyman, intends opening a school seven miles from Carlisle, on land of Paul Pierce, on Conodoguinet Creek.

May 14, 1771

Johann Michael Gruenewalt, tailor, Longswamp Township, Berks County.

Johannes Klinger, Yellow Springs, Chester County (now Chester Springs).

Johann Michel Kester, Easton.

May 21, 1771

Andreas Geyer, bookbinder, Second street, near Arch, Philadelphia.

Conrad Kerlinger, Plymouth Township (Montgomery County).

May 28, 1771

Georg Christoph Reinhold, bookbinder, Market street, Philadelphia, has removed to a house opposite his former house and next to the Black Bear inn.

Anthony Miller, Manor Township, Lancaster County, advertises that his servant, Thomas MacColly, ran away. He speaks English and German.

Peter Keiser, Worcester Township (Montgomery County), advertises that his German servant, Nicklas Neidel, 19 years old, ran away.

June 4, 1771

Johann Bernhard Fischer, brushmaker at the sign of the seven brushes, Second street, Philadelphia, next to the house where Christoph Curfesz, brushbinder, formerly lived, and opposite Christian Riffet, dyer.

Georg Valentin Reinhardt, Bedminster Township, Somerset County, N.J., advertises that his servant, James Morris, ran away. He is native born and 22 years old.

Caspar Singer, Lancaster.

June 11, 1771

Conrad Mohler, carpenter, near Lancaster, seeks his brother, Friedrich, born in Sulsbach, Alsace, who arrived in America two years ago last autumn. Conrad, who is now free, is employed with Georg Eberle, Lancaster.

Johann Philip DeHaas, trader, Lebanon.

June 18, 1771

David Watson, Leacock Township, Lancaster County, advertises that his servant, Daniel MacBride, 24 years old, ran away.

June 25, 1771

Christian Kehr, tobacco spinner, Philadelphia.

David Schaeffer, Second street, Philadelphia, advertises that his coachman, Peter Behler, or Bieder, ran away. He is native born, 25 years old, speaks English and German and formerly was coachman for Abraham Kensy, Market street, Philadelphia.

Christoph Kucher, Lebanon.

July 2, 1771

Stoffel Heyer, butcher, Lancaster.

July 9, 1771

William Skiles, Leacock Township, Lancaster County, advertises that his servant, Thomas MacCollaugh, 24 years old, ran away.

William Riegel, Albany, advertises that his German servant, Abraham Breitenducher, 40 years old, ran away.

July 16, 1771

Gottfried Klein, landlord of the Unicorn inn, Lancaster, advertises that his Irish servant, John White, 17-18 years old, ran away.

Israel Jacobs has removed from the White Horse inn, Market street, Philadelphia, to the Grape inn, Third street, where Mr. Davenport formerly lived.

July 23, 1771

Nicolaus Dschans, Brecknock Township, Berks County.

Jacob Billmeyer, Jun., collector of excise, York.

July 30, 1771

Johannes Haasz, cooper, Third street, Philadelphia, advertises that his German apprentice, Engelbert Ludwig, 14 years old, ran away.

August 6, 1771

Christoph Graffert, general store, Lancaster, opposite the Black Bear inn.

August 13, 1771

Martin Kreuder now conducts the Golden Swan inn in his own new house, on Third street, near Arch, Philadelphia, Adjoining Peter Miller and diagonally opposite the new Presbyterian Church.

Philip Henrich Rapp, Haycock Township (Bucks County), announces a public sale of his goods, as he intends going to Germany. He will undertake to provide pastors for congregations desiring them.

> (Rapp was a discredited Lutheran clergyman who at this time was deposed from the pastorate of the Tohickon charge. He did not go abroad, but some years later committed suicide).

August 20, 1771

Dietrich Welker, Salford iron hammer, Old Goshenhoppen, (Montgomery County), advertises that his German servant, Bernhard Heens, ran away. Heens was 19 years old and had been in America two and a half years.

Wilhelm Bettle, tanner, end of Second street, Philadelphia.

September 3, 1771

William Edmonds, Plainfield, Northampton County.

September 10, 1771

David Levy, shopkeeper, Upper Hanover Township (Montgomery County).

September 17, 1771

Henrich Stuber, drug store, Lancaster, sign of the golden mortar and pestle, Queen street, several houses from George Ross and near the court house.

Nicolaus Miller, store, Lancaster, King street, where Mr. Diffendorfer, innkeeper, lives, opposite Mr. Lauman.

September 24, 1771

Johann Engel Jung, Bethlehem on the Delaware in Hunterdon County (New Jersey), or his brothers in Easton, or his brother-in-law, Joh. Engel Gondermann.

Abraham Dauber, schoolmaster, Worcester Township on Skippack Creek (Montgomery County).

Joh. Conrad Weyell, Frankford road, Philadelphia County.

Johann Beltz, tile kiln, Philadelphia.

Wendel Zerban, tanner, Second street, Philadelphia, adjoining the White Swan inn.

Ran away from Samuel Mifflin's snow Rebecca, at Philadelphia, three German indentured servants--Anthon Wellfley, shoemaker, 28 years old; Maximus Remberg, 20 years old, and Friedrich Klein, a mason, 26 years old. They speak Spanish and Portugueish. Two were born in Switzerland, near Ulm, and the other in Nassau-Saarbruecken.

October 1, 1771

Michael Kraemer, cooper, Queen street, Lancaster, advertises that his apprentice, Michael Ley, 19 years old, ran away.

October 8, 1771

John Marshall, sign of the Seven Stars, Passyunk road, near Philadelphia, advertises that his German servant, Johann Christian Risler, ran away. He is a tailor, 28 years old.

Cornelius Hains, at Christiana Ferry, Newcastle County, Delaware, advertises that his German servant, Georg Williams, ran away.

Adam Gunter, Kingsessing, Philadelphia County.

Georg Scheer, on Mr. Morris' place, Moyamensing Township, Philadelphia County.

Henrich Guntermann, manufacturer of weaving frames, Germantown.

October 15, 1771

Jacob Sunday, Paradise Township, York County.

Martin Niszli, Mount Joy, near Donegal, Lancaster County.

October 22, 1771

Henrich Bitting, Lower Milford Township, Bucks County, advertises that his Irish servant, Robert Patrick, 17 years old, ran away.

October 22, 1771

Johann Bernhard Fischer and Christoph Miller have entered into partnership in the brushmaking business on Second street, Philadelphia, adjoining the house where Christoph Churfes, brushmaker, formerly lived and near Mr. Stellwagon's sign of the Seven Brushes.

October 29, 1771

Jacob Schaefer, Southwark, Philadelphia County, near the sign of the Sheep and Lamb.

November 5, 1771

Daniel Kunbordt, Conestoga Township, Lancaster County, advertises that his servant, Johann Wenssel, ran away.

David Miererly, mason and stonecutter, Reading.

November 12, 1771

Melchior Wisinger, wire worker, Front street, several doors from Arch, Philadelphia.

David Wagner, at Butler's mill, Bucks County (Chalfont).

November 19, 1771

John Wilkins, Carlisle, advertises that his German servant, Georg Dobler, ran away. He is 30 years old, speaks good English and has a wife in Lancaster.

Martin Kreuder, Golden Swan inn, Third street, between Arch street and Cherry alley, Philadelphia.

November 26, 1771

Ebenezer Mackie, Baltimore, and James French, Elk Ridge Landing, advertise that three servants ran away. They recently arrived from Bristol on the ship Restoration, Captain Thomas. They are: Georg MacCarty, 30 years old, who says he has a wife at Duck Creek; John Hinton, gardener, 25 years old, and William Rudge, locksmith, 27 years old.

December 3, 1771

Johann Anderson, Salisbury Township, Lancaster County, advertises that his apprentice, George Doyle, 15 years old, ran away.

Isaac Jung, dealer in dry goods, Reading.

Georg Adam Weitner, Manatawny, Berks County.

December 3, 1771

Philip Becker, Lancaster, has removed from Queen street to King street, taking the well known inn, the George III, that Michael Gaertner conducted, near the court house and adjoining Adam Simon Kuhn's house, near Paul Zantzinger and opposite the market house. He will continue the inn. He also conducts the shoemaking business and wants to employ a lastmaker.

January 7, 1772

Joseph Budd, hatmaker, removes from Water street to Second street, Philadelphia, adjoining the English Church and opposite Pewterplatter alley.

Ludwig Lauman, Lancaster, sells bolting cloth.

Zacharias Paulson, Greenleaf alley, near Market street, Philadelphia, sells ink powder.

Henry Funck, Manor Township, Lancaster County, advertises that his driver, Philip Jacobs, has disappeared.

Jacob Daubendistel, butcher, Third street, Philadelphia, advertises that his German apprentice, Conrad Faunder, 16 years old, ran away.

January 14, 1772

Philip Graffert, Lancaster, has removed nearer to the court house, the second house below the Black Bear, where Adam Reichart lives. He will continue the inn at the sign of the White Horse.

Joh. Georg Zeisinger, now scrivener in English and German, Quarry street, next to Moravian alley, Philadelphia.

Johannes Rup, shoemaker, Second street, Philadelphia, advertises that his German servant, Johann Justus Bernscheuer, a shoemaker, 25-26 years old, ran away. He arrived in America last July. He was caught in Allentown on December 17, through Mr. Hauch, a butcher, of Easton, who took him to Jacob Heisser's inn, the Ship, twenty-two miles from Philadelphia, on the North Wales road (Gwynedd). There he was kept over night, but in the morning he again ran away.

Georg Wack, shoemaker, Third street, Philadelphia.

Daniel Levan, dry goods, Middletown, Heidelberg Township, Berks County; also sells rum, sugar, coffee, tea, etc.

Johannes Zeller, brandy burner, Vine street, near Third, Philadelphia, formerly John and Peter Chevalier. Residence, Race street, at the sign of the buffalo.

January 21, 1772

Johannes Froely, on Mrs. Master's place, on Germantown road, near Philadelphia, advertises that his Irish servant, Nicolaus Bauer, 24-25 years old, ran away.

January 21, 1772

John Roberts, Manchester Township, York County.

January 28, 1772

Michael Bertsches, Lancaster, near the court house, adjoining Wilhelm Kuber, offers a tannery for rent on the west side of Queen street, adjoining Henrich Zank's tannery.

February 11, 1772

Michael Beck, great hammersmith, Goshenhoppen.

Joh. Jacob Beck, smith, Frederick County, Maryland.

Jacob Busch, tailor, Germantown.

Peter Ehrenmann, Warwick Township.

Paul Geiger, over the Schuylkill.

Christoph Heibel, York County.

Friedrich Henop, German preacher in Frederick, Md.

Joh. Rudolph Heuntz, Germantown.

Joh. Andreas Hieronimus, Mecklenburg (North Carolina).

Joh. Jacob Honold, North Wales (Gwynedd Township, Montgomery County).

Jacob Jentzle, Weisenburg Township (Lehigh County).

Hans Georg Ihle, York County.

Georg Lohnes, Lower Milford Township, Bucks County.

Joh. Jacob Lorenz, Codorus Township, York County.

Everhard Luttman, Lancaster.

Michael Miller, Lebanon.

Martin Obermiller, York Township, York County.

Anna Catharina Probstin, care of Stephen Hornberger, Lancaster County.

Conrad Rattenauer, Tulpehocken (Berks County).

Sophia Catharina Reilerin, Earl Township, Lancaster County.

Christoph Rein, Maxatawny (Berks County).

Martin Roeber, North Wales (Gwynedd Township, Montgomery County).

Rudolph Rohr, Frederick, Md.

Michael Rossel, Culpepper County, Virginia.

February 11, 1772

Diederich Rudt, Bucks County.

Philip Schumacher, Frederick, Md.

Gertraut Schumaennin, North Wales (Gwynedd, Montgomery County).

Andreas Staiger, organist and schoolmaster in New Goshen-hoppen.

Elisabeth Margretha Hafnerin, Stone Arabia, on the Mohawk River (New York).

Johannes Stoercher, Whitpain Township (Montgomery County).

Margretha Spicker, Tulpehocken (Berks County).

Ludwig Wagner, Tulpehocken (Berks County).

Jacob Wunder, near Germantown.

Joh. Georg Hoff, maker of tall clocks, Lancaster.

Ludwig Traber, Drumore Township, Lancaster County.

February 18, 1772

Wilhelm Schaeffer, papermaker, on the fresh water, New York, offers a new paper mill for rent.

April 7, 1772

Henrich Hebener, born in Hanover and now working with Johann Andreas Rohr, locksmith, Second street, Philadelphia, came to America many years ago with his brothers, Georg and Caspar. Georg now lives in Carolina. Information is sought about Caspar, who formerly worked in Richard Wister's glass house in New Jersey (Salem).

Augustin Neiszer, clockmaker in Germantown, gives notice that he removed last summer from his former dwelling into Georg Hittner's house, immediately opposite the White Horse inn, conducted by Adam Haas, and two houses above Baltes Roeser, tanner. He continues to make all kinds of new house clocks and repairs clocks and watches. * * He wishes to be relieved in cases where he gave security for debts. * * The cause and outcome of the court proceedings between John Wister and Augustin Neiszer will be laid before an unprejudiced public for its judgment.

April 14, 1772

Johann Philip Reitz seeks information about his brother, Georg Henrich Reitz, who was indentured in West Caln Township, Chester County, in Culbertson's mill.

April 21, 1772

Jacob Weisz the younger has a store on the east side of Second street, Philadelphia, second door above Chestnut.

Philip Conrad Christ, linenweaver's apprentice, born in Beuerbach, Nassau-Usingsehen, the son of Johan Philip Christ, linenweaver, arrived in America last autumn to visit his friend, Mr. Bott, master smith, from Stoeckenroth, Amt Idstein. Christ is now serving with Thomas Saunders, at the mouth of Mantua Creek, Deptford Township, Gloucester County, New Jersey, and he seeks news of Bott and also of Tobias Haberstock, who left Germany six years ago.

Johann Nicolaus Waltman, with Daniel Clark, Bucks County, three miles from Trenton ferry, seeks his brother Ludwig, who came to America a year ago. Their cousin, Johannes Waltman, has also arrived in America.

April 28, 1772

Jesse Bonsall and John Pearson, Darby, Chester County (now Delaware County), advertise that a German servant, Georg Paul Fryer, 21 years old, ran away. He writes well, and might pretend to be a schoolmaster.

Jacob Eckfeld, sicklesmith, south side of Market street, Philadelphia, adjoining Mr. Geyer, stone cutter.

May 5, 1772

Georg Miller, Windsor Township, Berks County, advertises that his German servant, Carl Schmidt, ran away. He is 29 years old, was born at Heilbrun and is a shoemaker and basket-maker.

Johann Steinmetz has a store on the south side of Market street, fourth house above Fourth street, Philadelphia.

May 12, 1772

Johann Gilbert, apothecary, and his partner, Jacob Hoff, have removed from the upper end of Reading to the market place, near the court house, in Isaac Levan's house, where Dr. Diemer formerly lived. Johann Gilbert has practiced his craft for twelve years.

Jacob Hausser, Philadelphia; wife, Kunigunda, born Hoell-mannin.

Jacob Shoffner, store, Lebanon.

May 19, 1772

Abraham Sahler, Perkiomen Township (Montgomery County), advertises that his German servant, Joh. Georg Bremer, 52 years old, ran away.

May 19, 1772

Gottfried Richter, Second street, Philadelphia, in the corner house at Vine street where Friedrich Dominick, clockmaker, lives, teaches English and German.

May 26, 1772

Elisabeth Willin, widow of Christian Will, Elizabeth Township, Lancaster County, three miles from Heidelberg.

Carl Hoffman, Blue Ball inn, Campingtown (Northern Liberties of Philadelphia).

Christoph Reborg, King street, Lancaster, second house below Johann Hopson.

Adam Hersperger, Lancaster.

Johannes Madoeryn, Lancaster.

June 9, 1772

Jacob Graeff died on June 4 in Philadelphia, aged 80 years, 5 months and 11 days. For more than thirty years he was a member of the Lutheran Church Council. He is survived by three sons, one daughter, thirty-one grandchildren and three great-grandchildren. Burial took place on June 6 in the Lutheran grounds.

Christian Wertz, store, Lancaster.

William Giddis, Chestertown, Kent County, Maryland, advertises that Johann Bernhold, a butcher born in Germany and reared in Philadelphia, has disappeared.

Johann Overholt, Tinicum Township, Bucks County, advertises that his Irish servant, William Mansfield, 24 years old, ran away.

June 16, 1772

Henrich Kaemmerer, Third street, Philadelphia, several houses above the King of Prussia inn, buys linen rags.

Johann Bergthaler, Roxborough Township, Philadelphia County, eight miles from Philadelphia.

Elisabeth Lehr, Moyamensing Township, Philadelphia County, near Henrich Leppicks.

Johann Georg Blumer, Campingtown (Northern Liberties of Philadelphia), adjoining the Blue Ball inn.

June 23, 1772

Nicolaus Kohler, farmer, from Muehlhofen, two hours above Landay, arrived in America last autumn. His father is Andreas Koehler. He seeks information about his brother Jacob, who has

June 23, 1772

been in America twenty years and nine years ago lived on a farm near York but is now believed to be in Virginia.

June 30, 1772

Johann Berndt, carpenter and instrument maker, removes from Race street to Campington (Northern Liberties of Philadelphia), on Third street, opposite Mr. Coates' burial ground.

Christian Curfesz, brushmaker, Vine street, near Second, Philadelphia, advertises that his German servant, Heinrich Meiszner, 40 years old, ran away.

July 7, 1772

William Bailey, coppersmith, York, is now conducting his business opposite his former place. Since beginning, on June 27, he has made 47 kettles of various kinds and has done much other copper work. He worked for ten years at his trade with Francis Sanderson, Lancaster. He will be in Frederick, Maryland, at court time, with Samuel Swearingain, and in Carlisle with Johann Poakes.

July 21, 1772

Christoph Simon, Kensington, Philadelphia County, born in Markbreit, is going abroad.

Jacob Daubendistel, butcher, Third street, Philadelphia, advertises that his German apprentice, Conrad Faunder, 17 years old, ran away.

July 28, 1772

Friedrich Kertz, butcher servant in Pennsylvania, came from Dornstatt, Wurtemberg, twelve years ago.

Christoph Hirth, needlemaker, from Geildorf, Wurtemberg.

Christian Fachler and Johannes Besserer, from Doeffingen, Wurtemberg.

Joh. Georg Behringen, from Sachsen-Fluhr, near Mergenthal.

Jost Markin, born at Traben, near Trarbach.

Martin Ziegler, from Malsem, Wurtemberg.

Georg Wagner, from Ruthesheim, Wurtemberg, said to be in Anweil (New Jersey).

Jonas Epple, of Leonberg, Wurtemberg, seeks news of his brother Andreas, who is said to be in Philadelphia.

Philip Leonhard Schwartz, from Duehrn, one-quarter hour from Brackenheim, wants to know where his brother Bernhard lives.

July 28, 1772

Johannes Metzger, linenweaver, from Vaihingen, Wurtemberg, is believed to be in the Shenandoah Valley, Virginia, with the Dunkers.

Elisabeth Wuestin, from Lomersheim, Wurtemberg, is said to be indentured with Georg McCall, in the country near Reading (Douglass Township, Montgomery County).

Zachariah Reis, Pikeland Township, Chester County, near Yellow Springs (Chester Springs).

August 4, 1772

Johannes Fritz, on the Hill, Southwark, Philadelphia.

August 11, 1772

Jacob Fimpel, Merion Township (Lower Merion Township, Montgomery County); wife, Margreth.

Johann Gilbert, doctor in Reading, has discontinued his partnership with Jacob Hoff in the apothecary shop, and Johann Gilbert is now in charge of the shop.

Information is wanted about Ludwig Bauer, from Oderdrunn, Alsace, linenweaver, who arrived in America several years ago and is believed to be in or near Philadelphia.

August 18, 1772

Abraham Staut, Rockhill Township, Bucks County, advertises that his English servant, Edward Higgins, 27 years old, ran away.

September 29, 1772

Georg Miller, Upper Alloway, Salem County, N.J., advertises that his German servant, Christoph Furman, 35 years old, a linenweaver, ran away.

Ernst Ludwig Baisch seeks information about Friedrich Lentz, a butcher from Dornstatt, Wurtemberg, who came to America twelve years ago.

Matthias Schlauch, storekeeper, Lancaster, opposite the court house.

Jacob Schroeder, near the ropewalk, on Front street, in the Northern Liberties of Philadelphia.

Christoph Schwartz, butcher, arrived at New York ten years ago.

Georg Adam Schmaltzhof seeks Friedrich Bickel, whose wife is the sister of Michael Mueller's wife.

Two brothers named Huebler, from Sendfeld, near Adelsheim, in the Odenwald.

October 6, 1772

Dr. Jonathan Potts has opened an apothecary shop in the former store of Thomas Dundas, Reading.

Dr. Johann Gilbert, Reading has removed from the house of Jacob Hoefele, barber, into old Isaac Levan's house, near the court house and opposite Ludwig Emler, the blue dyer. His former drug store was maliciously ruined but he now has a new shop.

Joh. Georg Schick, Heidelberg Township.

October 20, 1772

Elisabeth Willin, widow of Christian Will, "Sprengler," one mile from Schaefferstown or Heidelberg (Lebanon County).

Anthony Schaefer, Heidelberg Township (Berks or Lebanon County).

Joh. Friedrich Rohr, smith, adjoining the Red Lion inn, Second street, Philadelphia.

Hans Georg Scheiermann, Maxatawny (Berks County).

Heinrich Ritter, on Pequea Creek.

Jacob Billmeyer, Jun., York; wife, Maria.

October 27, 1772

Joh. Philip DeHaas, Lebanon, dealer in bolting cloth, wine, rum, etc.

November 3, 1772

William Man, Warminster Township, Bucks County, near Elliott's inn.

Information is wanted of Joh. Michael Duell, born in Neustadt, an der Aisch, near Nurnberg, who learned business in Erlang. On May 3, 1764, he came to New York by way of Hull, and for a time he was with Adam Simon Kuhn, in Lancaster, then he went to Reading and announced himself as an apothecary and doctor. After two years he returned to New York and worked at the iron works of Peter Hasenclever. Then he came again to Pennsylvania, where trace of him was lost. His sister seeks him. Notify Joh. Sebastian Stephani, chemist, New York.

November 10, 1772

Joh. Christoph Hayne, tinsmith, King street, three houses below Dr. Kuhn and opposite Georg Graf, Lancaster.

William and Isaac Clarke, near Princeton (New Jersey), advertise that two German servants ran away--Henrich Berger, 27 years old, who speaks German, Dutch and English, and Joerg Wortmann, 20 years old.

November 10, 1772

Andreas Wiester seeks information about his brother Philip, who was born at Geislingen, near Schwabisch Hall and arrived at Philadelphia several weeks ago with Captain Smith. Andreas Wiester lives by the Great Swatara Creek, in Paxton Township, Lancaster County (Paxtang Township, Dauphin County).

Johann Eberman, Jun., dealer in clocks and watches, Lancaster, has removed from King street to a house opposite the Black Bear inn.

November 17, 1772

Wilhelm Schmidt has opened a new German apothecary shop on the east side of Second street, between Vine and Race streets, Philadelphia, opposite Ludwig Farmer's inn, The Stag, in the house formerly occupied by Henry Miller, printer.

Peter Schmidt, born in Carlsruh im Durlachischen, who arrived in Philadelphia recently with Captain Smith, inquires for Friedrich Nester, living in the vicinity of the Blue Mountains. Peter Schmidt is in the employ of Andrew McGlone, merchant, at the lower bridge (drawbridge), Philadelphia. He is a son of Sigmund Schmidt, who is still in Germany.

Maria Lenora Weicherd, now married to Andrew Heillens, Cumberland County, in Shireman's Valley, seeks news of her two brothers, the older, Friedrich Weicherd, and the younger, Hans Bartel Weicherd. The two brothers and their sister came to America eight years ago, at which time the sister was 12 years old, and all three were indentured to pay for their passage. They were born in Mechelsen, Hanover.

Elisabeth Catharina Artinin, who arrived at Philadelphia five weeks ago on the ship Crawford, Captain Smith, seeks news of her brother, Joh. Heinrich Clement, who came to America six or seven years ago and in York County married a daughter of Lorenz Schweiszgut. They are from Mittelfischbach, in the Darmstadt region, in the Nieder Grafschaft Catzenellbogen, and their father is Christoph Clement.

December 8, 1772

Johannes Ostertag arrived this autumn in Captain Smith's ship, and he seeks his mother's brother, Johann Ulrich Keyser, who came to America twenty years ago, with his wife and child. Johannes Ostertag's wife died on the voyage, and he is not yet free from the ship. He is a linenweaver, from Hohen Meiningen, Wurtemberg.

Sebastian Muffler, sugarbaker and cook, has removed from Second street to Cherry alley, Philadelphia, into the house where Georg Mayer formerly lived, between William Dickinson and Benjamin Loxle, opposite the Rev. Mr. Weyberg and near the Lutheran Church.

Joh. Georg Mueller, born in St. Gallen, Switzerland, is asked to send word of his whereabouts to Jacob Ehrenzeller, at the Brown Horse inn, Fourth street, near the Academy, Philadelphia.

December 22, 1772

Joh. Melchior Raeff, born in the city of St. Gallen, Switzerland, is now with Mr. Murglt, Fourth street, Philadelphia, near the Academy.

Georg Stahly, Earl Township, Lancaster County.

December 29, 1772

Christian Huck, lawyer, removes from Second street to Race street, Philadelphia, between Front and Second streets, near Peter Paris and opposite Christian Schneider.

January 12, 1773

James Christee, Jr., Baltimore, advertises that his German servant, Johannes Gottschall, ran away. He arrived five weeks ago in the ship Betsy, Captain Bryson, from Rotterdam. He has been with the soldiers, and he has a sister in Philadelphia.

February 9, 1773

Joseph Kaighn, Newtown Township, Gloucester County, New Jersey, advertises that his German servant, Carolina DePool, ran away. She arrived in America last autumn and is 23 years old.

Christopher Saur, Germantown, and later Michael Keyser, advertise that a German servant, Elisabeth Prugelin, 26 years old, ran away. She is from Hesse Marburg, and arrived several weeks ago on the ship Sally, Captain Osman.

February 16, 1773

His sister asks for news of Adam Christian Hoffman, born in Berlin, who was employed in business in Hamburg, then in London and later in Kingston, Jamaica, until 1760. He left Jamaica without telling where he was going. Address Johann Carl Hekker, merchant, Londonderry Township (Dauphin County).

Abraham Koerper, Reading.

Gabriel Kron, shoemaker, Reading.

Joh. Michael Wolf, master tailor, Baltimore.

Johannes Weitzel, doctor of medicine, Lancaster.

Johann Nickel Korndoerffer, Goshenhoppen (Montgomery County).

February 23, 1773

Jacob Daubendistel, butcher, Third street, Philadelphia, advertises that his German apprentice, Conrad Faunder, 18 years old, ran away.

February 23, 1773

Heinrich Reinhardt will remove on March 10 from Race street to Second street, Philadelphia, into the former house of Valentin Schaunz, where he will continue his inn.

March 9, 1773

Anna Maria Schumannin, 34 years old, and her daughter, 10-12 years old, redemptioners, left the brigantine Morning Star, Captain Dempster, at Philadelphia, by permission, but failed to return.

March 16, 1773

Georg Honig and Carl Maus have formed a partnership as auctioneers and have rented the house where Jonas Philips formerly held auctions, at the upper end of Second street, Philadelphia, the seventh house on the west side above Vine street. Sales will be held every Wednesday and Saturday.

March 23, 1773

Adam Fleck, North Wales Township (Gwynedd Township, Montgomery County), advertises that his German servant, Carl Wittman, 23 years old, ran away.

Heinrich Roosen, sugarbaker, Second street, between Chestnut and Market street, Philadelphia, has an advertisement in verse.

April 7, 1773

His father, Daniel Schmoltze, seeks information about Peter Schmoltze, born in Zweybruecken, who has been in America for two or three years. Notify David Grim, New York.

April 13, 1773

Johannes Fromberger, Philadelphia, advertises that Henrich Reemer, sugarbaker, 30 years old, ran away.

April 20, 1773

Jacob Muszgnug, Heidelberg Township.

Philip Otto Wagner, Heidelberg Township.

Gottlieb Weydau, Oley Hills (Berks County).

Christoph Friedrich Weyler, Rancocas, New Jersey.

Joh. Martin Teis, Wahnkill, New York Province.

April 27, 1773

John Van Etten, Forks Township, Northampton County, advertises that his servant, Abraham Fitsched, or Fischer, ran away. He is 34 years old, and was born on Long Island, of English parents.

Marcus Bird, Birdsboro (Berks County), advertises that his German servant, Christian Metz, 45 years old, ran away.

Information is wanted about Johann Roetgu Miller, one of three brothers who came to America six years ago. They were born in Womelsdorf, in Berleburg. Two of the brothers were indentured to pay for their passage. Notify Johann Jost Mueller, care of the Ship inn, Lancaster. Joh. Georg Fischer, a step-brother, is in Rapho Township (Lancaster County), with Ludwig Metz and Ulrich Strickler.

Sebastian Muffler, sugarbaker, Philadelphia, advertises that two servants ran away--Johann Friedrich Hoeninger, 36 years old, born in Speyer, a baker and miller, who is lame, and Johann Sebastian Fitz-Charles, 16 years old.

May 25, 1773

Juliana Kummerlin, who arrived in America last autumn and is now with Jacob Bartsch, formerly landlord of the White Lamb inn, Market street, Philadelphia, seeks information about her grandfather, Melchior Schartle, born in Lobrunn, Zabergen, Wurtemberg, who came to America about thirty years ago and settled in the Blue Mountains. His youngest daughter, Maria Barbara, is the mother of Juliana Kummerlin.

June 1, 1773

David Han and Christian Setzer, Whitehall Township (Lehigh County).

Jacob Schallus, merchant, Second street, Philadelphia, adjoining the Red Lion inn.

Martin Graff, Lancaster.

Georg Stroh, Daniel Stroh, Lebanon.

Hans Nickel Duszing, master mason, Frederick (Md.?).

Jacob Nonnemacher, Goshenhoppen.

Johann Thiebolt, smith, Lancaster.

Johann Schweighauser, merchant, Second street, Philadelphia, inquires for the Sarasin family, from Basel, Switzerland.

Jost Ebert, landlord of the Conestoga inn, Race street, Philadelphia.

Jacob Schoch, Haycock Township, Berks County.

Jacob Fischer, brushmaker, has removed from Philadelphia to Lancaster, where his place of business is on King street,

June 1, 1773

between the court house and the prison, but he will continue his store in Philadelphia on Second street at the sign of the seven brushes.

Reinhart Rahmer and Philip Stein, beer brewers, Philadelphia, announce that they will dissolve their partnership at the end of August.

Theodore Memminger has removed from Second street, Philadelphia, to a place several houses farther up the street, at the sign of the tea chest, where he will continue in business as a cordial distiller.

Robert Patton and John Williams, Lebanon, have dissolved their partnership, and Robert Patton continues the store.

June 15, 1773

Solomon Brumfield, Amith Township, Berks County, advertises that his German servant, Maximus Remberger, 20 years old, ran away.

Jacob Dieterich, Waterford Township, Gloucester County, N. J., advertises that his Irish servant, John Wharton, 36 years old, ran away.

Simon Peter Baideman, cooper, with Isaac Paris, Stone Arabia, on the Mohawk River, in the Province of New York, seeks information about his brother, Johann Henrich, a cooper and beer brewer, born in the Rhine Grafschaft Daun, who came to America and was apprenticed with ---- Frick, brewer, in Lancaster. Address Peter Paris, merchant, Philadelphia, or his brother, Isaac Paris, Stone Arabia.

Peter Schaerer, Maxatawny Township, Berks County.

Jacob Latschar, Colebrookdale, Berks County, advertises that his servant, named Conrad, ran away. He came from Hanover, and arrived six weeks ago.

June 23, 1773

Dr. J. Gilbert, Front street, Philadelphia, between Arch and Race, adjoining Mr. Drinker, has studied many years on sea and land, and visited hospitals connected with the late war in Europe. He has been in Pennsylvania four years.

Solomon Sell, Northern Liberties of Philadelphia, one mile from Germantown, near Georg Losch's powder mill and near Falls of Schuylkill.

Henrich Zurhorst advertises that while he was in Surinam Joseph Schreiber, son-in-law of Joseph Kauffman, merchant, of Philadelphia, died there.

June 29, 1773

Henrich Buehler, Lebanon.

June 29, 1773

Georg Friedrich Dockenwadel, Upper Saucon (Lehigh County).

Michael Dieffenbach, Baltimore, Md.

Jacob Robel, shoemaker, Frederick, Md.

Leonhart Wolf, tanner, Philadelphia.

July 6, 1773

David Schneider, Lower Dublin Township, Philadelphia County.

Christopher Marshall, Jun., Philadelphia, advertises that his German servant, Georg Pfotzer, 20 years old, ran away.

July 13, 1773

Johannes Sauter conducts a dry goods store on Second street, Philadelphia, above Vine street, near the German auction house, in the house where Nicolaus Schreiner formerly lived.

Jacob Moser, in the service of Adam Erben, brandyburner, Philadelphia, born in Langenau, near Ulm, seeks information about his two sisters, Walburga and Margretha, who went to South Carolina about twenty-two years ago and married. They are now believed to be in Ebenezer, Georgia.

July 20, 1773

Georg Zeller, livery stable, sign of the Germantown stage, has removed to the northwest corner of Third street and Cherry alley, Philadelphia. The Germantown stage arrives in Philadelphia every Wednesday and Saturday and returns the same day.

Adam Hold, Oxford Township, Philadelphia County.

July 27, 1773

J. Georg Zeisinger, stationery, Quarry street, near Third, Philadelphia.

Georg Lechler, weaver, Market street, between Sixth and Seventh, Philadelphia, third house above the sign of the three kings, on the left side going toward the Schuylkill.

August 3, 1773

Bodo Otto, medical and chirurgical practitioner, Front street, Philadelphia, intends removing from the city.

August 10, 1773

Daniel Oldenbruch, medical and chirurgical practitioner, will remove from Philadelphia to Lebanon in a few weeks.

August 10, 1773

Bernhard Lawersweiler, landlord of the Half Moon and Seven Stars inn, Second street, Philadelphia.

August 17, 1773

Jesse, only son of Edward Milnor, Roxborough Township, Philadelphia County, was killed on August 13 by falling into the wheel of his father's mill.

Johann Huber, baker, Lombard street, near the new market, Philadelphia, advertises that his Irish servant, Michael Nicholson, 18 years old, ran away.

August 24, 1773

Michael Herzel, Hill Township (Hilltown?), Bucks County, advertises that his servant, Jacob Rubberd, ran away.

August 31, 1773

Curtis and Peter Grubb, Hopewell Furnace, Lancaster County, advertise that three servants ran away--John Ryan, 17-18 years old, born in Ireland; Samuel Jones, 18 years old, born in England, and Joseph Eyers, 20 years old, born in England, who recently arrived in America with Jones.

Ludwig Kuhn, Arch and Third streets, Philadelphia, advertises the disappearance of Friedrich Uebelin, silversmith, born in Basel, Switzerland.

Friedrich Hoffman, from Hintzweiler, in Oeszweiler Thal, Zweibrueckischen, seeks Johannes Lang, a smith, from the same place, who came to America 26-27 years ago.

Georg Merckel, Richmond, Berks County, advertises that his German servant, Leonhard Miller, left to seek another master and failed to return. He is 20 years old, and was born in Switzerland. He speaks German, French and Latin.

September 7, 1773

Rudolph Bonner the younger on September 15 will open a store in Worcester Township (Montgomery County), on Manatawny road, in the house where Rudolph Bonner formerly lived.

Michael Croll, Upper Salford Township (Montgomery County), advertises that his German servant, Catharina Tillin, ran away. She is 20 years old and came from the Ruckelschen land.

Ulrich Otto, chemist, who arrived in America from Germany last October, seeks information about his uncle, Hermann Ritzmann, a smith, who is past 80 years of age. He was born am Sester Deich, four miles from Hamburg, established a factory in Moscow under Czar Peter I, and later came to America, having been in New York fifty years ago. His four sisters and a brother whom he left in Germany are all dead. Send information to Dr. Adam Simon Kuhn, Lancaster, or Mr. Wiltberger, Market street, Philadelphia.

September 7, 1773

Robert Paul, Bensalem Township, Bucks County, advertises that his German servant, Johann Theobold Steffee, ran away. He is 18-19 years old, was born in Strasburg and arrived in America last August on the ship Sally, Captain Osman.

September 14, 1773

Henrich Dippenberger sells guns, Second street, Philadelphia, opposite the Stag inn, in the house where Heinrich Miller, printer, formerly lived.

Henrich Schaff, who had a store on Second street, Philadelphia, has removed to Baltimore.

September 21, 1773

Dr. Bodo Otto is now in Reading, where he has taken over Dr. Kuhn's apothecary shop and continues to practice medicine.

September 28, 1773

Lorentz Howard, Marlboro Township, Chester County, advertises that his Irish servant, Michael Linch, 28-30 years old, ran away.

Valentin Bauer, New Holland, Earl Township, Lancaster County, advertises that his English servant, James Dowlin, ran away. He is a tailor, 19 years old.

Philip Becker, Lancaster, advertises that his apprentice, Thomas Plunket, ran away. He is 18-19 years old, and was recently apprenticed with John Kelly.

October 19, 1773

Johann August Leonhardt, from Hitzenhahn, bey der Gentzbacher Muehl, near Dillenburg, notifies his cousin, Johann Peter Schaaf, Lebanon, of his arrival in America and that he is very sick on Abel James' place, Frankford, five miles from Philadelphia.

Ludwig Sprogell has a store on Second street, Philadelphia, six houses above Arch and opposite Michael Hillegass.

Christoph Pittsmayer, Dutchess County, New York, inquires for Adam Hauber, supposed to be in South Carolina.

Joh. Leonhart Goettman, from Kirchbrunndach, aus dem Obenwald, notifies his brother-in-law, Johannes Niclas Arnold, who came to America seven years ago, that he came to America this summer from Germany and is very sick on the ship Union, Captain Bryson.

John Pool, Burlington, N. J., advertises that his German servant, Anna Margretta Froelichin, ran away. She is 22 years old and arrived on the ship Britannia, Captain Peter.

October 19, 1773

   Adam Bender, Providence Township.

   Johann Michael Conrad, from Wurtemberg, who arrived recently, seeks a position as barber, bloodletter, organist, scrivener, or accountant.

   Wilhelm Eckhart, Lombard street, Philadelphia, advertises
that his German servant, Johannes Scheller, ran away. He was
born in Speyer and arrived in America less than a year ago.

October 26, 1773

   Johannes Rup and Georg Leib, Philadelphia, advertise that
two German servants have run away--Justus Bornscheier, a shoemaker, and Catharina Mum, 30-40 years old.

November 2, 1773

   Georg Boerstler, Maidencreek Township, Berks County.

   Georg Christian Reinholdt, bookbinder, Market street,
Philadelphia, adjoining the Black Bear inn, sells books.

November 9, 1773

   Johann Jung, Vincent Township, Chester County, advertises
that his Irish servant, Patrick Bryan, 19-20 years old, ran
away.

   Philip Mueller, barber, and his father-in-law, Johann
Sommerohr, tailor, Baltimore, Md.

   Conrad Seip, near Easton.

November 23, 1773

   Johanna Maria Lueckhardtin, on the ship Union, Captain
Bryson, Philadelphia, from Gelnhausen, seeks her brother, Bernhard Lueckhardt, who has been in America 19-20 years.

   Georg Hausel, Passyunk Township, Philadelphia County, advertises that his German servant, Elisabeth Ungerin, ran away.

   Georg Strehly, landlord of the Half Moon inn, King street,
Lancaster, has removed to the well known inn on King street
where the late Friedrich Jaiser lived and afterward Adam Reichert, and he will continue the inn.

   Christian Schultz, Strasburg Township, Lancaster County.

November 30, 1773

   Johann Martin Puff, Bristol, Bucks County, indentured with
John Hutchinson, from Nassau-Itstein, the son of Joh. Peter
Puff, seeks Philip Henrich Klein or Fritz, both of whose wives
are sisters of Johann Martin Puff's mother. Klein was born in
Limbach and Fritz in Warsdorf, Itstein.

128   GERMAN SETTLERS OF PENNSYLVANIA

November 30, 1773

Jacob Hiltzheimer, Seventh street, Philadelphia, advertises for information about Johannes Liebenstein, born in Duern,
near Sinsheim, cooper, who was married in Laudendach an der
Bergstrasse and came to America eighteen years ago.

Johann Meyer, tanner, Campingtown, Northern Liberties of
Philadelphia, by the rope walk, advertises that his German
servant, Sarah, or Sally, Albrecht, 13 years old, ran away.

Gideon Gilpin, Birmingham Township, Chester County, at the
ford in Brandywine Creek, advertises that his German servant,
Johann Jose, alias Johann Jose Maerk, ran away. He is 19 years
old, and his parents live 30-40 miles above Harris' ferry on
the Susquehanna.

December 7, 1773

Peter Viehl, Richmond Township, Berks County.

December 14, 1773

Maria Schweitzerin, Horse Mill alley, Philadelphia, between Second street and Cable lane, near Mr. Sitgrave's auction
house, buys linen rags.

Johann Andreas Krauel, Golden Swan inn, Third street,
Philadelphia, born in Grossen Bernden, Brandenburg, seeks his
brother, Johann Conrad Krauel, a miller, who came to America
from London four years ago.

December 21, 1773

Christoph Schmidt, joiner, west side of Front street,
Philadelphia, several houses from Race street, with Mr. Heyman,
tailor.

Jacob Hetherling, Coventry Township, Chester County, advertises that his English servant, William Williams, 19 years
old, ran away.

Georg Mayer, Penn Township, Cumberland County, advertises
that his German servant, Joseph Kunly, 21 years old, ran away.

January 4, 1774

Christian Ilgner, Lancaster, advertises that his apprentice, Caspar Ziegler, hatmaker, 16 years old, ran away, in
company with his brother, Michael Ziegler, tailor, 15 years old,
apprentice of Andreas Schenk, Manor Township, Lancaster County.

Henrich Becker, Frederick County, Maryland, one mile from
Solomon Miller, on the road from Frederick to Baltimore, advertises that his Irish servant, John Martingale, ran away.

STAATSBOTE, PHILADELPHIA
129

January 11, 1774

Peter Lowry, butcher, Philadelphia, advertises that his German servant, Georg Koch, 20 years old, ran away.

January 18, 1774

Carl Gemberling, Market street, Philadelphia, advertises that his German servant, Anna Juliana Rothin, ran away. She is 23 years old, and arrived last autumn from Nassau-Dillenburg.

February 15, 1774

James Nevil, landlord of the Rainbow inn, Campingtown, Northern Liberties of Philadelphia.

Willing & Morris, Philadelphia, advertise that Christian Mertle, dyer, from Herborn, Germany, and his wife decamped after coming to Philadelphia on the ship Crawford, Captain Smith.

Jacob Ludewig Videbant, former royal Prussian coin assayer, is now prepared to test metals, at the Golden Swan inn of Widow Kreyberin, Third street, Philadelphia.

Samuel Read, hatmaker, has removed from Market street, Philadelphia, into the house where Mr. Bingham formerly lived, on the east side of Water street, below the lower new bridge (drawbridge), at Stamper's wharf.

February 22, 1774

William Scott, mill, Strasburg Township, Lancaster County.

Abraham Mason, Philadelphia, advertises that his German servant, Elisabeth Hendricks, ran away. She is 33 years old and has been in America fifteen months.

March 8, 1774

Johann Georg Kuhmle continues the practice of medicine in the house where his father lived, on Third street, Philadelphia.

March 15, 1774

Wilhelm Schwartz, blacksmith, 50 years old, and his wife, who arrived last autumn on the ship Britannia, Captain Peter, left Henrich Haen's inn, Third street, Philadelphia, three months ago.

Adolph Strohl, 30 years old, tanner or pantsmaker, arrived last spring in the ship Pennsylvania Packet.

Dorothea Muellerin, 40 years old, arrived in the ship Pennsylvania Packet.

Johann Carl Hebigt, 27 years old, dyer, arrived in the ship Pennsylvania Packet.

March 15, 1774

Georg Ludwig Helmold, 25 years old, capable of teaching school, arrived last autumn in the ship Montague.

March 22, 1774

Dr. Anthon Yeldall has opened a drug store on Front street, Philadelphia, three houses from the Quaker meeting house.

Emanuel Grubb and Charles Robinson, Brandywine Hundred, Newcastle County, Delaware, advertise that two German servants ran away--Johann Christoph Busser, 21 years old, and Johann Braun, 20 years old.

Christian Derick, Passyunk Township, Philadelphia County, advertises that his German servant, Catherina Moserin, ran away.

April 5, 1774

Anna Catharina Nollin, alias Weberin, middle aged, German, has disappeared from the inn of Widow Kreiderin. She arrived last autumn in the ship Union, Captain Broson.

Ludwig Schultz, Hempfield Township, Lancaster County.

Susanna Kreyderin, Third street, Philadelphia.

April 12, 1774

Johannes Rup, shoemaker, Second street, near Race, Philadelphia, advertises that two German servants, both shoemakers, ran away--Georg Han and Friedrich Broner.

Jacob Heff, innkeeper, Springfield Township (Montgomery County).

Carl Hecker, Londondery Township, Lancaster County (now Dauphin).

William Dewees, Philadelphia, advertises that his servant, Jan Peterson, ran away.

Georg Frank, augur smith, Lancaster, is going to Germany.

Nicolaus Hauer, Frederick, Maryland.

April 19, 1774

Christian Christian, butcher, Abington (Montgomery County).

Conrad Escher, Passyunk Township, Philadelphia County.

Michael Bauszman, Lancaster.

Matthes Brueck, Macungie.

April 10, 1774

Adolph Gillman has removed to the Half Moon and Seven Stars inn, Second street, Philadelphia, where Bernhard Lawertsweiler formerly lived, adjoining Michael Hillegass, and he continues the inn.

Johann Beemer, Bethlehem Township, Hunterdon County, N. J., advertises that his German servant, Wilhelm Nickel, ran away. He is 24 years old, and says he was a soldier in Germany.

Peter Martiny, Upper Milford Township (Lehigh County).

Jacob Friedrich Carl Neundorf, Maxatawny, Berks County.

Johann Heinrich Orthgis, Lampeter Township, Lancaster County.

Johann Heinrich Schneider, North Wales Township (Gwyneed, Montgomery County).

Joh. Conrad Schlupp, Upper Salford Township (Montgomery County).

Gertraut Schuhmaennin, Gwynedd Township (Montgomery County).

Johann Jacob Weber, schoolmaster, Upper Milford Township (Lehigh County).

Ulrich Fischer, farmer, near Lancaster.

Matthes Gorth, Lower Saucon, Northampton County.

Michael Keller, Lancaster.

Johann Caspar Klock, behind Carolina.

Philip Otenwaelder, Easton.

Christian Saermann, Macungie (Lehigh County).

Conrad Strasser, Macungie (Lehigh County).

Joseph Schmeull, Mount Holly, New Jersey.

Ludwig Traber, Derry Township (Dauphin County).

Daniel Wunderlich, Hanover Township.

April 26, 1774

Georg Schranck, on Jacob Duberry's place, Ridge road, Philadelphia County.

Henrich Wilhelm Steigel, Manheim, Lancaster County, advertises that his German servant, Johann Barnickel, ran away.

Leonhard Jenawein, Manheim Township, Lancaster County, advertises that his German servant, Gottlieb Fuhrmann, ran away. He is 27-28 years old and was born in Eisleben, Mansfeld.

April 26, 1774

Philip Becker, Lancaster, advertises that his apprentice, Thomas Plunket, shoemaker, ran away. The Philadelphia overseers of the poor had indentured him to John Paul.

May 3, 1774

Kaspa Baltzer, Baltimore, advertises that his servant, Johann Henrich Staut, 33 years old, ran away eighteen months ago and is now believed to be in Philadelphia. He is a dyer.

Wilhelm Storck, Oley Hills (Berks County), near Hans Loescher.

Johann Conrad Bauer, Goshenhoppen.

Georg Strausz, master smith, Frederick, Maryland.

Alexander Klinger, Reading.

Anna Elisabeth Muellerin, Oley, Berks County.

Joseph Buettner, Reading.

Joh. Georg Schaeffer, John Henrich Schaeffer, Tulpehocken, Berks County.

Johann Caspar Schneer, Oley Hills, Rockland Township, Berks County.

Johann Wendel, Oley Hills, Rockland Township, Berks County.

Johann Conrad Menges, Rockland Township, Berks County.

Johann Hendrich Heist, Goshenhoppen.

Michael Kerber, Saucon Township.

Johann Adam Heist, Goshenhoppen.

May 10, 1774

Johannes Brunck, mill operator, is laying out the town of Westminster, on the Susquehanna, two miles from Middletown, Newberry Township, York County.

Conrad Schwartz, saddler, Lancaster, has removed to a house opposite Ludwig Lehmann's house, on the south side of King street.

May 17, 1774

Baltzer Stretzer, Lancaster, sells molasses, rum, oil, scythes, whetstones, etc.

May 27, 1774

Jacob Hosterman and Peter Groff, near Sunbury, Northumberland County.

May 27, 1774

Johann Guiliam Kals, minister of the gospel, conducts a school in the house of John Colbert, Chestnut street, between Front and Second street, Philadelphia.

Theodor Memminger recently opened a German apothecary shop at the sign of the golden pelican, Second street, adjoining David Schaefer and opposite where Leonhard Melcher formerly lived, Philadelphia.

May 31, 1774

Georg Knerr, baker, Philadelphia, advertises that his German servant, Carl Wentzel, ran away. He is a baker and was born in Alsace.

Martin Nestell, Stone Arabia, Tryon County, Province of New York, advertises that his servant, Adam Kuhn, 40 years old, ran away.

Maria Eva Elgertin seeks her daughter, Susanna Elgertin, who came to America from Wales in May, 1751, with George May.

June 7, 1774

Johann Dietrich Heist, house carpenter, Lancaster, advertises that his apprentice, Johann Johnson, 17-18 years old, ran away.

Johann Andreas Rohr, Philadelphia, advertises that his apprentice, Johann Heinrich Buehner, weaver, 20-21 years old, ran away.

Davis Bevan, Philadelphia, advertises that his German servants, Johannes Vandersteen and Johann Valentin Kinberger, 18-19 years old, ran away.

Johannes Honecker, near Peter Hegner, Passyunk road, Philadelphia County. Peter Hegner is landlord of the Two Tuns inn.

Anton Lechle, smith, Campingtown, Second street, Philadelphia.

Conrad Kraul, miller, near Lebanon, seeks his brother, Andrea, who arrived in America last autumn.

Peter Mierken, sugarbaker, on the Hill, Philadelphia.

June 14, 1774

Adam Kuester, boatman, Vine street, Philadelphia; wife, Margretha.

June 21, 1774

Christoph Becker, north side of Race street, between Third and Fourth, Philadelphia, three doors above Christian Lehman, notary public, and opposite Rudolph Bonner's inn, sells rum, wine, molasses, chocolate, etc.

June 21, 1774

Christian Eggert, Bethlehem.

June 28, 1774

Georg Wider, Earl Township, Lancaster County, advertises that his German servant, Lorentz Dihm, 35 years old, ran away.

Adam Painter, Providence Township, near Skippack Creek (Montgomery County).

July 5, 1774

Friedrich Hagner and Henrich Schlesman, master tailors, Philadelphia, advertise that their German servants, ---- Bruecher and Oswald Dewalt, have run away.

John Paul, Vincent Township, Chester County.

July 19, 1774

Johann Adam Rau, with Johann Schellenberger, Hempfield Township, Lancaster County, is going abroad.

August 2, 1774

Wilhelm Hembel, master tailor, Water street, Philadelphia, advertises that his German servant, Friedrich Brick, ran away. He is a tailor, 27 years old, and arrived last autumn from Hesse.

Daniel Udrie, proprietor of Moselem iron works, Berks County.

August 9, 1774

Valentin Stillwagen, hatmaker, has removed to the house where Blasius Bayer had a tavern, several houses above Race street, Philadelphia (sic).

Johann Georg Jacob, Race street, between Second and Third, Philadelphia, is going to Germany. He was born in Alsace.

Wilhelm Haus, Frederick, shoemaker.

Philip Wiltzheimer, baker, York.

Georg Biegler, landlord of the Angel inn, Lancaster.

August 16, 1774

Robert Paul, Bensalem Township, Bucks County, advertises that his German servant, Johann Theobold Steffe, 19 years old, ran away.

August 16, 1774

Joseph Pemberton, dealer in cattle, Kingsessing, Philadelphia County, advertises that his German servant, Caspar Mergel, 18 years old, ran away.

Andreas Engel, landlord of the Angel inn, Reading.

August 30, 1774

Jonathan Ingham, Solebury Township, Bucks County, advertises that his German servants, Cornelius Schnell, 24 years old, and his wife Lena, 23 years old, ran away. They came to America with Captain Mease, from Hamburg.

Joseph Barth, Bethlehem, has begun to print linen and cotton goods in colors and also dyes yarn.

John Klein, Paradise Township, Lancaster County.

September 6, 1774

Conrad Alster, near the Barracks, Philadelphia, buys honey.

Adam Poth, Market and Sixth streets, Philadelphia, advertises that his servant, Catharina Green, ran away.

September 13, 1774

Johannes Fuchs, Chestnut street, corner of Seventh, Philadelphia, advertises that his German servant, Georg Roofe, ran away. He is a shoemaker, 30-40 years old, and arrived in America last autumn.

Johann Ulrich Pommer, who arrived in America August 14 in the ship Sally, Captain Stephen Jones, has disappeared from Widow Kreiderin's Golden Swan inn, Third street, Philadelphia, where he was while sick. He is about 30 years old, and he worked for a time in a sugar house in London.

September 20, 1774

Johannes Fritz, landlord of the Green Tree inn, Race street, Philadelphia.

Johannes Feller is going to Germany. He was born at Kirchheim an der Deck.

Philip Ammen and Hans Stohr, Earl Township, Lancaster County.

Andreas Borner has a new tannery on Frederick street, Baltimore, Md., adjoining William Lavely's brew house.

Christiana Diebuschin, from Nassau-Dillenburg, who arrived in America last autumn and is now in New York, seeks information about her father's brother, Albert Diebusch.

Abraham Hauswirth, Bowery, New York.

September 27, 1774

Daniel Schmidt, Franktown road, Bedford County.

October 4, 1774

The following are from the Heilbrun region: Ludwig and Hansz Philip Neutz, from Flein; Tobias Hohrein, Johann Georg Hag, Johann Peter and Joh. Bernhard Kuder, of Frankenbach; Johann Georg Wageman, Johann Martin Wageman and Johann Michel Hoffman.

Georg Nailer has entered into partnership with Rudolph Haines to conduct a nursery five miles from Lancaster on the Charlestown road.

Rudolph Haines and Jacob Haines, Uwchlan Township, Chester County.

Wilhelm Engelfried, shoemaker, Race street, Philadelphia.

October 11, 1774

Ludwig Prahl, Second street, near Vine, Philadelphia, advertises that his German apprentice, Abraham Horn, 12 years old, ran away.

October 18, 1774

Jacob von Lahnen has opened a German school in the Northern Liberties of Philadelphia, adjoining Mr. Stillwagen's house. He has day and night classes.

Johannes Wickel, from Eyershausen, Nassau-Dillenburg, now schoolmaster in Vincent Township, Chester County, seeks his mother's sister, Anna Christina Blumin, and her children, who arrived 10-11 years ago. Her father, Johann Georg Blum, died on the voyage.

Michael Diffendoerfer, Lancaster, seeks information about Johann Peter Hest, born at Rohrbach, near Heidelberg, a cooper, who came to America in 1750.

Samuel Lein, Conestoga Township, Lancaster County.

October 25, 1774

Johann Heinrich Krum, tailor, Byberry Township, Philadelphia County, replying to the advertisement of Johannes Wickel in the issue of October 18, says Anna Christina Blumin is Krum's mother-in-law and she lives in Virginia, one mile from Straffordtown.

Ludwig Kuhn, landlord of the Rose inn, Third street, Philadelphia.

November 1, 1774

Official inquiry from Pfortzheim, in Baden-Durlach, for Philip Drescher and Friedrich Drescher's widow, who, with several children, left Ellmendingen several years ago for Pennsylvania; also for Hansz Martin Voltz, from Bockingen.

Robert Aitken, bookseller, Front street, Philadelphia, opposite the London Coffee House, advertises that his Scotch servant, Andrew Ure, ran away. He is a bookbinder.

Wilhelm Van Phul continues the brandy business formerly conducted by Johannes Zeller, in Philadelphia.

November 8, 1774

William Brown, baker, Vine street, Philadelphia, advertises that his English servant, William Tully, ran away. He is 17 years old and came from Bristol, England, with Captain Hood nineteen months ago.

November 15, 1774

Valentin Hagner advertises that his apprentice, Johannes Weisz, 10-11 years old, ran away.

November 29, 1774

Georg Palsgrove, New Hanover Township (Montgomery County), advertises that his German servant, Jacob Biver, ran away. He is 22 years old, and calls himself Jacob Mude.

Wendel Spring and Jacob Spring, brothers, formerly of Lancaster County, who have been absent many years, are asked to appear in Cocalico Township and receive a legacy of their brother Paul. If they fail to claim it the legacy will go to their three sisters.

Philip Angelberger, tanner, Conestoga (Lancaster County).

Sebastian Friedrich Mayer, schoolmaster, near Philadelphia.

December 6, 1774

Adam Protzman, Limerick Township (Montgomery County), advertises that his Irish servant, Margaretha Burris, ran away.

December 13, 1774

Carl Christian Ludwig, born at Seybersbach, near Creutznach, in the Palatinate, studied medicine and is now at Mrs. Kreiderin's Golden Swan inn, Third street, Philadelphia.

Johann Dieter, on Christoph Kleintop's plantation, Chestnut Township, behind the Blue Mountains (Monroe County).

December 27, 1774

Johannes Sauter, Second street, Philadelphia, between Vine and Callowhill streets, occupying the house which he bought from Nicolaus Schreiner, is going to Germany and to Zurich to obtain an inheritance from his father.

Catharine Tillin, from Munster, in Ruckelschen, came to America two years ago with the late Johannes Becker.

Wilhelm Flick, dyer, has removed from York to Lancaster, on Prince street, near the prison.

Caspar Michenfelder, Lancaster, advertises that his German apprentice, Johannes Marx, 17½ years old, ran away.

January 3, 1775

Andreas Mayer, now on Fourth street, Philadelphia, opposite the new Lutheran Church, will open a bakery on January 9. He will also cook dinners and conduct an inn.

January 10, 1775

Margaretha Steinin, German brew house, Northern Liberties of Philadelphia, near Vine street.

January 24, 1775

C. L. Boehme, Reformed pastor in Lancaster, seeks information about a man named Haffner, formerly "Churfaeltzlicher Renovator in Heidelberg," who went to Holland two years ago and then came to Pennsylvania.

January 31, 1775

Johann Martin Schweickart, serving with Henrich Eckel, Bucks County, thirty miles from Philadelphia, seeks his sisters, Eva Margaretha and Elisabeth, who came from Alsace to Pennsylvania seven years ago and were servants six miles from Lancaster, in Warwick Township.

February 7, 1775

David Ettlin, Middletown, Paxton Township, Lancaster County (now Dauphin).

Caspar and Georg Fries, Whitemarsh Township (Montgomery County).

Joh. Michael Bauszmann, shoemaker, King street, Lancaster.

Johannes and Peter Steigerwaldt, Albany Township, Berks County.

Christian Schternach, tailor, Strasburg Township, Lancaster County.

February 7, 1775

Bartholomew Metz, on the Mohawk River (New York).

Joh. Michael Wolf, tailor, Baltimore, Md.

Peter Schammer, Reading.

Peter Bauszmann, Albany, on the still water.

Michael Klippel, Dunmore County, Virginia.

Barbara, born Spintlerin, Winchester, Va.

Henrich Messerschmidt, Steffensburg, Va.

Daniel Cramer, Manheim Township, York County.

Christian Koch, Tulpehocken Township, Berks County.

Johannes Pfaffenberger, Conegetschick (Maryland).

Christian Schetla, York County.

Philip Peter Rodenhaeuser, miller, near York.

Christoffel Schenck, Frederick County, Md.

Carl Schmidt, Elizabeth Township, Lancaster County.

Simon Schetle, Maytown, Lancaster County.

Johannes Brubaker, on Mill Creek, Lancaster County.

February 14, 1775

Caleb Hartman, Bart Township, Lancaster County, advertises
that his Irish servant, Brien MacDonnel, ran away. He arrived
last autumn from Newry on the ship Liberty, is 21 years old and
a joiner by occupation.

February 21, 1775

Georg Paulus Merckel, from Wimpfen am Berg, near Heilbrun,
Wurtemberg, arrived this year and is now with his cousin, Mr.
Kurtz, tobacco manufacturer, Second street, Philadelphia, but
he intends going home in March and expects to return with his
family in the autumn. He is a smith.

Robert Kirkwood, Mill Creek Hundred, Newcastle County,
Delaware, advertises that his Irish servant, James Sweney, 25
years old, ran away.

Jacob Weber, Johann and Matthias Wentz advertise the
disappearance of Jacob Winzler, 22 years old, a German who had
been the servant of Peter Wentz, Worcester Township (Montgomery
County), but became free last April.

February 28, 1775

Widow Casey, Front street, Philadelphia, between Chestnut and Walnut streets, opposite Gray's alley, cures epilepsy.

Johann Behrent, joiner and instrument maker, Third street, Campingtown (Northern Liberties of Philadelphia), opposite Coats' burial ground, offers for sale a pianoforte which he has made.

Aaron Martson, Easttown Township, Chester County, advertises that his German servant, Conrad Bernard, ran away. He is 24 years old and arrived last autumn from England with Captain Stephen Jones.

March 7, 1775

John Dunlap, printer, Philadelphia, seeks information about Carl Klein, locksmith, from Zweibruecken, who came to America a year and a half ago with his son Georg, 12 years old, who was indentured to Dunlap.

Georg Stosz, Germantown road, Philadelphia County.

William Bodley, Charlestown Township, Chester County, advertises that his servant, James Thomson, ran away. He is 35 years old and speaks English and German.

Uly Fischer and Hannes Holty, three miles from the Dunker Cloister (Ephrata, Lancaster County).

Peter Irion, Jacobs Valley, Virginia.

Heinrich Theobald, Manheim Township (Lancaster County? York County?).

Johannes Mertz, Oley (Berks County).

Leonhard Goesel, Little Conewago (York County).

Jacob Musselmann, Rapho Township, Lancaster County.

Georg Stahlin, innkeeper, Conestoga (Lancaster County).

----- Mueller, barber, Trappe (Montgomery County).

Joh. Graff, distiller, Fourth street, near the Methodist Church, Philadelphia.

Conrad Schmidt and Peter Franck, Baltimore.

Peter Lang, Cocalico Township, Lancaster County.

Joh. Valentin Krauch, carpenter, South Carolina.

Michael Lauermann, Weisenburg Township (Lehigh County).

Wendel Koenigsfelt, Lower Merion Township (Montgomery County).

Michael Ohl, Heidelberg Township.

March 7, 1775

Frantz Jacob Hoffman, Lutheran schoolmaster in the Rev. Mr. Jung's parish.

Michael Scherb, Campingtown, Northern Liberties of Philadelphia.

Christian Gilbert, with Christopher Sauer, Germantown.

Johann David Schaadt, York.

Wolfgang Pfister, Allentown, twenty miles from Easton.

Conrah Bohner, Frederick County, Virginia.

Johann Michael Nagel, Allentown.

Jacob Balmer, Lancaster.

Peter Ulrich, Lancaster.

Anna Salade, born Weyermuellerin, Lancaster.

Abraham Schlegel, Baltimore.

Abraham Saeler, on Perkiomen Creek, Philadelphia County (now Montgomery).

Johannes Ritzman, shoemaker, South Carolina.

Joh. Hasz, tanner, Frederick, Md.

Wendel Winand, New Goshenhoppen.

Martin Christophel Roeder, tailor, Philadelphia.

Gottlieb Waeida, Pike Township, Berks County.

Johannes Sommerauer, Baltimore.

Martin Lang, on Little Conewago Creek, two miles from McAllistertown, Md.

Frantz Christian Daffe, Strasburg Township, Lancaster County.

Johann Michael Breitenbach, with Philip Gruenenwald, innkeeper, Lancaster County.

David Eschler offers to sell or rent a brew house in Allentown, the only one within thirty miles.

Joh. Wendel and Joh. Jacob Engel, near Easton.

Jacob Katz, Conegetschick, Hagerstown, Maryland.

Johann Georg Geiger, Lancaster.

Joh. Henrich Guterman, "Stuhlschlosser," Germantown.

Philip Walter, Philadelphia.

Joh. Nicolaus Rothenwalter, Philadelphia.

March 7, 1775

Isaac Hornecker, Rockhill Township, Bucks County.

Georg Bauer, near the Barracks, Philadelphia.

March 14, 1775

The firm of Honig & Mausz, Philadelphia, is dissolved, and Georg Honig, Jr., continues the business.

Peter Geyer, Raccoon Bridge, on the road to Salem, Gloucester County, N. J., advertises that his Irish servant, Matthias Cane, 23-24 years old, ran away.

March 21, 1775

Notice is given that Adam Stam, 30 years old, born in Alsace, who arrived in America last autumn on Captain Bryson's ship, has decamped from Widow Kreider's inn, Third street, Philadelphia, together with his wife. Notify Robert Ritchie, merchant, Philadelphia, or Ludwig Gordon, Easton, of their whereabouts.

Jeremias Mueller, Manheim, Lancaster County, advertises that his Irish servant, ---- Deveng, ran away. He is 22-23 years old, a shoemaker, and he arrived in America last summer. He and his wife were indentured to ---- MacColly, Lancaster, who sold them.

March 28, 1775

Caspar Diller, Middletown Township, Cumberland County (Middlesex Township?), advertises that his English servant, Edward Preston, ran away. He is 20 years old and a native of Shropshire.

John Chestnut, Springfield Township, Philadelphia County (now Montgomery).

Johann Kling, auctioneer, upper end of Second street, corner of Vine, Philadelphia, holds auctions on Tuesday, Wednesday and Saturday.

April 4, 1775

Bernhard Renschmidt, in the service of Jacob Frisch as furnacemaster at Mount Hope, Morris County, New Jersey, who married Maria Dorothea Michel and came to America about ten years ago, seeks his two brothers-in-law, Carl and Caspar Michel, who came to Pennsylvania from Germany three years ago.

Bernhard Humbert, St. Augustine, East Florida, seeks his brother Philip, born at Haetten, Lower Alsace, near Cronweissenburg, who came to America in 1773 and is believed to be in Maryland.

April 18, 1775

Jacob Neff conducts an inn in Springfield Township (Montgomery County), at the foot of Chestnut Hill, which was formerly in charge of Henrich Junken, who now has a tannery on the same place.

Jacob Schenckel, born at Faroldorf, Zurich, a butcher, came to Philadelphia twenty years ago, and later returned to Europe for his family, but through a misunderstanding his children had sailed for Nova Scotia before the father arrived. He then returned to Philadelphia, and his relatives heard nothing further from him. His daughter Elisabeth married Johann Rudolph Schmidt, butcher, in Quebec, and she seeks information about her father.

John Vance, Guilford Township, Cumberland County (now Franklin), advertises that his German servant, Christian Friedrich Streit, 18 years old, ran away.

April 25, 1775

Bartholomaeus Setzlein, on Samuel Powel's place, on the road to the lower ferry in the Schuylkill, Philadelphia County.

Johannes Lind opens a store for the sale of clocks and watches at Arch and Second streets, Philadelphia, formerly occupied by Edward Duffield, clockmaker.

May 9, 1775

Johannes Straub, Second street, near the new market, Philadelphia.

Friedrich Rohroe, Hagerstown, Md.

May 16, 1775

Marmaduke Cooper, Newtown Township, Gloucester County, N. J., advertises that three of his German servants have run away--Henrich Oberkirch, 27 years old; his wife, Barbara, 18 years old, and Jacob Krips, 27 years old.

John Elder, Paxton (Dauphin County), advertises that two of his servants ran away--William Mock, 40 years old, and John Alexander, Scotch, 22 years old.

Catharina Lippincott, Evesham Township, Burlington County, N.J., advertises that two of her servants ran away--Matthes Braun, 30-40 years old, from the Palatinate, and Gertraut -----, 20-30 years old.

Philip Weisz, sausage maker, Sixth street, between Arch and Race, Philadelphia.

Christian Lutz, Passyunk Township, Philadelphia County.

May 23, 1775

Johannes Jung, Vincent Township, Chester County, advertises that his Irish servant, Patrick Drowell, ran away. He
speaks German.

May 26, 1775

Christian Gally, tobacco spinner, Market street wharf,
Philadelphia, advertises that his servant, Peter Capes, ran
away. He was born at Muehlheim, near Cologne.

Christopher Ansley, Greenwich Township, Sussex County,
N. J., advertises that his French servant, Louis Demery, 25
years old, ran away.

Abraham Steiner, Sr., and his son, Abraham Steiner, Jr.,
17 years old, disappeared from their home at Schoeneck, near
Nazareth.

May 30, 1775

Michel Immel, innkeeper, Third street and Cherry alley,
Philadelphia, at the inn formerly kept by Daniel Steinmetz, and
later by Georg Zeller, where the Germantown stage stops.

June 2, 1775

Caspar Horsch, Turners lane, three miles from Philadelphia.

June 23, 1775

Matthias Scheiffele, near Mayberry's furnace, Marlborough
Township (Green Lane, Montgomery County), advertises that his
German servant, Magdalena Fuhrmannin, 24-25 years old, ran
away.

June 30, 1775

Joseph Smith, Wilmington, Del., advertises that his German
servant, Johann Plowmann, ran away. He is a sugar baker, 30
years old, and worked in London for ten years.

William Sarnighausen, doctor of medicine, Fifth street,
between Market and Arch, Philadelphia, with Peter Weber, pantsmaker, opposite the Kouli Khan inn.

His father seeks Johannes Lort, born at Grimberg, Darmstadt, who came to America twenty-one years ago.

July 4, 1775

Jacob Ehrenzeller, Brown Horse inn, Fourth street, Philadelphia, seeks Johann Georg Mueller, born at St. Gallen,
Switzerland.

July 4, 1775

Christian Van Phul, baker, Partition street, New York, advertises that his German servant, Johann Henrich Riese, a baker, ran away.

July 18, 1775

Henrich Marsteller, Providence Township (Montgomery County).

July 28, 1775

Peter Carlton, doctor according to the Indian method, lives on Christopher Mussel's plantation, Donegal Township, Lancaster County, near John Bealey's mill, on the road from Anderson's ferry to Reading. While held captive by the Indians for fourteen years he learned their medical methods, and he now gives treatment and also instruction.

August 1, 1775

Franz Jung, in the Neck, Passyunk Township, Philadelphia County.

August 4, 1775

Simon Keppler, Douglass Township, Berks County, is going to Germany. He was born at Aidlingen, Boeblinger Amt, Nurnberg, and has made the voyage across the ocean six times.

Johannes Rock, born at Rohrum, near Frankfort-on-the-Main.

Baltzer Widemeyer, born at Nordheim, near Heilbrun.

August 11, 1775

James Logan, Philadelphia, advertises that his English servant, George Field, ran away.

Sharp Delany, Philadelphia, advertises that his German servant, Joh. Michael Kirchbauern, ran away. He is 18 years old, and arrived in September, 1773.

August 13, 1775

Wilhelm Eckart, baker, Lombard street, Philadelphia, advertises that his German servant, Andreas Meyer, 19-20 years old, ran away.

August 22, 1775

Georg Bickham, store, King street, Lancaster.

August 29, 1775

William Lawrence, Deptford Township, Gloucester County, N. J., advertises that his German servant, Adam Lauer, 17 years old, ran away.

Peter Deshong, at the Governor's Mill, Northern Liberties of Philadelphia.

September 5, 1775

William Temple, Pennsbury Township, Chester County, advertises that his servant, John Wilmoth, ran away. He is a saddler, 30 years old, who served his apprenticeship in East Jersey and speaks German and Dutch.

September 8, 1775

William Drewry, Philadelphia, advertises that his German servant, Regina Burgmiller, ran away. She is 20 years old, and arrived two years ago in Samuel Howell's ship, Captain Osman.

September 12, 1775

Henrich Junken and Henrich Wynkoop, Second street, Philadelphia, adjoining the Red Lion inn, in the house where Jacob Schallus formerly lived, sell rum, wine, sugar.

September 19, 1775

Friedrich Greiner, Philadelphia, advertises that his Irish servant, Peter King, ran away. He is 20 years old, and arrived in July in the ship Betsy.

Johannes Weng, on Mr. Turner's place, Passyunk, Philadelphia.

September 22, 1775

William Forster, coppersmith, Second street, Philadelphia, eight houses from Market street, opposite the old English church.

Peter Dick, Front street, Philadelphia, advertises that his German servant, Johannes Niebel, ran away. He is 21-22 years old and a joiner by trade.

September 26, 1775

John Hess, Hagerstown, Md., advertises that his German servant, Leonhard Miller, 22 years old, ran away.

September 29, 1775

William Hannum, Concord Township (Delaware County), advertises that his German servant, Christoffel Knoflerink, 40-50

September 29, 1775

years old, ran away.

October 3, 1775

Jonathan Cuester, Limerick Township (Montgomery County).

October 20, 1775

Johannes Ellinger, Reestown, Bedford County, seeks Elisabeth Noerlingerin, born in Wurtemberg, aus dem Kloster Boeben-
Hauser Amt, who came to Pennsylvania about twenty-two years
ago.

John Harley, Joseph Lloyd and Jacob Ginther, near Yellow
Springs (Chester Springs, Chester County), advertise that two
Irish servants ran away—Alexander MacQuilen, 20 years old, and
John Horner, 20 years old.

October 24, 1775

Dorsey & Halling have settled in Hanover, York County to
practice medicine, and have opened a store adjoining the house
of John Spitler, merchant.

Johannes Ollinger, Vincent Township, Chester County, two
miles from Yellow Springs (Chester Springs).

Michael Dieterich, hatmaker, Albany.

October 27, 1775

William Bauszmann, Michael Deffendoerfer, P. Zantzinger,
Caspar Singer and Friedrich Kuhn continue the manufacture of
glass at Manheim, Lancaster County, and also offer building lots
for sale.

Michael Kuser, Colebrookdale Township, Berks County.

October 31, 1775

Jacob van Lahnen has opened a night school in the Northern
Liberties of Philadelphia, where German, French, English and
music are taught.

William Becker, Lower Saucon Township, Northampton County,
advertises that his German servant, Philip Suppert, ran away.
He is 20 years old, and has been in America three years.

November 3, 1775

Johann Salter, Water street, near the new ferry, Philadelphia, advertises that his servant, Peter Walter, ran away,
taking along his wife, Antonetta, known as Hannah, and their
child, 9-10 weeks old.

November 10, 1775

    Johannes Keller, Haycock Township, Bucks County.

November 14, 1775

    Peter Summer, Second street, Philadelphia, above the barracks, opposite the Rainbow inn.

    Johann Kirlin, Amity Township, Berks County.

November 17, 1775

    Georg Reichert, Allen Township, Northampton County.

November 24, 1775

    Simon Klas, Lower Merion Township (Montgomery County), advertises that his German servant, Philip Kolb, ran away. He is 18-19 years old, and he left with Johannes Fritz.

    Nicolaus Kayser, Vincent Township (Chester County).

    Johannes Maennchen, Second street, Northern Liberties of Philadelphia, adjoining Carl Maus' auction house.

November 28, 1775

    Conrad Rosch, Kensington, Philadelphia County.

December 1, 1775

    Christopher Weidman, Cocalico Township, Lancaster County.

December 5, 1775

    Jacob Geiger, living with Nicolaus Weber, Third street, Philadelphia, seeks information about Johann Caspar Berlen, who came to America in 1750 from Steinheim an der Murr and left his three children in New York--Justinia Magdalena, who married Seckler Falckenhan; Sophia Catharina, who married Dreher Wohl-haupt, and a son, Johann Caspar, a shoemaker. The father's sister, Eva Agnes Durstin, died in 1774.

December 15, 1775

    Widow Scheigin, Campingtown (Northern Liberties of Phila-delphia), between Second and Third streets, near Coates' burial ground.

December 26, 1775

    Melchior Steiner and Carl Cist have opened a printing shop on Second street, Philadelphia, at the corner of Coates alley, above the Race street, opposite the Stag inn.

December 26, 1775

Stephen Goodman, Lower Merion Township (Montgomery County).

Tobias Greider, Lampeter Township, Lancaster County.

December 29, 1775

Benjamin Mueller, Manor Township, Lancaster County.

January 26, 1776

Georg Strieper, sign of Adam and Eve, Callowhill street, Philadelphia.

January 30, 1776

Jacob Leech, Cheltenham Township (Montgomery County), near Shoemaker's mill, advertises that his German servant, Georg Philip Gruber, 19 years old, ran away.

Maria Memminger, sign of the golden pelican, Second street, between Arch and Race, Philadelphia, sells wine, vinegar, turpentine, cordials, etc.

February 2, 1776

Nicolaus Seidel, Worcester Township (Montgomery County), advertises that his German servant, Philip Peter Miller, 28 years old, ran away.

February 6, 1776

Michael Bauer, Fourth street, corner of Vine, Philadelphia, advertises that his German servant, Philip Diebaut, ran away. He is a butcher, 25-26 years old.

February 16, 1776

Heinrich Kurz (sic) seeks Elisabeth Barbara Kurtzin(sic), born in Ober Amt Kayserslautern, Dorf Katzenbach, who came to Philadelphia eight years ago, served in Lancaster and married Johannes Ziegler. Notify Friedrich Dietz, tailor, Philadelphia.

Philip Becker, innkeeper, Lancaster, has removed from the King of Prussia inn, King street, opposite the market, to the house on Queen street where Christian Wertz had a store, between Bernhard Hubly, coppersmith, and Christoph Breidenhard, where he will conduct an inn with the old sign. He also continues shoemaking.

February 20, 1776

Caspar Graff, Second street, Philadelphia, advertises that his German servant, Peter Koehler, ran away.

February 20, 1776

Jacob Schnell, windmillmaker, near the lower bridge (draw-bridge), Philadelphia, advertises that his German servant, Joseph Faetsch, 20 years old, ran away.

March 22, 1776

Johann Friedrich Kuecherer, Raccoon Creek, Gloucester County, N.J., twenty miles from Philadelphia, seeks two brothers, Georg Friedrich Riehle, who has been in America twenty years, and Johann Michael Riehle, a flour miller, who has been in America four years.

Jacob Zoll, Chestnut Hill, Philadelphia County.

March 29, 1776

Matthias and Georg Graeff, hatmakers, Lancaster, have formed a partnership and begun business in the house and shop of Matthias Graeff, corner of Orange street (sic).

Caleb Barrat, new post rider, leaves Philadelphia every Wednesday at 11 A.M., and stays over night in Vincent Township, Chester County, arriving on Thursday at Michael Wittmann's, Ephrata, Lancaster County.

William Jenkins, store, at Bangor Church, Caernarvon Township, Lancaster County.

April 2, 1776

William Hembel, Water street, near Market, Philadelphia, advertises that two servants ran away--Friedrich Brick, 29 years old, born in Hesse, a tailor, and his wife, Magdalena, from Wurtemberg. They took with them their child, a girl six months old. The man ran away once before and was caught at Fort Augusta.

April 5, 1776

Michael Hausman, German, 30 years old, coppersmith, Windsor, York County.

April 9, 1776

Henrich Walter, coppersmith, York.

April 12, 1776

Ralph Allen, Hanover Township, Burlington County, N.J., advertises that his English servant, Marshall Hall, alias Thomas Marshall, 23 years old, ran away.

William Schaeffer has a new paper mill at Spotswood, New Jersey, which will be completed in two months.

April 23, 1776

Jacob Scheppach, Philadelphia, advertises that his German servant, Georg Michael Keller, ran away. He is a baker, 18 years old, and was born three miles from Heilbrun.

May 14, 1776

Conrad Ledermann, York, advertises that his apprentice, Peter Baer, shoemaker, 16 years old, ran away.

May 21, 1776

Johann Georg Keller, who arrived in America nineteen years ago, and, with his mother, Maria, served with Jacob Fries, Gohansey (Salem County, N.J.), seeks his mother, who went to Virginia three years ago. Notify Johannes Fries, Race street, Philadelphia.

May 24, 1776

Jacob Abel, courier, travels weekly in summer between Philadelphia and Easton and bi-weekly in winter. He leaves from Peter Hey's, Third street, Philadelphia.

Christian Wolff, Bethel Township, Berks County.

Christoph Hegner, Lancaster.

June 4, 1776

Dr. L. Butte, dentist, has removed from Second street, Philadelphia, near the new market, to Chestnut street, opposite the sign of the Great Turk, in the house where Mr. Wallace formerly lived.

Christian Grever, on Wilton's plantation, belonging to Joseph Turner, Passyunk Township, two miles from Philadelphia.

Conrad Meyer, innkeeper, Heidelberg, Lancaster County (now Lebanon), advertises that his Irish servant, Charles MacNeal, ran away. He is 16 years old, and speaks English and German.

Jacob Wollschlaeger, Southwark (Philadelphia).

June 7, 1776

Simon Krausz, six miles above Harris' ferry, at the English meeting house, Cumberland County, who came to America twenty-six years ago from Konsheim, in the Palatinate, seeks information of his sister, Elisabeth, who is believed to have come to America the same year that her brother did.

Johannes Schneider, back of the Blue Mountains, Chestnut Hill Township, Northampton County (now Monroe), came to America in 1764, with his two sons, whose whereabouts he would like to know. The sons were indentured with Joseph Morrison, Cumberland

June 7, 1776

Township, Marsh Creek Settlement, York County (now Adams). The older, Johann Georg, was free August 14, 1773, and the younger, Georg Peter, August 14, 1776.

June 14, 1776

John Stokes, Haycock Township, Bucks County, advertises that his Irish servant, Bryan Burn, 22 years old, ran away.

Adam Eckert, Market street, Philadelphia, advertises that two German servants ran away--Alexander Otto, 20 years old, and Henrich Loes, 18 years old.

June 18, 1776

John Wickoff, Readingtown, Hunterdon County, N. J.

June 21, 1776

Jacob Schell, on Caleb Foulke's place, at the upper ferry in the Schuylkill, Philadelphia.

June 25, 1776

Wendel Zerband, Second street, Philadelphia, adjoining Blasius Beyer.

July 9, 1776

Thomas Kennedy, Carlisle, advertises that his servant, James Dorman, ran away. He is a mason, 27-28 years old.

July 12, 1776

Jacob Haderich, Codorus Township, York County, advertises that his English servant, Thomas Rief, 20 years old, ran away.

July 19, 1776

John Hinde, Adamstown, Lancaster, sells sugar, coffee, rum and dry goods.

July 23, 1776

Christiana Riesin, King of Prussia inn, Market street, Philadelphia, advertises that her German servant, Jonathan Conrad, called John, 18 years old, ran away.

Carl Gemberling, Market street, Philadelphia, advertises that his German apprentice, William Peter, 14 years old, ran away.

July 26, 1776

Conrad Schneider and Aquilla Weilly, Manheim Township, York County, advertise that two servants ran away--Peter McTonahugh, 28 years old, and an English woman.

Georg Schneider, baker, Strawberry alley, Philadelphia, advertises that his apprentice, Jacob Saurman, 12 years old, ran away.

July 30, 1776

Jacob Dauttel, York, advertises that his Irish servant, Jane Shepherd, 23 years old, ran away.

August 13, 1776

Melchior Kiener, Baltimore, advertises that his German servant, Benjamin Belcher, a cooper, ran away.

August 27, 1776

Peter Maison, at the Glass House, Bucks County, advertises that his German servant, Eberhard Meyer, ran away for the sixth time.

September 3, 1776

Joseph Caufman, Second street, Philadelphia, advertises that his German servant, Christian Signitz, 45 years old, ran away.

September 10, 1776

Johann Meyer, Third street, Northern Liberties of Philadelphia, advertises that his apprentice, Tobias Herberger, ran away.

Henrich Dippelberger, Philadelphia, advertises that his apprentice, Richard Evans, ran away.

Esther Meyer, Elfrith's alley, Philadelphia, advertises that Adam Plom, a potter's apprentice, ran away. He is 20 years old, and was born of German parents.

September 24, 1776

Ludwig Stork, tanner, Spring Garden, near Philadelphia, advertises that his servant, Friedrich Beyerlein, 19-20 years old, ran away.

Joshua Lampater, butcher, Vine street, Philadelphia, advertises that his apprentice, Johann Peter Paul, 16-17 years old, ran away.

October 15, 1776

Michael Croll, Upper Salford Township (Montgomery County), advertises that his German servant, Catharina Thillin, ran away. She is more than 20 years old and was born in the Grafschaft Ranckel.

October 29, 1776

Rees Peters, Aston Township, Chester County (now Delaware County), advertises that his German servant, Nicolaus Dertscher, 47 years old, ran away.

Philip Hahn, New Hanover Township (Montgomery County), advertises that his German servant, Philip Jung, ran away. He is middle aged and was born in the Palatinate.

Michael Schmidt, Lower Merion Township (Montgomery County), advertises that his servant, Elisabeth Soelheimerin, 28 years old, ran away.

November 12, 1776

Joseph Honigkam, on Mr. Lightfoot's place, near the Almshouse, Philadelphia.

Abraham Lang, Third street, Philadelphia, adjoining the White Swan inn, cures dysentery.

Johann Michael Fuchs, Second street, Philadelphia, opposite the Red Lion inn.

November 19, 1776

Johannes Kreiter offers for sale a furnace in Upper Salford Township (Montgomery County), with 370 acres.

November 26, 1776

Henrich Liber, North street, near Fifth, opposite the burial ground, Philadelphia, prints blue on linen.

Matthis Kaehler, tanner, Philadelphia, in care of John Haworth, tanner, Fourth street, who has been in Philadelphia one year, seeks information about his relative, Michael Weber, who came to America 13-14 years ago from Wetmuehe, near Heilbrun.

December 3, 1776

Gottfried Schmidt makes and sells colored and uncolored thread, New street, Philadelphia, the first red board house on the right hand side from Second street, between old Mr. Weiszmann's dwelling and smith shop.

Anthon Weitzel, Stone Creek, eleven miles from Woodstock, or Millerstown, Dunmore County, Virginia.

January 2, 1777

Conrad Zorn, Warrington Township, Bucks County, advertises that his cooper apprentice, Henrich Bony, 16 years old, ran away.

January 8, 1777

Philip Jung, Moyamensing Township, Philadelphia County, advertises that his servant, Anna Maria Jaegerin, ran away. She is 30 years old and was born in Hesse.

January 15, 1777

Johann Rudel, Fourth street, Philadelphia, second house on the west side from Race street, buys linseed.

February 5, 1777

Sebastian Hoffmann, on Joseph Fox's place, Northern Liberties of Philadelphia.

Georg Straehly, on John Morgetreith's place, near the Hospital, Philadelphia.

February 12, 1777

Jacob Butland, braid weaver, has removed from Front street to Second street, between Arch and Market, Philadelphia.

Casper Reide, on Thomas Roschy's place, Northern Liberties of Philadelphia.

Georg Leib, Northern Liberties of Philadelphia, advertises that his German servant, Patty Brannas, 25 years old, ran away.

Richard Steer, Abington Township (Montgomery County), advertises that his servant, Mary Jamison, 20 years old, ran away.

March 12, 1777

Dewald Stork, corner Third and Brown streets, behind the barracks, Philadelphia.

March 26, 1777

Georg Keszler, with Henrich Landes, Lampeter Township, three miles from Lancaster. He has a brother, Johannes.

Conrad Scherer, Vincent Township, Chester County, advertises that his German servant, Friedrich Loewenberg, 21 years old, ran away.

Johannes Laubach, Pikeland Township, Chester County, advertises that his German servant, Peter Jacob, 19 years old, ran away.

March 26, 1777

Nicolaus Walter, Campingtown, Northern Liberties of
Philadelphia, advertises that his apprentice, Johannes Geisz-
bach, alias Jung, ran away. He is 17 years old, and is a
brother-in-law of Joseph Wagener, pantsmaker, of Adamstown,
Lancaster.

April 2, 1777

Anthony Berkenbeil, at the lower ferry in the Schuylkill,
Philadelphia, advertises that his servant, Jacob Lehr, ran
away.

April 9, 1777

Philip Wiltberger has removed from Market street and
Strawberry alley to the old and well known house in Strawberry
alley, Philadelphia, where the late Johann Lukens kept an inn,
and he will continue the inn.

Jacob Leech, Cheltenham Township (Montgomery County), advertises that his German servant, Georg Philip Gruber, 21 years
old, ran away.

Georg Senneff, tailor, Front street, near Race, Philadelphia, opposite Mr. Rush's blacksmith shop.

John Weinland, saddler, Lititz, Lancaster County.

April 16, 1777

Georg Friedrich Pflueger has begun the dyeing business in
Reading, in the house where Jacob Mayer formerly had an inn,
opposite Henrich Hahn.

Christoph Haenszmann, tailor, Second street, near Vine,
Philadelphia, advertises that his German servant, Jacob Henrich
Bast, a tailor, ran away. He is 20-21 years old, and was out
twice with the militia last year and recently worked at his
trade at Widow Gerhart's inn, on Bethlehem road.

Felix Lang, Charleston, South Carolina.

Johann Joachim Doelke, tanner, Charleston, S.C.

Johann Jacob Fansch, Mount Hope Furnace, near New York.

Johann Melchior Werle, Charleston, S. C.

Johannes Rahn, smith, Tulpehocken (Berks County).

April 30, 1777

Michael Gingerich, Jr., Lebanon Township (Lebanon County).
His mother is named Anna.

May 21, 1777

Johannes Miller, on Benjamin Harbeson's place, Moyamensing (Philadelphia).

June 18, 1777

Bartholomaes Schaertzlein, on Samuel Bowl's place, on the road to the lower ferry (Philadelphia).

Leonard Duer, on William Paul's place, at Point No-Point Philadelphia.

July 2, 1777

David Schneider, Lower Dublin Township (Philadelphia), advertises that his German servant, Jacob Schweitzer, ran away. He is 17-18 years old, and the son of Ludwig Schweitzer, of the Northern Liberties of Philadelphia.

William Bastian, on Lewis Davis' place, in the Neck (Philadelphia).

August 12, 1778

Valentin Hagener, cedar cooper, Third street, Philadelphia, advertises that his apprentice, Johannes Weisz, ran away.

August 19, 1778

Jacob Durant has come to Philadelphia and established himself on Fifth street, between Market and Arch, near Jacob Bartsch, where he is engaged in bloodletting, the pulling of teeth, hair cutting and barbering.

September 9, 1778

Georg Kinsinger, tailor, after two years' absence, has returned to Philadelphia and is located on Third street, near the northwest corner (sic).

September 16, 1778

Steiner & Cist remove their printing shop to the northeast corner of Race and Second streets, Philadelphia.

November 18, 1778

Johann Bergenthaler, Norriton Township (Montgomery County), on David Knox's place.

Andreas Boszhart, Third street, Philadelphia, advertises that his German apprentice, Philip Sauermann, ran away. He is a shoemaker, and was born in America.

January 20, 1779

Philip Jacob Becker and Georg Jacob Becker, father and son, from Pfortzheim, in Baden-Durlach.

Joh. Friedrich Boehmer, school teacher, Cohansey (Salem County, N.J.).

Joh. Henrich Jacob Locher, journeyman tanner, Falckner Swamp (Montgomery County).

Catharina Dorothea Stauchin, New Hanover Township (Montgomery County).

Elias Wieand, school teacher, Goshenhoppen.

Jacob Weber, school teacher, Upper Milford (Lehigh County).

Cornelius Mutz, from Buttenhausen, near Graveneck, Wurtemberg.

Michael Reiner, from Schweigern, near Heilbrun.

Joh. Martin Voltz, from Boeckingen, near Heilbrun.

Joh. Henrich Hepp, from Geiszlingen an der Steig, Ulm.

Wilhelm Lorentz, over the river, near Philadelphia.

Joh. Ernst, master smith, South Carolina.

February 17, 1779

Joshua Dudley, Evesham Township, Burlington County, N.J., advertises that his German servant, Johann Georg Wanner, 21 years old, ran away.

February 24, 1779

Gottlieb Weidau, Maxatawny, Berks County, seeks Friedrich Weidau, born in Durlach, who came to America many years ago.

March 3, 1779

Godfried Schwing, goldsmith and jeweler, removes from Second street to the south side of Market street, between Third and Fourth, opposite the sign of the King of Prussia, Philadelphia.

Anna and Maria Stuberin, who came to America seven years ago and were with Emanuel Zimmerman, Jr., Earl Township, Lancaster County, seek their mother, Elisabeth Stuberin.

March 10, 1779

Daniel Goodman, Arch street, between Second and Third, Philadelphia, treats mad dog bites.

March 24, 1779

Sebastian Hoffman, on Carl West's place, Kensington, (Philadelphia).

March 31, 1779

Dr. Janus, trained in Germany, is with Nicolaus Jacob, opposite the German Reformed Church, Race street, Philadelphia.

Peter Oberscheimer, corner house, opposite the former Sower printing shop, Germantown, at the sign of the Conestoga Wagon, where Georg Losch, powdermaker, formerly had an inn, now conducts the inn, and he will continue also to operate his tannery in Allentown.

April 14, 1779

Jost Susse, Douglass Township, Berks County, advertises that his servant, Johann Henrich Steinseifer, 19-20 years old, ran away.

PHILADELPHISCHE ZEITUNG

Published by Benjamin Franklin.

March 6, 1756

Anton Witt, Batterstown, near Rahway, New Jersey.

Michael Walter, school teacher, New Hanover (Montgomery County).

September 23, 1756

Weirich Bensz, near the Dunker Cloister (Ephrata, Lancaster County).

December 30, 1756

Johann Georg Schneider, German apothecary, Race street, Philadelphia, at the sign of the silver bullet, has been established for several years and is now enlarging his place of business.

Jacob Pfister, Sassafras street, Philadelphia (now Race street).

Henrich Keppele, merchant, Market street, Philadelphia.

Michael Grosz is about to leave Lancaster.

Johannes Baer, Lancaster.

February 11, 1757

Widow Ulrich, Second street, Philadelphia, near the George inn.

Peter Ox, Falckner Swamp (Montgomery County).

February 26, 1757

Jacob Franck, glazier, and his wife, of Lancaster, have both died. Friedrich Danbach, Johannes Ebermann and Kraft Roeser, Vormunder (administrators), notify Stophel Franck, Henrich Franck, Andreas Franck, Anna Maria Franckin, Maria Gertraut Mollin, Michael Moeller and Christian Moeller to appear for the settlement of the estate.

May 20, 1757

Dr. Conrad Schultz, Springfield Township, Philadelphia County (now Montgomery).

June 3, 1757

   Johann Ringer, New Hanover Township (Montgomery County).

June 17, 1757

   Joseph Jol begins the manufacture of stockings on the Hill, in David Ronan's house, Philadelphia.

July 15, 1757

   Samuel Berry, Bristol, seeks Walter Fryson, formerly of Schnailwell, near Barnwell, or New Market (Virginia), farmer and later woolcomber.

   Inquiry for Gudman Lyngberg, born at Helsinggeoer, near Copenhagen.

July 29, 1757

   Leonhard Lescher, Market street, Philadelphia.

   Jacob Hur, innkeeper, Market street, Philadelphia.

September 9, 1757

   Andreas Brochell, furrier, Third street, near Market, Philadelphia.

October 21, 1757

   Adam Wilheld, in the burned house on the Schuylkill, Philadelphia.

November 4, 1757

   Michael Baertges, innkeeper and tanner, Germantown road, near the Governor's mill, Philadelphia County.

   Bernhard Hubele, Lancaster, sells almanacs.

   Bernhard Holtzinger, York, sells almanacs.

November 18, 1757

   Georg Friedrich Bayer, dealer in cutlery and hardware, Water street, between Market and "Erd" street, Philadelphia.

December 17, 1757

   Georg Meyer, York County, near York.

PHILADELPHISCHE CORRESPONDENZ

Published by Melchior Steiner.

June --, 1781

Inquiry for Johann Michael Beyerfalck, who, with his wife
and one daughter, came to Pennsylvania about forty years ago
from Zweibruecken and settled near Georgetown, in the Holz
Schwamm. The daughter married a European.

July 23, 1781

Jacob Ulrich Siltzel, baker, Fourth street, adjoining
Zion Church, Philadelphia, born in Neckergroeningen, Wurtemberg,
is going to Germany.

Maria Armbruester, midwife, after thirty years' experience
in Albany, N.Y., has established herself in Philadelphia, on
the south side of Race street, between Front and Second, opposite Christian Schneider and adjoining Mrs. Pinyard.

August 22, 1781

Georg A. Becker, general store, Arch street ferry, Philadelphia.

August 29, 1781

Anton Stiemer, dealer in leather, returns to Philadelphia
and is engaged in business on Second street, at the corner of
New street, between Race and Vine and adjoining Georg
Schlosser.

Anna Elisabeth Eigen seeks her cousin, Johann Dewalt Lei-
brock, who was born in Zweibruecken, in Vogelbach, and came to
America eleven years ago.

September 26, 1781

Jacob Herman, Maxatawny, Berks County, seeks the children
of his brother Friedrich, last known to have lived near Wister's
glass house (Salem, N.J.).

October 24, 1781

Philip Jacob Lischer, with Conrad Hess, Race street, Philadelphia, seeks his mother's brother, Paulus Maerker, a miller,
born at Langen Sulzbach, Lower Alsace, who came to America about
thirty years ago.

November 28, 1781

Adam Franck, medical doctor, who lived on the Mohawk River
for fifteen years and for the past four years was regimental
doctor under Colonel Gleyd, is now practicing medicine in
Philadelphia, being located with William Jordan, on Eighth
street. Dr. Franck's wife was murdered by Indians a year ago,
and last summer his buildings were burned and he lost his
cattle.

February 13, 1782

Dr. Bodo Otto, for several years a surgeon in the hospitals
of the Continental army, is now practicing medicine in Philadelphia, being located on Fifth street, opposite the old
Lutheran Church.

February 20, 1782

Friedrich Doersch has begun to ride post between Philadelphia and Lancaster, leaving Philadelphia on Thursday at
2 P. M. and arriving in Lancaster on Friday afternoon, and
leaving Lancaster on Tuesday morning and arriving in Philadelphia Wednesday afternoon, at William Geisses King of Prussia
inn, Market street, between Third and Fourth.

March 27, 1782

Conrad Boyer, Limerick Township (Montgomery County), advertises that his German servant, Matthias Preis, 18 years old,
ran away.

Daniel Preisz, South Branch of the Shenandoah River,
Virginia.

Michael Lahinger, Winchester, Va.

April 10, 1782

Johann E. Schweighaus, Second street, Philadelphia, seeks
Barbara Maerkly, born Tschoppin, who came to America from
Switzerland ten years ago, with her husband, Hans Maerkly, who
was born in Dueren. They brought their seven children with
them.

A mother in Tuebingen, Wurtemberg, seeks her son, Johannes
Haupt, who several years ago was the servant of a captain in
Philadelphia.

May 29, 1782

Georg Zeisieger, experienced schoolmaster in German and
English, will open a German and English school on June 3, on
Stein street, Philadelphia, entrance on Moravian alley, second
house from Third street.

July 2, 1782

    William and Christian Butz and Moses Yarman dissolve their
partnership at Chelsea iron works, Sussex County, N. J.,
August 1. Yarman will thereafter operate the Oxford iron works,
in Sussex County, and William and Christian Butz will operate
Mount Pleasant Furnace, Berks County, Pa.

July 16, 1782

    Nicolaus Yont, Earl Township, Lancaster County, gives
notice that Daniel Morton has absconded. He is a saddler, 23
years old, was born in New England, and has a brother, Joseph,
also a saddler.

July 23, 1782

    Friedrich Schinckel resumes business as a tanner on Market
street, between Third and Fourth, Philadelphia, opposite the
King of Prussia inn.

August 6, 1782

    Georg Lehman opens an apothecary shop on Second street,
Philadelphia, between Race and Vine, opposite Colonel Farmer's
house. He learned the business in one of the leading houses of
Philadelphia.

September 3, 1782

    Information is sought as to John Christian Thielmann, who
is believed to be in Pennsylvania. His father died in Dresden
in 1781.

September 10, 1782

    Ludwig Steigner, on Captain Fortner's place, at Falls of
Schuylkill (Philadelphia).

October 1, 1782

    Dr. Bodo Otto is now located with Widow Tripolet, in
Baltimore, and has opened an apothecary shop.

October 22, 1782

    Jacob Lahn will open a night school for instruction in
the French language, on October 28, on Arch street, in Chancery
lane, between Front and Second streets; a lamp before the door.
Limit, twelve students.

October 29, 1782

    William Green has opened a store in Reading, opposite
William Reeser.

December 24, 1782

The widow of Johann Jost Metzeler is notified that her
father, Georg Ludwig, of Herborn, in Ocanien Nassau Dillenburg,
died some time ago, leaving her 2000 gulden.

January 21, 1783

Andreas Huck, dealer in "wet goods," has removed from
Water street to Fourth street, Philadelphia, seven houses below
Walnut.

Leonhard Schwengel, grist and saw mill, Washington County,
Maryland, five miles from Hagerstown.

June 3, 1783

Leonhard Bauer seeks information about his wife's brother,
Peter Dormeyer, born in Diemringer Amt, Dorf Deringer, who in
1764 came to America, with his sister, Carolina Christina, and
her husband, and was indentured. Dormeyer is believed to be in
the dry lands near Bethlehem. Notify Jacob Friesz, innkeeper,
Salem County, N.J.

Christiana Nufferin, from Rothenburg, on the Necker, who
came to America about thirty-four years ago and lived at Allentown, seeks her son Christian and her three daughters, Christiana, Catharina and Veronica.

June 10, 1783

Henrich Hauptmann, born in Alsace, near Strasburg, who
came to Philadelphia in 1773, is asked to visit his brother in
New York, No. 8 Bowery lane.

Andreas Herzog, Water street, near Chestnut, Philadelphia,
advertises that his apprentice, William Bender, ran away. He is
12-13 years old and is well acquainted in Germantown.

June 24, 1783

Johannes Weber, born in Rodenbach, Amt Heyger, Nassau-
Dillenburg, is going to Germany.

July 8, 1783

Dr. Joseph Schmitt, who recently arrived from Germany to
study botany in America, is practicing medicine at the Golden
Swan inn, Third street, between Arch and Race, Philadelphia.

Philip Schwartz, born in Weingarten, Oberamt Germersheim,
in the Palatinate, is going to Germany.

July 22, 1783

Jacob Marx seeks Philip Klein, born in Adenbach, who served
his time as a redemptioner fifteen miles from Philadelphia.
Notify Jacob Ableiter, seven-mile stone, Germantown.

July 29, 1783

Andreas Weiler, Douglass Township, Philadelphia County (now Montgomery), seeks his cousin, Friedrich Weiler, who was born at Sprengingen, two hours from Kreuzenach. As a redemptioner he was in the service of Matthias Schlauch, Lancaster, five years ago.

August 12, 1783

Dr. Jacob Rieger & Company open a store in Lancaster at the corner of King and Queen streets, near the door of the court house and opposite Matthias Schlouch.

September 9, 1783

P. E. Delius, Philadelphia, with Peter Whitesides & Company, seeks A. H. Willmans, from Bielefeld, Grafschaft Sparenberg, Prussia.

Johann Nicolaus Hagenau, from Hamburg, opens a store in Mrs. MacFunn's house, Second street, between Race and Vine, Philadelphia.

Daniel Braeutigam removes from Second street to Race street and Moravian alley, Philadelphia. He sells cutlery, books and stationery.

Johann Friedrich Langenbein & Company, from Hamburg, open a store on Front street, between Market and Chestnut, Philadelphia, in Charles Risk's house.

Michael Trautman, Frederick County, Md., twelve miles from Frederick.

September 16, 1783

Joseph Schober & Company open a grocery store on Second street, above Race, Philadelphia, adjoining the store of Waeger & Habecher.

Ludwig Denig, Lancaster, advertises that his German apprentice, Leonhard Krumbein, ran away. He is a shoemaker, 19 years old.

Johannes Rheiner, from Frankfort on the Main, opens a dry goods store on Third street, Philadelphia, in the house of Jacob Dieterich, tobacco manufacturer.

September 30, 1783

Notice to Johann Meli, born at Baar, Alsace, that his sister, Catharina Meli, single, died in February, in Brussels.

October 7, 1783

Friedrich Doersch and Georg Haas operate the post wagon between Philadelphia and Lancaster, leaving Philadelphia on

October 7, 1783

Monday and returning on Tuesday, leaving again on Thursday and
returning on Friday. The Philadelphia terminus is at the King
of Prussia inn, Market street, between Third and Fourth, and
the Lancaster terminus is at the Black Horse inn, Queen street.

Philip Steinmetz, Macungie Township, seven miles from
Allentown (Lehigh County), is going to Germany in June, 1784.
He was born in Salmschen an der Nah. He seeks information about
Henrich Strom, from Hoff in Winter an der Nah, with whom he
came to America about eighteen years ago.

October 28, 1783

Johann Christian Pieters, Philadelphia, born in Harburg,
Lunenburg, has been in America a long time.

Friedrich Wilhelm Jericho, doctor and eye specialist, from
Eisenach, Saxony, recently arrived in Philadelphia, and may be
consulted at his lodgings, with Mrs. Elliott, Second street,
opposite the Black Bear inn.

December 23 Dr. Jericho announces his removal to the house
of Robert Scott, adjoining Sharp Delany.

Reuben Haines, Philadelphia, advertises that his German
servant, Johann Michael Meyer, ran away. He is a brewer and
brandy burner, about 35 years old, and arrived recently from
Holland.

November 4, 1783

Thuun & Boden, from Hamburg, conduct a bookstore on Second
street, Philadelphia, the second house below South street. They
seek information about Gerhard Meyer, born at Geren, Amt Kahl-
enberg, near Hanover, who left for America October 21, 1772.

Bache & Schee sell Saxon mineral products, Chestnut street,
near Front, Philadelphia.

Georg Schaeff, on John Bissel's place, Ridge road, between
the third and fourth milestones, Philadelphia County.

November 11, 1783

Georg Vogel, dry goods merchant, removes from Arch street
to Third street, the second house above the Golden Swan inn,
Philadelphia.

Jacob Wismer, Gwynedd Township (Montgomery County), advertises that his servant, William Gordon, 19 years old, ran
away.

Peter Heist, Marlborough Township (Montgomery County), advertises that his German apprentice, Friedrich Leitzel, ran
away. He is a wheelwright, 22 years old, and the son of Parson
Leitzel, fifteen miles above Reading, Berks County.

Johannes Schnell sells dry and wet goods, Reading, one door
below Mr. Hahn.

November 25, 1783

Adam Seitz, Market street, between Third and Fourth, Philadelphia, inquires for Georg Albrecht Stierle, a tanner's apprentice, born at Sinzheim, in the Palatinate, who left Nancy,
France, last Easter Monday for America.

December 16, 1783

Dr. Maus, Cherry street, between Third and Fourth, Philadelphia, near the Lutheran school house, served the country
throughout the war and has now resumed the practice of medicine.

Henrich Schucht, on Robert Morris' place, two miles below
Philadelphia, near the Schuylkill.

December 23, 1783

Valentin Muendel, Earl Township, Lancaster County, announces his intention to remove from Pennsylvania.

December 30, 1783

Samuel Schober, druggist, removes from Race street to
Third street, between Arch and Race, opposite the Golden Swan
inn, Philadelphia.

Andreas Rieth, Marlborough Township (Montgomery County),
advertises that his apprentice, Samuel Rossel, ran away. He is
10-11 years old, and speaks English and German.

January 6, 1784

Georg Greber, Macungie Township (Lehigh County), has a
son, David Greber, a nailsmith.

January 20, 1784

Friedrich Vogel, New Hanover Township (Montgomery County),
advertises that his servant, Jacob Raab, ran away. He is 30
years old and a deserter from the Hessian troops. Notify Georg
Vogel, Third street, Philadelphia.

January 27, 1784

Daniel Koerschner, Head of Elk, Maryland, is going to
Germany. He is a native of Landau.

February 10, 1784

Johannes Cress is going to Germany in March. He is a
native of Steinau an der Strasse.

February 24, 1784

Henrich Seytel, Bern Township, Berks County, near the Reformed Church, is going to Germany in March. He is a native of Breischdorf, Alsace.

March 2, 1784

Andreas Weiler, Douglass Township, Philadelphia County (now Montgomery), is going to Germany. He is a native of Sprenglingen, two hours from Creutzenach.

Jacob Kugler, innkeeper, Frederick Township, Philadelphia County (now Montgomery).

March 9, 1784

Jacob Keller, Jr., Cocalico Township, Lancaster County, inquires for Friedrich Dobelbauer, son of Christoph Dobelbauer, a dyer.

Christian Knob, Christian Bauman, Adam Brua and Christian Gut, millstone cutters, Cocalico Township, Lancaster County.

March 17, 1784

Johann Stein removes from the George Washington inn, Vine street, to the Black Bear inn, Market street, near Fifth, Philadelphia, which he will conduct.

March 30, 1784

Jacob Mytinger begins business in the George Washington inn, Vine street, between Second and Third, Philadelphia where Johann Stein was.

April 6, 1784

Berthold Henrich Giese, just arrived from Hamburg, 30 years old, writes a good hand, can shave and wait on table, seeks employment for pay for his passage.

April 27, 1784

Paul Merckle, living in Skippack (Montgomery County), with his relative, the well known Abraham Merckle, has become a resident of this country, with his family. He has letters for various persons which he brought with him from Germany last autumn. He is going to Germany this summer, leaving on June 24.

May 11, 1784

Carl Gemberling, Market street, Philadelphia, advertises that his shoemaker apprentice, Abraham Krausz, ran away. He is a native-born German, 20 years old.

May 11, 1784

Johannes Noecker, Bern Township, Berks County, nine miles from Reading, advertises that his servant, Henrich Kirsch, ran away. Kirsch was a Brunswick soldier, nearly 50 years old, who was sold to Noecker.

May 25, 1784

Johannes Schmidt, Donegal Township, Lancaster County, inquires for Henrich Stauffer, his brother-in-law, a son of the late Daniel Stauffer, of Mount Joy Township, Lancaster County.

June 15, 1784

Philip Zeller, dealer in dry goods and wet goods, removes into the former house of Mr. Spiegel, Race street, between Third and Fourth, Philadelphia, on the north side, opposite the King of Prussia inn, Michael Hay, landlord and near the German Reformed Church.

Gottfried Haga, dry and wet goods, removes into the house where Colonel Jacob Morgan formerly lived, adjoining Mr. Steiner, publisher of this paper, Race street, between Second and Third, Philadelphia.

June 29, 1784

Alexander Benson, Water street, Philadelphia, advertises that his shoemaker apprentice, Andreas Debre, 17-18 years old, ran away.

Johannes Schmidt, Springfield Township, Philadelphia County (now Montgomery), inquires for the brother of his father, Jost Schmidt, who has been in America thirty years and who was born at Amt Wetter, Nieder Espy, Hesse.

July 6, 1784

Johann Jacob Flenne gives notice to his brothers and sisters, Johannes Flenne, Johann Henrich Flenne, Elisabeth Miller, Catharina Flenne and Maria Flenne, that he is in Cheltenham Township (Montgomery County), living with Rynier Hallowell, and has heard nothing of them for ten years.

July 13, 1784

Dr. Bodo Otto and Son have stocked their apothecary shop in Reading with fresh drugs.

Balthaser Vettermann, Upper Milford Township (Lehigh County), notifies Philip Peter Huft that his father, Johannes Georg Huft, has died and left his children £10.

October 19, 1784

Jacob Lehre, German and English scrivener, Callowhill street, near Second, Philadelphia.

October 19, 1784

Philip Rothenhauser, Luneburg, Nova Scotia, inquires for Johann Philip Manweit, who was with a Philadelphia baker several years ago.

Johannes Scheibely, organ maker, New Holland, Lancaster County.

Johannes Rheiner, from Frankfurt on the Main, conducts a store in Jacob Dieterich's tobacco manufactory, Third street, opposite the Eagle inn, between Vine and Race streets, Philadelphia.

October 26, 1784

Inquiries for

Johannes Manner, from Geiszlingen, near Ulm, merchant.

Johann Christoph Hochetsen, Ulm, clockmaker.

Friedrich Riedel, Bareuth, former officer with the Anspach troops.

Johann Schweitzer, or Schwizki, Zurich, former French officer.

Georg Wachter, merchant, of Memmingen, who was married in 1769 at Upper Hanover (Montgomery County) to a daughter of Michel Rith, shoemaker.

Maria Barbara Hennerin, Ulm, believed to have been in Philadelphia at some time since 1774.

Joh. Christoph Ehninger, from Goeppingen, Wurtemberg, believed to own a brandy distillery in interior Pennsylvania. His sister-in-law is the widow of Johann Georg Vetters, butcher, from Goeppingen, who died in Philadelphia several years ago.

Johann Wasser, experienced doctor from Canton Zurich, Switzerland, has settled in Philadelphia and may be consulted at the Golden Swan inn, Third street.

Inquiry for Friederich Herman van Gemund, born in Hanau, enlisted in the Jaegercorps in Heilbrun at the beginning of February, 1776, and later was transferred to the Thirty-third English Regiment, but since September, 1777, he was for some time in Albany.

November 2, 1784

Inquiry for August Johannes Fricke, who came to America as a cadet with the Brunswick troops in 1776, was captured in 1777, and in 1778 joined the American army. His relatives in Wolfenbuettel inquire for him.

Georg Friedrich Boehmer, Reformed schoolmaster in Cohansey (Salem County, N. J.).

November 2, 1784

Elias Wiand, Reformed schoolmaster in Goshenhoppen.

Georg Friedrich Bockenwadel, Berks County, one mile from the Warm Springs.

Joh. Georg May, horseshoer, twelve miles from Philadelphia.

Joh. Jacob Solzer, from Hausen, near Frankfort on the Main.

Adam Schweiggert, from Worms.

Joh. Martin Voltz, from Boeckingen.

Dr. Hornbaum, Charleston, South Carolina.

Nicolaus Suter, Lebanon.

November 16, 1784

Joh. Friedrich Langenberg & Company, from Hamburg, remove their store from Water street to Second street, between Vine and Race, Philadelphia, in Mrs. MacFan's house, opposite the Black Bear inn.

Johannes Dentzel advertises that his servant, Johannes Hamman, ran away. He is 35 years old and arrived recently on the ship Van Berkel, Captain William Campbell.

Sebastian Roth, livery stable, Fifth and Walnut streets, Philadelphia; sign of the Volunteer.

December 14, 1784

Philip Bayer, with William Jones, two miles from Philadelphia, inquires for Matthias Bayer, "Kaercher," believed to be in Philadelphia, and Michael Bauer, linenweaver, believed to be in New England. Both were born at Liebenstadt, near Heilbrun, Wurtemberg, and came to America thirty years ago.

Information is sought about Ludwig Carl Hausmann, born in Hesse Hanau, son of the late Hesse Cassel First Lieutenant Franz Theodor Hausmann. He came to America with the Hesse Hanau troops as fire worker, was at the Albemarle Barracks, Virginia, left there in June, 1780, and is believed to have been in Rockingham County, Virginia, with the brothers Zeller and later with Colonel Schmidt, but after he left there nothing further is known about him.

February 22, 1785

Peter Krub, Williams Township, Northampton County, is going to Germany. He was born in Gettenbach.

Jacob Fischer, Reformed schoolmaster at the stone church, Bern Township, Berks County, eight miles above Reading, inquires for Sebastian Schuechen and Jacob Duenschman, born in Niedermerschbach, near Hochenburg. They left Amsterdam on May 29 last for Philadelphia.

March 8, 1785

Redemptioners who fled from the ship Capellentot den Pol, Captain Hermann Ryding, Baltimore, October 3, 1784:

Joh. Jacob Gnawau, German, 34 years old, tailor.

Joh. Martin Schmidt, Jager, 36-38 years old.

Joh. Henrich Diehle, German, 28-30 years old, laborer.

Friedrich Elb, German, 26-28 years old, sugarbaker and seaman.

G. R. Ulrich von Castel, German, 36-38 years old, left on October 2.

Philip Ernst Brendel, German, and his wife, Catharine Barbara, escaped from the ship North American, Captain T. deHaas, Baltimore.

May 3, 1785

Residents of Charleston, South Carolina: Georg Hahnbaum, Christian Stroit, Anna Maria Werlein, widow.

Conrad Roth, Philadelphia, from Bornheim.

June 14, 1785

Peter Martinus von Steuben has settled in Philadelphia to practice medicine among his German countrymen. He is with Valentin Schmidt, south side of Arch street, second house from Front street.

Justus Fuchs (Fox), Germantown, advertises that his apprentice, Friedrich Becker, ran away.

Adam Eckhart is laying out a new town, New Philadelphia, on the northeast side of the Susquehanna River, in Dauphin County, adjoining Harrisburg.

His brothers and sisters inquire for Remigius Serazino, born in or near Strasburg, who was last heard from in 1761, when he wrote a letter from New York. He was then living with Mrs. Daniel Wittib, leather worker.

Tench Coxe, Philadelphia, advertises that his German servant, Johann Lorenz Bicking, or Buecking, ran away. He is 30 years old, a baker, and arrived in America last autumn.

January 10, 1786

Died, January 6, Catharina Keppele, only single daughter of the Rev. Dr. (J.H.C.) Helmuth (Lutheran pastor in Philadelphia). Burial took place Sunday afternoon in the Lutheran grounds.

Jacob Gerwer and Georg Ritchie, dealers in clocks and watches, remove to Front street, Philadelphia, two houses above the drawbridge.

January 10, 1786

The city of Windau inquires for Johann Wilhelm Goebell, son of Johann Heinrich Goebell, one of the magistrates and a merchant of that city. The son left home some years ago, supposedly for Philadelphia. He is entitled to a legacy from his mother, Maria Elisabeth, who has died, and from his late father-in-law, Berend Heinrich Coht, who died in 1783.

John Vandaren, Jr., opens a real estate office on the north side of Market street, Philadelphia, opposite the Coffee House. He was formerly surveyor along the Pennsylvania-Virginia border.

Michael Miller, Second street, Northern Liberties of Philadelphia, near the former barracks, advertises that his German servant, Leonhart Mayer, 19-20 years old, ran away. He arrived in America nine months ago, from Hesse, and was first indentured to William Bell, and then transferred to Miller.

January 17, 1786

Adam Lewer, with David Sickel, Market street, between Eighth and Ninth, Philadelphia, is going to Germany. He was born in the Palatinate, near Mannheim.

January 24, 1786

Conrad Grosch, Frederick (Maryland).

January 31, 1786

Balch, Buerger & Schouten, Baltimore, call upon the following to pay their obligations for ship passage, they having arrived at Baltimore in the autumn of 1784 on the ship Capellen tot den Pol, Captain H. Reyding, and the ship North America, Captain T. deHaas, both from Holland, and as they could not obtain employment in the usual way they were permitted to go free upon signing an agreement to pay the costs of the passage:

Johann Georg Winter	Christoph Gaertner
Johann Henrich Capiton	Johann Aug. Harter
Johann Georg Capiton	Christoph Kesselbach
Peter Winzweiler	Johann Henrich Schwartz
Philip Rauer	Jacob Schmidt
Anton Miller	Jacob Grosz
F. Folweiler	Michael Metz
Anton Becker	Friedrich Wagner
Johann Henrich Brill	Franz Cayral
Gabriel Steinmetz	Stephen Voght
Michael Kempf	Joh. Henrich Eberhard
Georg Koch	Peter Oberbach
Samuel Weiser	Philip Schneider
Jacob Schoenenberg	Michael Bart
Joh. Peter Glasz	Joseph Wumps
Johann Fernburg	

Johann Philip Wald, shoemaker, Heidelberg Township, Berks County.

February 7, 1786

Johannes Eberhard, sixteen miles above Esopus, on the North
River, New York, with Abram Baer, inquires for his father,
Solomon, and his oldest brother, Georg, and his mother, who
sixteen years ago removed from Makus River, above Albany, leaving behind the son Johannes and his twin brother Jeremias.

Jacob Schnaebely, Leacock Township, Lancaster County, advertises that his Irish servant, John MacDonnel, ran away. He
is 20 years old, comes from Wicklow, and came to America in
Captain Alcorn's ship, from Dublin.

February 21, 1786

Daniel Sutter removes to the east side of Fourth street,
between Market and Arch, Philadelphia. He sells wine, sugar,
indigo, mackerel, etc.

Georg Blankenburg, post rider, proposes to ride from
Philadelphia through Germantown, Norriton, Pottsgrove, Reading
and Hamburg to Sunbury and Northumberland. His Philadelphia
terminus is at Henry Funck's inn, east side of Second street,
between Race and Vine. He arrives there on Thursday and leaves
on Friday.

February 28, 1786

Andreas Schmidt, Windsor Township, Berks County, advertises
that his apprentice, Georg Haas, 17-18 years old, ran away.

April 4, 1786

Johann Stark, dealer in salt, Market street, Baltimore.

April 11, 1786

Anthon Grosz, Baltimore.

Jacob Schmidt, Baltimore.

Philip Hof, Baltimore.

April 18, 1786

Heinrich Henschi, Cocalico Township, Lancaster County, advertises that his German servant, Andreas Wilhelm Schaeffer,
ran away. He is a smith, 22 years old.

May 9, 1786

Georg Schneider, Philadelphia, advertises that his servant,
Conrad Zeily, ran away. He is 25-26 years old and has a cousin
in Frederick (Maryland).

May 9, 1786

Joseph Muszi, Philadelphia, advertises that his German servant, Carl Philip Pannet, ran away. He is 25 years old, was born in Kaiserlautern, in the Palatinate, is a buttonmaker, and arrived last autumn with Captain Clarkson. He left in company with Henrich Thomas (See next paragraph).

James Bayard, Philadelphia, advertises that his German servant, Henrich Thomas, ran away. He is a tailor, 25-26 years old, and arrived last August with Captain Clarkson.

August 15, 1786

Peter Steltz, New Hanover Township, Montgomery County, advertises that his German servant, Christian Helm, ran away. He is 25 years old and was born in Hamburg.

Johann Huck, potter, Northern Liberties of Philadelphia, advertises that his servant, Georg Fee, ran away. He is 20 years old, and was born of German parents.

August 22, 1786

Died, August 17, the Rev. Ferdinand Farmer, of Philadelphia. He was buried at the Old Chapel, the funeral being attended by the Protestant clergy, the members of the Philosophical Society, the faculty of the University of Pennsylvania and a large number of people of all religions. He was a born German and a Roman Catholic pastor for many years. The Rev. T. Molyneaux conducted the funeral service, on Friday.

September 5, 1786

Notice to Johann Gottlieb Klingener that his wife, Maria Sophia Bidener, is on board the ship Condide, which recently arrived at Philadelphia from Amsterdam.

Jacob Herleman, Whitpain Township, Montgomery County; wife, Anna Maria, born Scherer.

September 12, 1786

Relatives in Germany inquire for Johann Hartmann Holzmann, born at Bonamus, near Frankfort on the Main, who went to New York in June, 1781, with the English 60th Regiment, under General Amherst.

September 26, 1786

Conrad Weber removes his board yard from Salter's wharf to Widow Williams' wharf, Front street, Philadelphia, above the hay scales and opposite his dwelling.

William Craig and Henrich Ries, Philadelphia, advertise that two German servants ran away--Henrich Wagner and Jacob Rosenkranz, the latter a baker 30 years old.

October 10, 1786

Inquiry for John Dresky, who came to America in 1776-7 with the Hesse-Cassel Jaeger Corps.

October 24, 1786

Christian Hagenbuch, Allen Township, Northampton County, advertises that his servant, Johann Offenbacher, ran away. He is 18 years old, was born in America and speaks English and German.

Andrew Pettit, Water street, between Market and Chestnut, Philadelphia, advertises that his German servant, Johann Henrich Offenstein, 20 years old, ran away.

Susanna Barbara Kriszheimerin, New Goshenhoppen, Montgomery County.

Johann Heinrich Hoegner, Long Island.

October 31, 1786

Georg Lescher becomes landlord of the Double Eagle inn, Third street, Philadelphia.

Jeremias Wadsworth, Hartford, advertises that his servant, Johann Georg Hosmann, ran away. He came from Hanover, was a British soldier in the war and was captured by the Americans.

November 21, 1786

William Stiles, stonecutter, Third street, near Spruce, and William Wood, tailor, Third street, near Market, Philadelphia, advertise that two German servants ran away--Johann Georg Geissel, 20 years old, a stonecutter and mason, and Tobias Schaubhut, 25 years old, a tailor. Both arrived recently from London.

November 28, 1786

Carl Cist, printer, removes to the north side of Race street, several houses below Second.

December 5, 1786

Johann Philip Molenhaupt, from Alsdorf, in Anspach, is now in New York, and he notifies his cousin, Heinrich Guntermann, that he came to America last year in response to a letter from Guntermann, promising to free him upon his arrival, but as he has heard nothing from Guntermann he has been compelled to go into service. He has three years more to serve, and he owes eight guineas.

December 26, 1786

Johannes Krick, Cumru Township, Berks County, advertises that his servant, Paul Dewies, 19 years old, ran away.

January 9, 1787

Nicolaus Kohl, Lancaster, inquires for Christian Kohl, a
baker, about 50 years old, born at Frankfort on the Main, who
left there thirty-four years ago.

Notice is given that two German passengers on the brigantine Dispatch, Captain Veder, recently arrived from Rotterdam, are to be indentured for the cost of their passage--Johann
Christoph Lelli, 30 years old, baker and farmer, and Nicolaus
Hauberger, 35 years old, stonecutter.

Johannes Schuesler, tobacco worker, Flourtown (Montgomery
County).

Johann Henrich Becker, in the service of Dr. Christell
Nohf, Lancaster.

Henrich Hemsing, from Etekum, near Frankenthal.

Caspar Schoeffer, Sussex County, New Jersey.

Ernst Schoeffer, Lancaster; from Mittelbruecken.

March 13, 1787

Passengers who arrived at Baltimore and owe for their
passage:

Johann Daniel Herrose, on the brigantine Candidus, Captain
A. P. deHaas, arrived August, 1786, from Rotterdam.

Margaretha Elisabeth Metzler, on the ship North America,
Captain T. deHaas, from Amsterdam, arrived September, 1786.

April 17, 1787

Friedrich Sebastian Marker, master tailor, Pine and
Seventh streets, Philadelphia, inquires for Joh. Georg and Adam
Keszler, Anna Margaretha and Eva Keszlerin, surviving children
of the late Wilhelm Keszler, of Nieder Husselbach, Ober-Amt
Herrstein.

April 24, 1787

Christian Bechtel, Cumru Township, Berks County, advertises that his servant, Samuel Koenig, ran away.

Jacob Heyer, Alsace Township, Berks County, advertises that
his apprentice, Friederich Filb, 16 years old, ran away.

May 1, 1787

Wilhelm Geisse removes from the King of Prussia inn,
Market street, Philadelphia, to Frankford road, at the third
milestone, where he has opened an inn.

Joseph Leiendecker, with Widow Reser, Race and Second
streets, Philadelphia, is going to Germany. He is a native of
Weiler an der Noh.

May 1, 1787

Inquiry for Ludwig Ludert, from Memel, Prussia, who left London for America fourteen years ago.

May 8, 1787

Christoph Raborg, Baltimore, advertises that his German servant, Johann Ernst Schwind, ran away. He is 35 years old and a coppersmith.

Georg Yentz, Baltimore, advertises that his German servant, Nicolaus Hitscher, ran away. He is 27 years old and a butcher.

June 5, 1787

John Kuehmle has removed to the corner of Moravian alley, opposite the publisher of this paper (Race street), Philadelphia, where he continues the practice of medicine.

Michael Hettinger, Baltimore.

Urbanus Hueffer, Millertown, Va. (Woodstock).

Jacob Moore, schoolmaster, near New York.

June 12, 1787

Andreas Stahl, aged 63 years, left Philadelphia eight months ago on a peddling trip, and nothing has since been heard of him.

June 19, 1787

David Hailer, surgeon, Appletree alley, between Fourth and Fifth streets, near the old Lutheran Church, Philadelphia.

Elisabeth Maag, widow, establishes a tobacco factory on Second street, Philadelphia, the second house above the Black Bear inn and opposite the Stag inn, above Race street. She was formerly Widow Braun.

Carl Gemberling, Philadelphia, advertises that his shoemaker apprentice, Benjamin Meyner, ran away. He is 18 years old, was born in Bucks County, speaks English and German, and is believed to have gone to Baltimore.

July 17, 1787

Carl Miller, Mount Pleasant Iron Works, Berks County, notifies Henrich Adam, a German, and his wife Elisabeth, to come and sign a redemptioner agreement. They arrived at New York at the end of 1785 in the ship Watson, from Amsterdam.

Jacob Waendel, Frederick, Md., advertises that his German servant, Nicolaus Hauberger, ran away. He is 38 years old and a stonecutter.

July 17, 1787

Peter Legaux, Spring Mill, Montgomery County, advertises that his German servant, Johann Georg Rindlaub, ran away. He is 25 years old, a baker and came from Northern Germany. He was tempted to leave by Joseph l'Eveille, a French deserter, who was recently freed from servitude.

Conrad Abel, Arch street, near Fourth, Philadelphia, advertises that his German servant, Ludwig Jeck, ran away. He is 25 years old, a baker, and arrived last autumn. He is believed to have left with Johann Henrich Henning, 45 years old, servant of Samuel Wetherill, who also arrived last autumn.

August 7, 1787

Joseph Kaufman, Providence Township, Montgomery County, advertises that his German servant, Elisabeth Vetnant, ran away. She is 30 years old and came to America two years ago.

August 21, 1787

Peter Eckert, Mill Creek, Leacock Township, Lancaster County, advertises that his Irish servant, Terence Smith, 18-19 years old, ran away.

August 28, 1737

Samuel Lehman, Front street, near Pool's bridge, Philadelphia, advertises that two blacksmith apprentices ran away--Jacob Errot, 19 years old, born in America, and Anton Margelaer, born in France.

September 4, 1787

Philip Hall, butcher, Race street, Philadelphia, advertises that his German apprentice, Johannes Boraf, 18 years old, ran away.

Christian Jung, Passyunk Township (Philadelphia), advertises that his German servant, Anna Louisa Moellerin, 25 years old, ran away.

October 2, 1787

Jacob Schuller removes from New street to Third street, Philadelphia, five doors above Vine street, at Mr. Morgan's sugar house, where he will conduct an inn.

Wilhelm Mohr, Catharine street, between Second and Third, Philadelphia, advertises that his carpenter apprentice, Andreas Elyert, ran away. He is 19 years old and speaks English and German.

October 30, 1787

Inquiry for August Friederich Meier, born in Amt Durlach, who came to America in 1773.
(In the issue of November 6 August Friederich Meier advertises that he is going to Germany in response to the preceding advertisement).

Peter Spruckman, organist, Lebanon.

December 18, 1787

Christian Hartman, Allen Township, Northampton County, advertises that his shoemaker apprentice, Wilhelm Hubach, ran away.

December 24, 1787

Joseph Middleton and Mr. Hunter, in an open boat, were on their way to Burlington, N.J., on the Delaware River, about two weeks ago, when a storm upset their boat and both were drowned.

February 5, 1788

Burkhart Presser is going to Germany. He was born in Ottweiler.

March 11, 1788

Henrich Henritzy, Flourtown, Montgomery County, advertises that his hatmaker apprentice, Michael Urweiler, ran away. He is 18-19 years old, was born in America and speaks German and English.

March 25, 1788

Friederich Weckerlin removes from Third street to the south side of Race street, the third house west of Third, Philadelphia. He sells mackerel, salmon, cod liver oil, etc.

April 1, 1788

Friederich Boullange, Bristol Township, Philadelphia County, six miles from Philadelphia, advertises that three German servants have run away--Johannes Hesselbach, 35 years old, and his wife, Anna Elisabeth, 27 years old, who had arrived in America recently, and who took with them their 18-month-old son, and Anna Regina Cauffman, 24 years old, who formerly was indentured with Captain Forrester for eighteen months.

April 8, 1788

Joseph Lehman opens a new German apothecary shop on Third street, between Arch and Race, Philadelphia, the second house above the Golden Swan inn.

April 15, 1788

     Richard Backhaus, Durham Iron Works (Bucks County), advertises that his servant, Daniel Walker, 26-27 years old, ran away.

May 20, 1788

     Three German servants, who arrived in America last autumn, ran away from Philadelphia--Johann Michael Baackner, indentured to Chief Justice McKean; Johann Horning, indentured to Thomas Lea, 19 years old, and Caspar Greiner, tailor, 21 years old, indentured to Edward Burd.

     Inquiry for Conrad Meyer, from Zurich, who came to America many years ago.

     Johann Leonhard and Georg Philip Borger, Frederick, Md.

June 3, 1788

     Hilarius Becker removes from Race street to the south side of Market street, between Second and Third, adjoining the Indian King inn, Philadelphia. He sells hardware and is also an English and German scrivener.

July 22, 1788

     Inquiry for Georg Stupsky, born near Danzig, West Prussia, who came to America about 1783.

August 12, 1788

     Philip Neisz, Haycock Township, Bucks County, advertises that Johannes Maier ran away. He is a miller 25 years old, and worked for five or six years at Levering's mill, on Wissahickon Creek (Philadelphia).

September 16, 1788

     Georg Esterly, Harrowgate, near Frankford (Philadelphia), advertises that his servant, Maria Morrey, ran away. She is 14 years old and speaks English and German.

September 23, 1788

     David Stiem, Nockamixon Township, Bucks County, advertises that his apprentice, Jacob Miller, 17-18 years old, ran away. He is a German weaver.

September 30, 1788

          Letters for

     Johann Georg Eisenlohr and Ernst Emanuel Seltz, from Durlach.

September 30, 1788

    Letters for

Jacob Kurz, from Jeccar-Deutzlingen.

Joseph or Philip Sommer, from Ober-Boyhingen.

Christian Fenstermacher, Johann Adam Heckardt and Christian Ringmacher, born in Iszuy, in Algoemo, near Ulm.

Hieronymus Heinzelman, from Augsburg.

Christoph Miller, from Goeppingen.

Andreas Reuschlen, from Wahlheim.

Martin Volz, from Boeckingen.

October 21, 1788

    Letters for

Fridolin Scharb, from Hauingen, near Loerrach, Baden.

Georg Jacob Becker, Pfortzheim, Durlach.

Johann Peter Kammerer, cooper, from Blaukenloch, Durlach.

Johannes Freuler, weaver, from Oberweiler, Durlach.

Rosina Dieszin, from Wolfartsweiler, near Durlach.

Joh. Franz Daniel, Franz Nicolaus Helm and his sisters, Maria Elisabeth and Anna Chatarina Helmin, near Birkenfeld.

Johann Friedrich Weiszhard, from Schmidthaueser Thal, near Loewenstein.

Catharina Graeszlin, married ---- Hofackerin, from Auggen, near Loerrach, Baden.

Georg Siliger, from Auerbach.

Andreas Backenstos, from Wolfartsmeyer, near Durlach.

Jacob Omberger, near Emendingen, Baden.

Hans Georg Klais, from Schopfheim, Baden.

Joh. Georg Hetler, from Enzvayhingen, near Stuttgard.

Johannes Zeiher, from Eichen, Baden.

Jacob Wohlschlegel, from Schutterzell, Baden.

Hans Michael Brand, from Koenig Schashausen, Baden.

Christiana Iarausin, from Schroeck, near Carlruh.

Hans Hangen, tailor, from Sprendlingen, Baden.

October 21, 1788

Georg Schroeder's wife, born Echterachtu, from Malbron, near Birkenfeld.

Nicolaus Schneider, from Burgbirkenfeld.

Georg Michael Lackner, tailor, from Sinsheim.

Christoph Herbster, from Graben, Durlach.

Philip Graeff, from Weinsheim.

Johann Nicolaus Wagner, from Gebrod.

Conrad Conradus, from Standernheim.

Johannes Leonhard, from Daubach, Baden.

Georg Veit Meister, from Hofheim, in dem Gemmingischen.

Joh. Heiderich, from Roetzweiler.

Conrad Moser, from Binzen, Baden.

Franz Beck, from Eningen, near Reutlingen; he served with John Ross.

Jacob Mayer, from Regensburg, Canton Zurich, mason.

Johann Jacob Schneider, from Ober-Constanz, near Kirchberg.

Johann Georg Bauer, from Gehlweiler, near Kirchberg.

Johann Conrad Bloede, with Peter Schuetz, Heidelberg Township, Lancaster County (now Lebanon).

Anna Catharine, widow of David Bruche, master butcher, Limerick Township, Montgomery County.

November 4, 1788

Died on October 25, near Kensington, Philadelphia County, Matthias Landenberger. Burial took place October 28 in the Lutheran grounds.

Johann Christian Grotian, schoolmaster of St. Michael's and Zion Lutheran Church, Philadelphia, proposes to open a German night school in the school house. His residence is with Georg Kuefer, Race and Fifth streets.

November 25, 1788

Samuel Wallis, Muncy Township, Northumberland County (now Lycoming), advertises that two German servants ran away--Carl Erdman Arndt, 25 years old, ship carpenter, and Jacob Stump, 25 years old, cooper.

Two travelers born in Germany ran away without paying for their passage on the ship Amsterdam Packet, November 15, at Philadelphia--F. Schwartz, hatmaker, 25 years old, and Johann Landler, cooper, 25 years old.

January 6, 1789

Carl Christoph Reiche opens an English, German and Latin school for older children; residence, south side of Cherry street, between Third and Fourth, Philadelphia.

May 26, 1789

Johann Wilhelm Otterbach and Anna Elisabeth Bucherin arrived September, 1785, on the ship Watson, from Amsterdam, consigned to Sears & Smith, New York.

Inquiry for Michael Gerst, who arrived at Philadelphia seventeen years ago from Oberhoffen, five hours from Strasburg, in Lower Alsace, and worked at his trade with Jacob Ritter, blacksmith, Third street, Philadelphia. His sister, Magdalena, who married ---- Volckel, is also sought.

Johann Georg Geiser, stonecutter, Philadelphia, from Breitenholz, Wurtemberg.

Johann Fausser, smith, with Georg Adam Schneider, North Wales (Gwynedd Township, Montgomery County).

Jacob Welker now conducts the Wagon inn, Race street, between Second and Third, Philadelphia, adjoining Steiner's printing shop, where the late Jost Ebert was landlord for many years.

August 18, 1789

Georg Baer, Frederick Township, Montgomery County, advertises that his servant, William Hallode, 26 years old, ran away.

Mrs. Schneider, master baker, born Grosz, from Hanau, now on the Delaware, in Philadelphia.

Ebenezer Branham removes from the Sheep and Lamb inn, Front street, near Pools bridge, to the south side of Market street, between Sixth and Seventh, occupying the inn that Thomas Craig formerly conducted, which is now named the Black Bear, Philadelphia.

September 1, 1789

Georg Jaeger, hatmaker, Reading, advertises that his apprentice, Philip Kuntzman, 18 years old, ran away.

September 8, 1789

William Lawrence, Philadelphia, advertises that his German servant, Johannes Andreas Pietz, a tailor, 30 years old, ran away.

Heinrich Clause, Philadelphia, advertises that his German apprentice, Johann Grosz, 14 years old, ran away.

September 8, 1789

Ran away--Friederich Ludwig Jaecky, born German, servant
of Peter Legaux, Spring Mill, Montgomery County, aged 10 years
and 9 months; speaks English, German and French well; is ac-
customed to work in a vineyard and around horses and also in
the house. He is a son of Lorenz Jaecky, who lives in the
German suburbs of Reading and has been in America four years.

October 13, 1789

Anna Margretha Regina Reinhardin, widow, born Hempele,
living in Wetzler, Germany, inquires for her only son, Johann
Theodor Reinhard. He studied for five years in the Gymnasium
in Weilburg, taking up French, English, Italian, Greek, Hebrew
and the Oriental languages. In his 16th year he went to the
University of Leipzig to study law, and after remaining there
two and a half years he left for Goettingen, where he intended
to spend a half year at the university. He traveled by way of
Hamburg and Bremen. At Bremen a ship was about to sail for
America. The young man had heard and read much about America
while in Leipzig, and on April 28 he wrote his mother that he
intended sailing for America the following day, but he did not
give the name of the ship nor the captain. His father, who
died in 1783, was assessor of the local court of justice. The
son was born in 1770 in Neustrelitz, Mecklenburg.

June 1, 1790

Martin Hausman has established a stage line between Philadelphia and Reading, leaving John Hartmann's house, Reading,
Monday at 5 A.M. and arriving Tuesday noon in Philadelphia;
leaving Jacob Meytinger's inn, the George Washington, Vine
street, Philadelphia, Thursday at 5 A.M., and arriving in
Reading at noon on Friday. Fare, $2 one way; letters, 3 pence.

Catharina Limken, Front street, near Race, Philadelphia,
advertises that her shoemaker apprentice, Jacob Klinger, 20
years old, ran away.

Johann Friederich Amerlung established a glass factory five
years ago near Frederick, Md. The place is now known as New
Bremen.

October 5, 1790

Adam Schnook, Frederick County, Md., eight miles from
Frederick, advertises that his German servant, Georg Miller, a
miller, ran away.

October 15, 1790

Ludwig Conrad Kuhn, born at Aldensimmern, innkeeper at
Mannheim, in the Palatinate, at the sign of the elephant, in
the house that formerly was a pipe factory, gives notice that
he arrived at Philadelphia on October 3 in the ship Mary, Captain Fitzpatrick, and he seeks information about his brother,
Franz Paul Kuhn, tanner, who came to America from Germany in
1764.

October 15, 1790

Heinrich Walter, cabinetmaker, and Mrs. Knochin, born Kimmerlein, from Wiesbaden.

Johannes Speckert, or Sperkert, arrived at Philadelphia in 1776 from Schriesheim, near Heidelberg.

Inquiry for Wilhelm Silber, from Erfurth.

October 29, 1790

Henrich Hoffwecker, tailor, born in Mannheim, in the Palatinate.

November 26, 1790

Anna Margaretha, only daughter of Balthaser Seltzer, inquires for him. She was left at home in 1752 when her father and his wife left Germany for America. The father was born in Rotheim, Hesse-Hanau, and was last heard from in Philadelphia in 1753.

Johannes Fausser, Third street, Philadelphia, born in Bodelhausen, is going to Germany.

Peter Bachman, Lower Saucon Township, Northampton County, advertises that his carpenter apprentice, Philip Gelnet, 23 years old, ran away.

Friederich Schuetz, papermaker, Lower Merion Township, Montgomery County, advertises that his German servant, Peter Wallauer, ran away. He is 19 years old, has learned papermaking, and speaks good English.

Adam Siter, Jr., removes from the Spread Eagle inn, Lancaster road, to the Spread Eagle inn, Market street, between Seventh and Eighth, Philadelphia.

February 4, 1791

Ludwig Conrad Kuhn, a citizen of Mannheim, is going to Germany in March.

February 18, 1791

Nicolaus Mayer, dyer and cloth printer, removes from Allentown to Philadelphia, and will conduct his business on Second street, in the Northern Liberties, in the house that formerly was the Blue Ball inn.

April 5, 1791

Michael Gundacker and Johann Gundacker, Lancaster, dissolve their partnership, and Michael Gundacker will continue the business in the same store.

April 8, 1791

Benedict Ludwig Schaufele (Schausele?), Campington, in the Northern Liberties of Philadelphia, is going to Germany. He was born in Stuttgart.

May 31, 1791

Johann Henrich Hoffecker is going to Germany. He was born at Mannheim, in the Palatinate.

September 9, 1791

Conrad Seybert, No. 390 Second street, Philadelphia (North), sign of the white cock and lion, corner Coates street, Campingtown, in the Northern Liberties, is going to Germany in October. He was born in the Palatinate.

Carl Erdman, scrivener, has removed from Fifth street to the north side of Callowhill street, No. 121, between Third and Fourth, Philadelphia.

Pfaffenhauser & Schwab remove their cotton printing and bleaching factory from Darby (Delaware County), to Second street, south side of the bridge, Campingtown, Northern Liberties of Philadelphia.

Henrich Schlonecker, Douglass Township, Montgomery County, inquires for Martin Zihan, weaver and saddler, about 50 years old, who left Schlonecker February 24, 1790.

Christlieb Baertling becomes landlord of the Stag inn, No. 130 Second street, above Race, Philadelphia.

Inquiry for Johann Leonhard Schloepp and Johann Maar, from Mt. Taschendorf, in Frankischen Kreis of Germany (Franconia), belonging to Reichsfreyherr von Kuenstberg, Amt Obersteinbach, who left there in 1766 for America. Schloepp wrote his parents, June 16, 1774, from the potash factory in New York, where he was employed as a cooper.

October 21, 1791

Conrad Zutter, a German passenger, 33 years old, who has relatives at Pottsgrove, escaped from the ship Philadelphia Packet, Captain Edward Rice, which recently arrived at Philadelphia from Amsterdam.

November 8, 1791

David Gotthilf Schmidt, from Altenfelt.

November 15, 1791

Johann Pfeil, Philadelphia, advertises that his German servant, Elisabeth Fornwald, 35 years old, ran away, taking along her child, 3-4 years old.

November 15, 1791

Ludwig Henrich Luering, 93 Race street, Philadelphia, inquires for Carl Diedrich Gustav Haekermann, former secretary of the council and court of justice at Barth, in Swedish Pomerania, who sailed from Amsterdam in 1780 for Charleston, with Mr. Buchholtz.

November 29, 1791

B. Bohlen, 7 North Water street, Philadelphia, inquires for Traugott Butze, apothecary, born in Saxony, who came to America seventeen years ago.

February 28, 1792

Georg G. Woelpper, Philadelphia, advertises that his German servant, Conrad Rothhasz, ran away. He is a butcher, 27 years old, was born at Berg-op-Zabern, and speaks French and English.

Wilhelm Von Phul, Philadelphia, advertises that his German servant, Johann Christoph Geil, ran away with Rothhasz, mentioned in the preceding advertisement. Geil is a cooper, 26-27 years old, and was born at Nierstein, on the Rhine.

March 23, 1792

Polly Laeckin, at the inn of Andreas Drumber, Lower Milford Township, Bucks County, inquires for her sister, Elisabeth Laeckin, daughter of Paul Laeck, who left the family twenty years ago and for a time was in Pottsgrove.

May 1, 1792

Peter Ridenauer, Heidelberg Township, Northampton County (now Lehigh), intends leaving on May 27 for Germany. He was born at Dieffenbach, Littel, Steiner-Amt.

Maria Krebs conducts a sewing school on New street, north of Fourth, Philadelphia.

May 29, 1792

Friederich Mayer, 92 Market street, Charleston, South Carolina, inquires for Christian Keeper, miller, born in Hanau, who came to America 18-19 years ago.

Henrich Haupt, Durham Township, Bucks County, advertises that his servant, Friederich Bries, 19 years old, ran away.

June 5, 1792

Magdalena Leinin, Salisbury Township (Lehigh County), offers $200 reward for the arrest of Johann Peter Nagel, whom she accuses of having killed her husband, Wilhelm Lein, by knocking him down on May 12.

June 5, 1792

On June 26, Hanna Nagelin, wife of Johann Peter Nagel, replies to the preceding advertisement, denying that her husband had killed Lein but asserting that Lein was the aggressor and that on May 12 the two men quarreled in a field, but no murder was committed, but that Lein died several hours afterward from the results of an old injury which became aggravated by his anger.

June 10, 1792

Michael Mueller, 172 Spruce street, Philadelphia, advertises that his German servant, Friederich Kabelmacher, ran away. He is a carpenter, 26-27 years old.

Carl Baumann, Northern Liberties of Philadelphia, advertises that his German servant, Jacob Stoer, ran away. He is a butcher 21 years old.

July 3, 1792

Inquiry for Johann Ludwig Daum, formerly a gamekeeper at Daaden, Sayn-Altenkirchen, who in 1785 went to the United Netherlands and thence to Philadelphia.

July 17, 1792

Elias Botner, Baltimore, near Griffith's bridge, advertises that his German servant, Johann Samuel Stein, ran away. He is a saddler, 30 years old.

July 31, 1792

William Higginbotham takes possession of the old inn, the Wagon and Four Horses, on the north side of Race street, between Second and Third, Philadelphia, formerly conducted by the late Jost Ebert and previously by Bernhard Haens.

August 14, 1792

Johann Philip Koerger, from the Palatinate, Dorf Erolsheim, near Bingen, notifies his sister, Anna Maria, wife of Anton Miller, and his sister's daughter, the wife of Valentin Gaul, her father being Matthias Best, who have come from Germany to Philadelphia, that he lives at Neudorlach, near Schoharie, forty miles west of Albany, in New York State.

August Koenig, merchant, Gay street, and Johann Fischer, brushmaker, Market street, Baltimore, inquire for

> Jacob Hubert, from Bomoln.
> Joseph Anton Walk, from Amsterdam.
> Johannes Neszler, from Amsterdam.
> Christian Folger, from Westphalia, Grafschaft Luettich.
> Georg Rayner, from Amsterdam.
> Johann Eugenius Folger, Ignatz Anton Schoch, the brothers Ruen and Joseph Wolk, from Amsterdam.
> Joseph Hubert and Joseph Jansen, from Rotterdam.

August 28, 1792

James Morrison, Baltimore, advertises that his German servant, Solomon Gottlieb Hinding, ran away last October. He is a painter and glazier, 20-25 years old, and came to America in the ship Republican, from Bremen.

September 18, 1792

Martin Miller, Kensington, Philadelphia County, inquires for Mathes Schempp, from Belinger Amt, Wurtemberg, who came to America about forty-five years ago.

Abraham Stiel, Salisbury Township (Lehigh County), two miles from Allentown, advertises that his German servant, Peter Stiel, 16-17 years old, ran away.

September 25, 1792

Johannes Schneider, Pikeland Township, Chester County, advertises that his shoemaker apprentice, Henrich Schmidt, 17-18 years old, ran away.

October 23, 1792

Abraham Sheridan, innkeeper, removes from the Golden Swan inn, Third street, to the White Swan inn, Race street, between Third and Fourth, Philadelphia.

January 8, 1793

Friederich Graemer, Annapolis, Maryland.

Christoph Hensman, Pensacola.

January 22, 1793

Inquiry for Magdalena Gutbrod, from Tuebingen, Wurtemberg, who came to America in 1754, with her husband and several children. The husband died on the voyage, and the others settled at Canajoharie, New York.

February 19, 1793

Died, February 3, Anna Catharina, wife of Daniel Sutter, lace merchant, Philadelphia, in her 44th year. The burial took place February 6 in the German Reformed grounds.

March 12, 1793

J. Williams, Jr., 244 North Front street, Philadelphia, advertises that two German servants ran away--Ferdinand Liebenstern, 23 years old, born in Prussia, and Christoph Schmidt, 19 years old. Both play the flute.

March 26, 1793

Inquiry for Jacob Stierle, baker, who left Baltimore
August 5, 1792.

April 9, 1793

Jacob Anspach, from Mentzinger, in the Middle Palatinate,
is going to Germany in June.

Engel Christina Getzin inquires for her brother, Andreas
Getz, formerly doctor with the Anspach troops and now believed
to be in Canada.

March 26, 1793

Henrich Eckel, Bucks County, advertises that his apprentice, William Muckelroy, 16 years old, ran away.

April 23, 1793

Michael Christman, at Martin Kirschner's mill, on the
Conococheaque, six miles from Hagerstown, Md., inquires for his
brother, Georg Christman, a shoemaker, who left the vicinity
of Kaiserslautern, in the Palatinate, about twenty years ago.

Jost Otterbach, Middle Paxton Township, Dauphin County,
nine miles above Harrisburg, inquires for his brother, Wilhelm
Otterbach, born in Amt Burbach, Nassau-Dillenburg, who arrived
at New York, in 1785 on the ship Watson.

May 7, 1793

Carl Hoeth, Upper Saucon (Lehigh County), on the late
Dr. Lynn's place, conducts a general store.

Georg Schleicher, Front street, between Vine and Callowhill, Philadelphia, advertises that his cooper apprentice,
Caspar Diel, 19 years old, ran away.

May 10, 1793

Inquiry for a family named Hepenstiel, from Grafschaft
Witgenstein, who have been in America more than thirty years.

May 14, 1793

Johannes Schroyer gives notice that Michael Cener has left
him. He is a German shoemaker who came from Albany and worked
in Philadelphia with Johannes Philips.

June 11, 1793

James Whitehead, 222 North Second street, Philadelphia,
advertises that his German servant, Georg Grall, 11 years old,
ran away.

July 5, 1793

John Andrews, residing on the grounds of the University of Pennsylvania, Philadelphia, advertises that his servant, Johann Philip Engel, a German, 15 years old, ran away.

July 16, 1793

Georg Eyre, Burlington, N. J., advertises that his German servant, Hartmann Scheir, ran away. He is a butcher, 20 years old, and has also worked in a tannery. He arrived at Philadelphia last September on the ship Columbia.

July 23, 1793

Carl Schroeder, formerly "Hofmeister, Canditor und Decorateur" with the minister of the King of France, has opened a confectionery store at 22 North Seventh street, Philadelphia.

August 20, 1793

Jacob Eckfeldt, 30 North Fifth street, between Market and Arch, Philadelphia, advertises that his smith apprentice, Christian Van Phul, ran away. He is 18 years old, of German descent, was born below Hagerstown, Md., and has relatives in that vicinity.

Johann H. Guenther, 30 Arch street, between Second and Third, Philadelphia, advertises that his German servant, Christian Ludwig Burger, a tailor, ran away.

Jacob Stang, Lower Salford Township, Montgomery County, advertises that his German servant, Adam Greulich, ran away. He is 21 years old, arrived in America last autumn, is well educated and might assume to be a schoolmaster.

December 17, 1793

Catharina M. Riedel advertises that her German servant, Johann Kieferdorf, ran away last September. He is a tailor, 19 years old.

January 4, 1794

Dr. Ritzinger, who recently arrived from Germany, is practicing medicine at 57 Race street, between Second and Third, Philadelphia.

February 7, 1794

Richard Potter, Thomas Bradford and Samuel Edwards, Philadelphia, advertise that three servants ran away--Philip Balthaser, tailor, 22 years old, born in Germany, arrived from Hamburg at the time of the yellow fever epidemic (in 1793); Johann Nonn, German, 20-21 years old, a printer, who arrived on the ship Polly, Captain Dryburg, and Friederich Loy, who was a silk weaver in Germany but worked in an herb store in America.

March 18, 1794

Johannes Biszbing takes possession of the Black Eagle inn, Third street, between Race and Vine, Philadelphia.

J. Friederich Reiche, gold and silver worker, who recently arrived from Germany, has begun business at 82 Fourth street, near Race, Philadelphia.

April 4, 1794

Johannes and Abraham Singer and Ludwig Farmer, Philadelphia, advertise that two German servants ran away--Michael Siebenlist, 19 years old, and Andreas Kurfix, 24 years old.

April 22, 1794

Henrich Scheiffele, 49 South Third street, and Anna Chaloner, 38 North Third street, Philadelphia, advertise that two German servants ran away--Georg Carl Benecke, 23 years old, locksmith, who assumes to understand medicine and surgery, and his brother, Ernst Julius Bencke, 19 years old, who served part of his apprenticeship with a jeweler in Germany. They were born in Hanover, and arrived in Philadelphia from Hamburg in the autumn of 1793.

Henrich Wellmig, who arrived from London two years ago and is now at 240 North Front street, near the new market, Philadelphia, offers to provide pianofortes for his German countrymen.

May 23, 1794

Joseph Rittenhouse and Adam Haines, 135 North Third street, Philadelphia, advertises that two servants ran away-- William Peter Carroll, 20 years old, who speaks English and German, and Franz Carolus Grum, carpenter, 24 years old.

August 19, 1794

Georg Ozeas, Water street, third house below South, Philadelphia, advertises that his German servant, Johann Georg Jaeger, ran away. He is a baker, 19 years old.

August 26, 1794

Dr. J. B. Risch, from Germany, lodges with Georg Graul, Second street, fourth house from Dr. Weber, Northern Liberties of Philadelphia. He specializes in the treatment of melancholia.

December 5, 1794

Dr. A. Hunnius, who studied medicine at the University of Nena, is practicing in Philadelphia, and is now at the Golden Lamb inn, Second street, with Mr. Johe. He gives free advice to the poor.

February 6, 1795

Johann Adam Ruppert, of Boston, inquires for his brother-in-law, Caspar Werner, who was born at Altengronau, is a cooper and came to America about two years ago.

April 10, 1795

Adam Haendel has removed to the King of Prussia inn, Market street, between Third and Fourth, Philadelphia, which Colonel Ludwig Farmer formerly conducted.

Christoph Hergesheimer, Germantown, advertises that his blacksmith apprentice, Jonathan Paul, 19-20 years old, ran away.

Dr. F. E. Risch removes from Georg Graul's to the Golden Plow inn, 240 North Front street, corner of Callowhill street, Philadelphia, with Mr. Geucke.

June 23, 1795

Dr. S. Kunckler removes from 147 North Third street to 115 Race street, between Third and Fourth, Philadelphia.

July 31, 1795

Carl Erdman, scrivener, residence, 121 Callowhill street, opens an office at 99 Race street, corner Third, Philadelphia.

Henrich Hummeler, Nicetown, five miles from Philadelphia, advertises that his German servant, Francis Einmann, 25-30 years old, ran away.

Inquiry for Johann Henrich Wagner, born in Hesse-Cassel, who left there thirty years ago and wrote his relatives in 1787 from Northampton County.

Carl Kayser opens an inn, the Flag and Arms of the United States, at 52 North Fourth street, Philadelphia, northwest corner of Appletree alley, in the house where Georg Reinhardt formerly lived.

Joseph Till, Bethlehem, advertises that his shoemaker apprentice, Johann Christ, ran away. He is 18 years old, and still has three years to serve.

September 15, 1795

Carl Miller and Friederich Schinckel, Jr., Second and Market streets, Philadelphia, dealers in herbs, dissolve their partnership.

September 22, 1795

Gottfried Lehnhoff, Plumb street, Philadelphia, advertises that his German servant, Christian Leiper, ran away. He is 26 years old and a butcher.

December 14, 1795

Abraham Cullman, Vine street, Philadelphia, advertises
that his shoemaker apprentice, Isaac Kaercher, 16 years old,
ran away.

Charles Grevoir, Bristol Township, Philadelphia County,
advertises that two servants ran away--Georg Roth, 38 years old,
and his wife, Anna Gusta, 40 years old. They took with them
their daughter, Anna Maria, 9 years old.

December 25, 1795

Conrad Axt, Frankford, Philadelphia County, advertises that
his German baker apprentice, Jacob Obersteg, 17-18 years old,
ran away.

January 8, 1796

Georg Spiesz, with Daniel Niesz, Bern Township, Berks
County, is going to Germany in February. He is at home in
Wittgenstein.

January 12, 1796

George W. Steinhauer, living on a plantation on Frankford
road, near Three-Mile Run, Philadelphia County, advertises that
his German servant, Anton Blume, ran away. He is a shoemaker,
25 years old. His wife, Austina, went with him.

German almanacs sold by

Henrich Lenthaeuser, 24 King George street, New York.
Johann Schultz, Schroeder & Company and Luke Tiernan,
Baltimore, Md.
Friederich Schwartz, Frederick, Md.
Mathias Zehring, Woodstock, Va.
Joseph Stover, Strasburg, Va.
Abraham Merkel, Charleston, S. C.
Justus H. Schruber, Savannah.

February 23, 1796

James Whitehead, 222 North Second street, Philadelphia,
advertises that his German servant, Christian Schleiter, ran
away. He is 11 years old and the son of Henrich Schleiter,
who formerly lived near Thomas Potts' iron works on French
Creek (Chester County), but is now at Lesher's furnace, Oley
(Berks County).

March 18, 1796

Nicolaus Marvereau, Union street, near Second, Philadelphia, advertises that his servant, Jacobus Hutchinson, ran
away. He is a coppersmith, 23 years old.

March 22, 1796

Conrad Brake, Caernarvon Township, Berks County, advertises that his German servant, Anton Pre, 35 years old, ran away.

May 20, 1796

John Rice, Kensington, Philadelphia County, advertises that his German servant, Garret Friezy, ran away. He is 23 years old and a carpenter.

June 7, 1796

Walter Leeve (Levy?), Tredyffrin Township (Chester County), and Isaac Moore, Upper Merion Township (Montgomery County), advertise that two German servants ran away--Johann Gunnen, 32 years old, farmer, served in the French army, and Conrad Freyberger, baker, 23 years old, born in Wurtemberg.

Johann David Hoechstaetter, sculptor, recently arrived from Germany, is now ready to receive commissions on Second street, adjoining the new German Catholic Church, Philadelphia.

Samuel Wallis, Muncy Township, Lycoming County, advertises that two servants ran away--Christian Singerling, German, 22 years old, who has been in America two years, and Friederich Schultz, born in Germany, 19 years old, who came to America when young and speaks good English.

Nicolaus Schaumburg, Hempfield Township, Lancaster County, three miles from Lancaster, with Peter Musselman, tanner.

Georg Johe becomes landlord of the White Swan inn, Race street, between Third and Fourth, Philadelphia.

Urbanus Huefer, care of Matthias Zehring, merchant, Millerstown, Shenandoeh County, Va. (now Woodstock).

Andreas Saulig, tanner, care of Catharina Drockgoedin, Neustadt (Newtown), near Baltimore.

June 21, 1796

George Leib, 445 North Fourth street, Northern Liberties of Philadelphia, advertises that his servant, Elisabeth Dermans, ran away. She is 26 years old, was born in Germany, but most of her life was spent in Flanders.

Veronica Muennich, 51 North Seventh street, Philadelphia, advertises that her German servant, Johann H. G. Pax, ran away. He is a baker and arrived from Hamburg nine months ago.

July 15, 1796

Anna Catharina Wilhelm, born Sporin, born in Neukirchen, near Ziegenhayn, Hesse, recently arrived in Philadelphia and is in Georg Water's house, Third street, near Market. She inquires for her brother, Conrad Spor, who has been in America twenty years.

September 20, 1796

Abraham Hendel opens an apothecary shop at 42 Arch street, near Second, Philadelphia.

October 7, 1796

Jesse Edwards, Oxford Township, Chester County, advertises that two servants ran away--Johannes Ingel Baltis Dascher, 30 years old, and his wife, Anna Maria Dascher, 22 years old. They are Germans who arrived last May from Amsterdam on the ship Columbia.

December 16, 1796

Gottfried Lahnhoff, 38 Plumb street, Philadelphia, advertises that his German servant, Johann Philip Spies, 20 years old, ran away.

May 8, 1798

Michael Heisly, Lancaster, advertises that his apprentice, Georg Bauers, ran away. He is a blacksmith, 19 years old, and speaks English and German.

May 29, 1798

Thomas Owens, York, advertises that his German servant, Johann Nicolaus Kolb, ran away. He is a tailor, 30 years old.

Friederich Greiner, Philadelphia, advertises that his apprentice, Friederich Long, ran away. He is 15 years old, and his mother is now the wife of Georg Weinhold, York Township, York County.

July 10, 1798

O. Hoagland, Willingboro Township, Burlington County, N. J., advertises that two German servants ran away--Johannes Meyners, a gardner, 48 years old, and his wife, Helena, 38 years old. They had many children, which they took with them.

September 18, 1798

Anna Barbara Seylerin, living at 81 Appletree alley, Philadelphia, received word from her husband two years ago, while she was in Germany, directing her to come to America, but she has not heard from him since. He lived in Baltimore for six years.

March 5, 1799

Died on February 8, in Frederick, Md., Melchior Geisser, 110 years old. He was born in Germany.

April 16, 1799

Married on March 9 in York by the Rev. Mr. Goering, Jacob Schmeisser, son of Commissioner Michael Schmeisser, and Miss Margaretha Jeszler, daughter of Henrich Jeszler.

April 23, 1799

Isaac W. Norris, Philadelphia, advertises that his German servant, Catharina Kochin, 22 years old, ran away.

June 11, 1799

Vincent Thuun, merchant, of Philadelphia, died March 13, in Hamburg.

Married, on June 3, the Rev. G. Lochmann and Miss Susanna Hoffman, daughter of Valentin Hoffman, of Philadelphia.

June 25, 1799

Friederich Keszler, North Front street, Philadelphia, advertises that his shoemaker apprentice, Samuel Hutch, 19 years old, ran away.

July 3, 1799

Christoph Heiszler, butcher, five miles from Reading, fell from his horse on June 21, and was killed.

Heinrich Peter Laporterie, from Hamburg, is notified to appear and claim a legacy from his father.

October 22, 1799

Died in Philadelphia, from the prevalent disease (yellow fever), Christian Staehly, printer, in his 45th year.

November 5, 1799

Johannes Valentin, Codorus Township, York County, who came to America in 1796, inquires for his brother, Peter Valentin, from the parish of Stahlau, in Hesse-Darmstadt, who came to America in 1772.

December 3, 1799

Died, November 24, Jacob Greiner, of Philadelphia, in his 70th year. Burial took place November 26 in the Lutheran grounds.

January 14, 1800

Johann Georg Grinsman, Hagerstown, Md.

January 21, 1800

Johannes Seider, 16-17 years old, while sledding on January 12, one mile above Reading, on Tulpehocken Creek, became overheated, sat down on the ice and died suddenly.

January 28, 1800

Abraham Kiefer, Bedminster Township, Bucks County, advertises that his apprentice, William Williams, 30 years old, ran away.

GERMANTAUNER ZEITUNG

Published in Germantown, Philadelphia County, Pa., first
by Leibert & Billmeyer and later by Michael Billmeyer.

March 22, 1785

Dr. Felix Lynn will remove on March 22, from his place in
Upper Saucon Township (Lehigh County), on the Great road from
Bethlehem to Philadelphia, to Lower Saucon Township, Northampton County, eight miles from the old place and two miles
from Bethlehem, to the place formerly occupied by James Cruick-
schank, where he will continue his former business. John Green
will continue to conduct the store at Dr. Lynn's old place, in
Upper Saucon.

November 29, 1785

Rudolph Miller, Lebanon Township, Dauphin County (now
Lebanon County), advertises that his recently purchased German
servant, Nicolaus Wilhelm, ran away. He is a cooper 27-28
years old.

April 18, 1786

Caspar Kirling, Hamburg, Windsor Township, Berks County,
cures cancer and fistula.

August 8, 1786

Mattheus Flack, Groenwich Township, Berks County, one
mile from the stone church, is going to Germany in August. He
was born at Rimhorn, near Hoechst, in the Odenwald.

Georg Weber, Caernarvon Township, Lancaster County, advertises that his servant, Henrich Seiler, also known as Bickel,
17-18 years old, ran away.

October 31, 1786

Simon Keppler, Little Oley, Berks County, one mile from
the old furnace, is going to Germany in five weeks. He was
born at Adlingen, Boeblinger Amt, Wurtemberg.

November 14, 1786

Reuben Haines, Philadelphia, inquires for proof of the
death of Adam Marggranden, cooper, from Eggenstein, Germany,
who lived with Reuben Haines for several years and left him in
1777. He was a substitute in the militia in the campaign
against the Indians at Shamokin, and on returning, two years
ago, it was reported he had been drowned in a millpond near
Northumberland.

December 12, 1786

Inquiry for Johann Lorenz Veil, baker, Johann Wilhelm Deinhart and the latter's sister, Christina Magdalena Deinhartin, both born at Gartsch, Wurtemberg. They came to America thirty-four years ago. The sister married Peter Haller, of York.

February 6, 1787

Died in Colebrookdale Township, Berks County, Franz Latschaar, a German Mennonite, in his 102d year. A few days before his death he traveled twenty miles to visit sick relatives. He frequently walked twenty to twenty-five miles a day.

May 20, 1787

Michael Eckert, from Eppingen, five hours from Heilbrunn, is going to Germany the middle of August.

April 3, 1787

Martin Apple perfects a process of printing on linen, in Upper Saucon Township (Lehigh County), and he solicits such work. He continues dyeing and fulling.

June 12, 1787

Valentin Wunder, Germantown Township, Philadelphia County, advertises that his apprentice, Georg Wealbanck, ran away. He is a butcher, 17 years old, and speaks English and German.

June 10, 1787

Thomas Kerr, Jr., Tulpehocken Township, Berks County, advertises that his German servant, Jacob Spangler, 16 years old, ran away.

September 18, 1787

Inquiry for Georg Carl Friederich Hartmann, formerly in the service of the Duke of Brunswick. The last information received from him came from Loudoun County, Va., in 1780.

November 13, 1787

Jacob Schnebbely continues the inn and store of his late father, Caspar Schnebbely, in Lebanon.

February 19, 1787

Heinrich Clement is going to Germany in March. He is at home in Frauenfeld.

August 19, 1787

Adam Hillegass, Upper Hanover Township (Montgomery County), advertises that his German apprentice, Phillip Kaufman, 20 years old, ran away.

William Tennis, Lower Salford Township, Montgomery County, advertises that his apprentice, James McCallister, ran away. He is 22 years old, of Irish ancestry but was reared in a German family.

October 14, 1787

Jacob Berto, Rockland Township, Berks County, advertises that his papermaker apprentice, Jacob Ginder, nearly 18 years old, ran away.

April 28, 1789

Balzer Weinberger, Lower Milford Township, Bucks County, advertises that his apprentice, Jonas Forre, 23 years old, ran away.

October 13, 1789

Wendel Koenigsfeld, Whitpain Township, Montgomery County, advertises that his servant, Johannes Treck, 14 years old, ran away.

October 27, 1789

Inquiry for Gottlieb Daniel Hoffman, born at Wertin, near Halle, his father being a clergyman. He went to Hamburg as the servant of a merchant and then emigrated to America several years ago. The only letter received from him came from Philadelphia, August 21, 1786, and said he was then in the service of Herbert & Potte, Alexandria, Va.

March 30, 1790

Georg Fetzer, Macungie Township (Lehigh County), advertises that his apprentice, Heinrich Boger, 18 years old, ran away.

May 25, 1790

Christophel Stoerner, Macungie Township (Lehigh County), is going to Germany in August. He was born in Odenwald.

Caspar Schoenebruck, Whitehall Township (Lehigh County), advertises that his apprentice, Anthony Moore, ran away. He is 17 years old and of Irish descent.

June 8, 1790

Lorenz Christ, Longswamp Township, Berks County, advertises that his apprentice, Heinrich Strohman, 19 years old, ran away.

INDEX

Baer, Abram 175
  Georg 185
  Hansz 37
  Jacob 28
  Jeremias 37
  Johannes 19, 94, 160
  Melcher 88
  Peter 14
Baeringer, Catharina
  72
  Nickel 72
Baernes, Joseph 24
Baertges, Michael 161
  Michel 50
Baertling, Christlieb
  188
Baertsch, Jacob 93
Baest, Nicolaus 39
Baeyerle, Michel 10
Baideman, Johann Henrich
  123
  Simon Peter 123
Bailey, William 116
Baisch, Ernst Ludwig
  117
Balch, (?) 174
Balljet, Paul 71
  Pool 60
Balmer, Jacob 141
Balthaser, Philip 193
Baltzer, Kaspa 132
Bamberger, Christel
  95
  Henrich 15
Barclay, James 50
Barel, Christophel 64
Bargards, Nicolaus 94
Baringer, David 65
Barnickel, Johann 131
Barrat, Caleb 150
Bart, Michael 174
Barth, Joseph 135
Bartholomae, Benedict
  48
  Johann 25
Bartsch, Conrad 36
  Jacob 93, 122, 157
Baser, Melchior 69
Baserman, Sigmund 23
Bast, Dorothea 12
  Georg 12
  Jacob Henrich 156
  Johannes 59
Bastian, William
  157
Baszel, Georg 81
  Johann Georg 69
Baszel, Juliana 69
Baszler, Peter 72, 76
Bates, Robert 7
Batz, Robert 7
Bauer, Abraham 25
  Christian 8
  Conrad 86, 88

Bauer, (cont.)
  Diel 21
  Georg 142
  Hansz 19
  Johann Conrad 132
  Johann DeWald 9
  Johann Georg 184
  Leonhard 165
  Ludwig 117
  Maria Elisabeth
    9
  Michael 149, 172
  Nicolaus 111
  Philip 174
  Valentin 126
Bauermann, Michel 89
Bauers, Georg 198
Baum, Jacob 28
  Susanna Margretha
    28
Bauman, (?) 29
  Abraham 22
  Christian 169
  Dietrich 41
  Jacob 8, 39
  Johann Dieter 64
  Johann Dietrich 18
  Johannes 37, 82
Baumann, Carl 190
  Georg Adam 53
  Henrich 90
  Johannes 39, 94
Baumgaertner, Anna
    Catharina 24
  Gottfried 24
Bausch, Joh. Adam 101
Bausum, Lorentz 59
Bausz, Johann 98
  Johannes 98
Bauszen, Johannes 46
Bauszman, Michael 130
Bauszmann, Joh. Michael
  138
  Peter 139
  William 147
Bayard, James 176
Bayer, Andreas 5
  Blaesz 20
  Blasius 134
  Christoffel 4
  Friedrich 51
  Georg 83
  Georg Friedrich
    66, 161
  Johannes 71
  Maria Chatarina 4
  Matthias 172
  Philip 172
  Valentin 98
Bayerle, Jacob 16, 25
Bayle, Johann 79
Bayly, Elisabeth 87
  James 87
Bealey, John 145

Bechtel, Christian 178
  Georg 22, 66
  Martin 66
Beck, Andreas 72
  Franz 184
  Jacob 1
  Joh. Jacob 112
  Johann Georg 51
  Martin 47
  Michael 112
Becker, Anton 174
  Christoph 133
  Dewald 61
  Elisabeth 34
  Friedrich 41, 43, 102
    173
  Georg 34
  Georg A. 162
  Georg Jacob 158, 183
  Henrich 87, 128
  Hilarius 182
  Jacobus Gerardus 3
  Joh. Hilarius 62
  Johann 95
  Johann Henrich 178
  Johannes 32, 89, 138
  Michel 56
  Peter 20
  Philip 111, 126, 132
    149
  Philip Jacob 158
  William 147
Beckers, Velten 18
Beehar, Joh. Jacob 79
Beemer, Johann 131
Beener, Johannes 21
Behler, Peter 107
Behrent, Johann 140
Behringen, Joh. Georg 116
Beil, Balthaser 3
Beiler, Conrad 52
  Jacob 94
Beisch, Sebastian 32
Beissel, Joh. Adam 88
  Peter 88
Beisser, Johannes 100
Beisserin, Anna Maria
    100
Beiszler, Johannes 80
Beiteman, Friedrich 58
Belcher, Benjamin 153
Bell, Elisabeth 93
  Johannes 93
  Samuel 87
  William 100, 174
Beltz, Jacob 81
  Johann 109
Bencke, Ernst Julius 194
Bender, Adam 127
  Catharine 28
  Georg 77
  Hansz Georg 26
  Jacob 28, 62
  Johannes 55

Bender (cont.)
  Michel 28
  William 165
Benderin, Appolonia 36
  Christina 36
  Maria 36
  Maria Johana 36
  Maria Margretha 36
Benecke, Georg Carl 194
Bener, Peter 89
Beneset, Daniel 5
Benezet, Daniel 55
  Stephen 26
Benner, Christian 23
  Ludwig 86
Benninghof, Johannes 80
Bennphilip, Thomas 65
Bens, Johann Eberhard 80
Bensel, Carl 24
Benson, Alexander 170
Bensz, Weirich 160
Bentzel, Johann Henrie 52
Beppler, Friedrich 96
Berckemeyer, Georg 69
Berckemeyerin, Anna
    Gertraut 69
Bercki, Jacob 95
Berend, Johann 103
Bergenthaler, Johann 157
Berger, Andreas 85
  Henrich 118
  Jacob 84
  Johannes 12
  Philippina 85
Bergey, Michael 60
Bergman, Hansz Georg 31
Bergmann, Johann Georg 11
Bergstraeszer, Georg 61
Bergthaler, Johann 115
Beringer, Catharina 85
  Ursula 85
Berkenbeil, Anthony 156
Berlen, Johann Caspar 148
  Justinia Magdalena 148
  Sophia Catharina 148
Berlet, Anna Maria 18,27
  Conrad 27
  Hans Wolff 16
  Johann Conrad 16, 18
Berlett, Paul 16
Bernard, Conrad 140
Berndt, Johann 116
Bernhart, Christian 21
  Stephen 50
Bernhold, Henrich 105
  Johann 115
Bernscheuer, Johann
    Justus 111
Bernthaler, Peter 88
Bero, Frantz 19
  Susanna 19
Berry, Samuel 161
Bershold, Anna Maria
    Elisabeth 25

Hoffmann, Johann Georg 65
  Peter 72
  Sebastian 155
Hoffschaar, Lorentz 93
Hoffsessin, Margretha 17
  Maria 17
Hoffwecker, Heinrich 187
Hohnecker, Marx 62
Hohrein, Tobias 136
Hold, Adam 124
Holl, Peter 44
Holland, Johannes 77
Hollebach, Matheus 31
Hollinger, Jacob 8, 88
Holteman, Nicolaus 79
Holty, Hannes 140
Holtz, Johannes 39
Holtzaeder, Peter 26
Holtzhauer, Abraham 52
  Caspar 86
  Casper 31
Holtzinger, Bernhard 161
Holzmann, Johann Hartmann 176
Honecker, Johannes 133
Honig, (?) 142
  Georg 47, 121
  Georg, Jr. 142
Honigkam, Joseph 154
Honold, Joh. Jacob 112
Hood, (?) (Captain) 137
Hook, Samuel 70
Hopson, Johann 115
Horein, Tobias 101
Horlacher, Michael 72
  Michel 72
Horn, Abraham 136
  Sebastian 96
Hornbaum, (?) (Dr.) 172
Hornecker, Isaac 142
Horner, John 147
Horning, Johann 182
Hosmann, Johann Georg 177
Hosterman, Jacob 132
Hottenstein, Henrich 84
  Wilhelm 77
Hoven, James 87
Howard, Lorentz 126
Howell, Samuel 146
Hubach, Wilhelm 181
Hubele, Bernhard 20, 161
Huber, (?) 30
  Christian 18, 31
  Daniel 18
  Henrich 5
  Jacob 44, 45, 53, 55
  Johann 125
  Johann Nickel 103
  Johannes 31
  John 76
  Michel 43, 44
  Ulrich 45
Hubert, Jacob 190
  Joseph 190
Hubly, Bernhard 149
Huck, Andreas 25, 165

Huck (cont.)
  Christian 120
  Johann 176
Huebler, (?) 117
Huefer, Urbanus 197
Hueffer, Urbanus 179
Huegel, Christian 46
Huenge, Ludwig 1
Huft, Johannes Georg 170
  Philip Peter 170
Hugel, Johannes 33
Huhn, Daniel 97
Hulings, Marcus 28
Humbert, Bernhard 142
  Philip 142
Hummeler, Henrich 195
Hundsberger, Christel 86
Hunnius, A. (Dr.) 194
Hunter, (?) 181
Hur, Jacob 161
Husar, Lorentz 8
Hussa, Dewald 16
Huston, John 87
Hutch, Samuel 199
Hutchinson, Georg 102
  Jacobus 196
  John 127
Huweler, Jacob 79
Huy, Uli 12
Iarausin, Christiana 183
Ickes, Johannes 66
  Nicolaus 23
Ihle, Hans Georg 112
Ilgner, Christian 128
Imler, Georg 82
Immel, Johann Michel 33
  Michel 144
Im-Ober-Steg, Abraham 54
Ingersheim, Grosz 53
Ingham, Jonathan 135
In Haeven, Geret 8, 12
Irion, Peter 140
Iserloh, Bernhart 39
  Johann Otto 2
Iserlohin, Maria 75
Iwans, Methusalem 60
Jacob, Bernet 77
  Bernhard 88
  Henrich 59
  Johann Daniel 12
  Johann Georg 134
  Nicolaus 159
  Peter 155
Jacobi, Christophel 47
  Conrad 84
Jacobin, Anna Maria 12
Jacobs, Israel 107
  Philip 111
Jaeckel, Abraham 57
Jaecky, Friederich Ludwig 186
  Lorenz 186
Jaeger, Antoni 17
  Antony 91
  Baltzer 62
  Georg 185

INDEX